Routledge Revivals

Modern Tendencies in World Religions

First published in 1933, *Modern Tendencies in World Religions* is the result of author's desire to find out what was happening in different religions and a long difficult search for materials to satisfy that interest. The sources of information have been various: books, newspapers, magazines, periodicals, in just so far as possible from the countries or religions represented. The book discusses themes like factors that produce change in religion; tendencies in Hinduism; modern tendencies in Japanese religion and China; religion in Russia; twentieth century tendencies in Islam and tendencies in Judaism.

In discussing the world religions, author felt that the probable familiarity of the readers of the book with the effect of the modern age on Christianity would warrant the omission of any discussion of that faith. This is an important historical reference work for scholars and researchers of religion and world religion.

Modern Tendencies in World Religions

Charles Samuel Braden

First published in 1933
by George Allen & Unwin Ltd.

This edition first published in 2025 by Routledge
4 Park Square, Milton Park, Abingdon, Oxon, OX14 4RN

and by Routledge
605 Third Avenue, New York, NY 10017

Routledge is an imprint of the Taylor & Francis Group, an informa business

© 1933 Charles Samuel Braden

All rights reserved. No part of this book may be reprinted or reproduced or utilised in any form or by any electronic, mechanical, or other means, now known or hereafter invented, including photocopying and recording, or in any information storage or retrieval system, without permission in writing from the publishers.

Publisher's Note
The publisher has gone to great lengths to ensure the quality of this reprint but points out that some imperfections in the original copies may be apparent.

Disclaimer
The publisher has made every effort to trace copyright holders and welcomes correspondence from those they have been unable to contact.

A Library of Congress record exists under LCCN: 33011134

ISBN: 978-1-041-05903-5 (hbk)
ISBN: 978-1-003-63281-8 (ebk)
ISBN: 978-1-041-05906-6 (pbk)

Book DOI 10.4324/9781003632818

MODERN TENDENCIES IN WORLD RELIGIONS

BY

CHARLES SAMUEL BRADEN, PH.D.
NORTHWESTERN UNIVERSITY

LONDON
GEORGE ALLEN & UNWIN LTD
MUSEUM STREET

FIRST PUBLISHED IN GREAT BRITAIN 1933

(All rights reserved)

TO
MY FATHER

PREFACE

ONE who is awake to what is happening in the big world outside his own limited section of it finds tangible evidence every day in his newspaper that humanity everywhere is amove. Here political revolution, there economic upheaval, yonder an intellectual awakening! Something interesting seems to be happening anywhere he turns his attention. "How fares religion amid all this change?" is a question that must occur many times to one who is interested in the faiths of mankind. Now and then an article appears purporting to discuss some phase of the question for a given part of the world. An occasional monograph on some one of the world's religions issues from the press. But where shall he go for a picture of the total world situation?

A desire to find out what was happening in different religions and a long difficult search for materials to satisfy that interest led to the preparation of this book. What a convenience it would be, I thought, if some one would survey the religions at the present time and bring together in concise form the result of this study. Believing that others would share that same thought the writer finally, after several times directing a Seminar on Modern Tendencies in World Religions, has brought together a brief statement of

PREFACE

the major tendencies that he, with the aid of his classes, has been able to discover.

Certain definite limits were set for the study. It should cover only the years of the twentieth century, bringing it down as near to the publication date as possible—1933. The approach should be that of a chronicler of what is occurring rather than an appraiser of what has occurred. The attempt would be made to keep only to the *trends,* that is, points at which some change of direction was apparent, and *change* should mean not merely progress, it might quite as well be *reaction.*

In discussing the world religions it was felt that the probable familiarity of the readers of the book, with the effect of the modern age on Christianity, would warrant the omission of any discussion of that faith. So many books of merit are available that a brief chapter, such as would fit into the plan of the book, would seem to be uncalled for. A special phase of what is happening to Christianity is discussed in the chapter on Religion in Russia, quite the most interesting and significant development anywhere in Christendom.

It seemed most convenient, instead of trying to isolate the specific religions for separate treatment in every case, to consider the main geographical areas, distinguishing where possible what is happening to each religion. Thus Buddhism, one of the greatest religions, does not appear separately. This may have been a mistake, for it does leave almost untouched Hinayana Buddhism, which does not figure in the areas under discussion. Mahayana Buddhism does,

PREFACE

however, come in for attention in both China and Japan, and it is in these two countries that Buddhism seems to be most aware of the fact of a modern world. Had Buddhism as a whole been given separate treatment, the bulk of the discussion would still have centered in these northern lands.

A brief suggestive bibliography is supplied for each chapter for the benefit of those who may desire to go more deeply into the subject. To include the entire bibliography of materials examined or even used directly or indirectly would require much more space than could profitably be allowed, since it would call for the listing of literally hundreds of newspaper and magazine articles.

The sources of information have been various, books, newspapers, magazines, periodicals, in just so far as possible from the countries or religions represented. Care has been taken to allow for the peculiar bias that any given writer might be supposed to evince. In each case the chapter on a given religion or country has been submitted for criticism to persons representing the respective religions or peoples, or to recognized authorities in each particular field. Personal interviews with representatives of some of the religions or with specialists in their study have been of very great help in assembling the material. Persons too numerous to mention by name have given much time and thought to the discussion of the movements here treated. Two former students, Mr. Glen Bruner and Miss Louise Hobart, who prepared Masters' theses on "The Twentieth Century Revival of Buddhism in Japan" and "Modern Trends in the

PREFACE

Religions of China since the Revolution," respectively, unearthed not a little material of value to the writer. Particular recognition is due Rabbi Felix A. Levy, Rabbi Solomon Goldman and Rabbi Meyer Waxman for help on the chapter on Judaism; Swami Gnaneswaranda and Professor Malcom Pitt on India; Dr. Matthew Spinka on Russia; on China, Dr. James M. Yard and Miss Mary Kesler, both residents of China for many years and keen students of Chinese life; on the Moslem world, Sufi M. R. Bengalee, a Hindu Moslem; and on Japan, Dr. Charles W. Iglehart, long time resident of Japan in close touch with its religious life. Two Japanese graduate students recently come from Japan also read the chapter and gave valuable suggestions.

The nature of this study has made a large use of quoted material desirable. The author hereby makes grateful acknowledgement to the following publishers for permission to quote from their various publications. Footnotes are used throughout, giving credit wherever quotations appear: Charles Scribner's Sons, New York; Geo. H. Doran, New York; The Abingdon Press, New York; G. Allen and Unwin, London; G. P. Putnam and Sons, New York and London; The Oxford Press, London; The Yale University Press, New Haven; The Missionary Education Movement; The Edinburgh House Press, London; The University of London Press, London; Jonathan Cape, London; Selwyn and Blount, London; Kegan Paul Trench, Trubner and Co., London; Farrar and Rinehart, New York; Little Brown and

PREFACE

Co., Boston; A. A. Knopf, New York; Harper and Brothers, New York; and The Macmillan Co., New York.

The author, of course, is solely responsible for what is here included. He dares not hope that he has succeeded in capturing all the trends observable in these great religions or that he has represented them all in true proportion. He reports here, what, on the basis of all the materials available, appear to him to be the trends within the period. If this rapid survey proves of interest or help to any student of religions the writer will feel himself richly repaid.

CHARLES S. BRADEN.

Evanston, Ill.,
December, 1932.

CONTENTS

		PAGE
PREFACE		vii

CHAPTER
I.	FACTORS THAT PRODUCE CHANGE IN RELIGION	1
II.	TENDENCIES IN HINDUISM	20
III.	MODERN TENDENCIES IN CHINA	87
IV.	MODERN TENDENCIES IN JAPANESE RELIGIONS	136
V.	TWENTIETH-CENTURY TENDENCIES IN ISLAM	177
VI.	RELIGION IN RUSSIA	231
VII.	TENDENCIES IN JUDAISM	272
	APPENDIX. SUGGESTIONS FOR FURTHER READING	329
	INDEX	333

MODERN TENDENCIES IN
WORLD RELIGIONS

CHAPTER I

FACTORS THAT PRODUCE CHANGE IN RELIGION

ON the question as to whether or not religion ought to change there is very wide difference of opinion. But the fact that religion does actually change is undeniable. It is necessary only to look at the religion of any given people as it was one thousand years ago and as it is today, to see that a religion does not remain static. Indeed the whole history of religion reveals a continuous process of change in the world's religions whether in the more primitive or in the more advanced stages. By this it is not meant that the fundamental basis of religion is changing, that is, that basic urge expressed variously as "The search of the soul for God," or "The quest for the good life," or "The quest for a completely satisfying life." That eager questing after the supreme satisfactions, expressed in a thousand different ways at different cultural levels seems to be a constant in religion. What is meant is that the forms which religion takes, its organization, its techniques for securing the sought-for ends, its intellectual expressions these are always changing. Contrast for example the luxuriant polytheism of the Vedic age and its very simple this-worldly ideal of salvation, with

MODERN TENDENCIES

the developed religion of philosophic Hinduism, with its emphasis upon escape from the wheel of existence. Or again contrast the narrow tribal religion of the early Hebrews with that of the developed Christian church. Yet these represent definite lines along which development has taken place.

Religion has always changed. Must it always continue to change or have we arrived finally at a stage beyond which religious progress may not go? The experience of recent years is evidence that we have not. The whole conflict between modernism and fundamentalism within Christianity is a clear indication that change is still going on within religion. Or again, that much more fundamental struggle between what may be called the mechanistic view of the universe and the religious or spiritual view of the universe shows quite clearly that religion has not arrived at a place of finality. Almost every number of the major magazines of America and the continent carries articles that are symptomatic of the change that religion is undergoing. For example, one asks "Does America Need a New God?", another, "One God or Many Gods?" One writer produces a book on "Religion Coming of Age," another on the "Twilight of Christianity," another on "Do We Need a New Religion," still another on "An Emerging Faith."

Far from being settled and static and incapable of variation it is probable that no single age has witnessed more profound movements in the direction of change in religion than our own twentieth century. It may therefore be worth while to attempt some

CHANGE-PRODUCING FACTORS

analysis of the factors that underlie religious change. Once these factors are gathered together it may likewise be interesting to see to what extent they are actually operating within the sphere of the world's great religions to produce change. Evidences of change are apparent within traditional Christianity whether it be Protestantism or Catholicism. Evidences of change within Judaism are clear to every one who is in close contact with the Jewish group within America. Do other religions outside of America, outside of Europe, feel the effects of these change-producing forces? Is there a modernism within Islam, in Hinduism, in Shinto? Have the sacred scriptures of Buddhism, of the Sikhs, of the Taoists been affected by the same forces that have brought about a change of attitude toward the Bible? Is the idea of the supernatural undergoing any modification within age-old Confucianism, or in Hinduism? In short, it will be the task of this study to inquire into the modern trends that have developed within the present century within the great ethnic faiths of the world.

Is it possible to make any general statement regarding the basis of change in religion? The writer thinks it is. Broadly speaking, will not anything that produces human progress ultimately affect religion? The history of the world's faiths is replete with illustrations of religions that have failed through having proven unable to adapt themselves to new conditions and to meet the new needs developed through human progress. For, of course, whenever religion does fail to satisfy human needs it is doomed to oblivion. It

MODERN TENDENCIES

seems to be the essential nature of religion to satisfy the deepest human needs at any given stage of human development. A man is not religious without a reason. Through religion, if through nothing else, he seeks certain supreme ends which he conceives of as desirable. When religion either fails to secure these ends or when in the course of human development it becomes possible for man to achieve them without the aid of religion there is little hope of religion surviving. What happens historically is that as man develops, new needs seem constantly to arise which only religion in some modified form seems capable of satisfying. If this general statement be true, that human progress [1] necessarily entails religious change, then any analysis of the factors making for progress would be also factors in the production of religious hange. Without attempting the pretentious task of analyzing all the factors in human progress there are five factors that affect religion in a very direct way. They are:

1. Scientific discovery.
2. Economic change.
3. Political evolution.
4. Intellectual change.
5. Cultural interchange.

These factors, it need hardly be said, are in constant interplay and it would easily be possible to argue that some of them are of primary and others of only secondary importance—that, for example,

[1] It would be more accurate doubtless to speak not of human progress but of human change since progress implies going forward while as a matter of fact a retrogression is quite as fruitful in producing religious change.

CHANGE-PRODUCING FACTORS

cultural interpenetration is merely an agency in causing economic change or providing new incentive to political evolution; or again that economic change produces political reorganization. Once more, and with very great plausibility, all the others might be held to be secondary to the first, scientific discovery, if this be very broadly interpreted as meaning some new increment of knowledge with reference to the world and its control by human intelligence. But for the present purpose of the writer these serve adequately to explain the major changes that religion undergoes.

Science aims at a more complete understanding and control of the world in which man lives. So also does religion. Historically it has dealt chiefly with those invisible forces of the world of spirit as contrasted with matter. By it man has sought to bend the spirit world to his ends, indeed to secure by its help a control of the world of things which seemed too much for his puny physical powers. Since among primitive peoples so much of the world is mysterious and so many of the forces beyond man's physical control, religion (or magic, since the two are not easily distinguishable on the lower levels of life) plays a dominant rôle even in such matters as the securing of food, shelter and protection from the dangers that threaten human life.

But as the rational understanding of the world advanced, much that to an earlier day seemed mysterious and inexplicable, and therefore unamenable to other than spirit control—i.e. religion or magic, was seen to be perfectly natural, and easily subject

MODERN TENDENCIES

to control if only the proper techniques were employed. To take a single example, men learned that a good yield of grain was dependent rather upon deep stirring of the soil, proper rotation of crops or artificial fertilization of the soil than upon the proper blessing of a field or the performance of fertility rites at time of planting.

As a result, the advance of science has progressively delimited the sphere of religion. Gradually the world of the supernatural has yielded to the discovery of the scientist, and the world of the natural has expanded its frontiers until some have come to think that in truth there is nothing that is not natural and that ultimately the most recondite secrets of the universe will yield to the mind of man. There are those who dream of the ultimate control of such vast forces even as those which make the earth to quake. In such a world, religion, in so far as it is wrapped up in a belief in the supernatural—and nine-tenths of religion or more rests back upon such a basis—is bound to encounter difficulties. It must yield, however reluctantly, reach after reach that it once claimed as distinctively its own field, and consequently, unless it find new realms unpenetrated by science, must gradually lose its place of commanding importance in the lives of men. It is no part of our purpose here either to defend religion or to condemn it. The author is by no means one of those who fear that religion is lost. On the other hand, he inclines to be grateful that religion has been freed from an almost intolerable burden and released at last for its real mission among men. Here we are only indicat-

CHANGE-PRODUCING FACTORS

ing that scientific advance means *change* in religion if it is to survive and play an effective rôle in the unfolding life of humanity.

Scientific discovery has affected religion in still other ways. Perhaps none has been more far-reaching in its effect than the application of the scientific method to the study of religion itself. An outstanding example here is the application of the method of science as used in its approach to history and literature to the sacred book upon which so much in authoritarian religion rests. The so-called higher criticism or the historico-literary method of studying the Bible has had a tremendous effect upon both Judaism and Christianity. It has completely modified the nature of the authority of the Bible for those who accept its results. For many it has redeemed the book and given it a genuine place of power; for many others it has caused a total abandonment of its use as in any sense an authoritative book. Christian doctrine has suffered not a few important changes as a result of the changed attitude toward the Bible.

But perhaps of even greater consequence has been the persistent objective study of religious phenomena by the use of psychology. Religion in an older day was something to be experienced. It has become now an object of the most painstaking study on the part of trained psychologists who are attempting to find the explanation of what really happens in the experiencing of religion. They have analyzed faith and prayer and the mystic experience of the presence of God. Nothing within the whole field has been passed

MODERN TENDENCIES

by. Little wonder that its results have profoundly affected our concepts of religion.

Going beyond religion itself, certain schools of psychology have undercut the very bases upon which religion rests by denying the reality of the soul or the self as anything other than the product of purely mechanical forces operating within the human organism. Can religion come to terms with any such results of scientific study as this? Of course it remains to be proven that such psychologists are right in their conclusion; but for those who accept them, what place can religion have? Can it be sufficiently modified to meet such a test? Or must religion go? Many, convinced of the truth of a mechanistic behaviorism have said that it must go. We are here concerned only to note that it is in a world in which such changes in thought are occurring that religion must make itself at home if it is to survive at all. Scientific progress is an important factor in producing religious change.

Thus far we have stressed what might be thought of as the more theoretical phases of scientific advance. Its practical outworking in the modification of the world of human relations has far-reaching consequences as well, upon the forms which religion takes. In a real sense the changes which we note under the influence of economic, political, and intellectual change may, as indicated above, be traced to the increased understanding and control of the universe which we have called scientific progress.

Economic change has brought about many modifications within the sphere of religion. First of all it

CHANGE-PRODUCING FACTORS

has resulted in a changed sense of need on the part of humanity. Vast numbers of new wants and necessities arise as a result of economic change, and since religion finds one of its major functions in the satisfying of human needs it must also of necessity change. Through promoting a larger prosperity and well-being in the here and now, economic progress has steadily undermined human interest in the hereafter. It is a notable feature of present-day society that any appeal on the basis of a future life has lost a great part of its effectiveness. It has been universally observed that where life is hardest in the here and now, hope for a recompense in another world has burned brightest. When life was hard and burdensome, men dreamed of a future life in which they should have much of what was here denied them. When, on the other hand, the present is rich in comfort and satisfaction there is comparatively little concern for an on-going life in the future. Not that it of necessity drops out completely, but it occupies a steadily decreasing place of importance. Religion grows increasingly this-worldly in its emphasis. Through the general advance in the economic field, largely due to the introduction of new tools and machinery, very much of what in the early days seemed to be accessible only through the aid of divine power is now to be secured by the use of the proper machine or through the right sort of coöperation with the social group. In other words, the dependence upon some power outside human control has decreased in direct proportion as man's conquest over the physical forces of nature has gone forward. From the

MODERN TENDENCIES

fact that much which had formerly depended upon a divine source was found to be due to some controllable force, it has been an easy leap for many a mind to the belief that, ultimately, nothing lies outside the sphere of man's control, and that, therefore, the need for God or for religion is gone.

Then again, economic change has produced vast movements of population. This in turn has created new sets of social relations, given rise to new social problems by which religion has been inevitably affected. Take, for example, the enormous population movements due to the shifting of our civilization from an agricultural to an industrial type. Great numbers of people are flocking to the cities, great bodies of population are built up in brief periods of time. New needs, new problems, new ideals are the natural fruit of such re-groupings. Religion, it has been repeatedly said, finds its chief function in the satisfaction of human needs. It must therefore adapt itself to this new situation. By way of example, note that for the building and maintenance of the institutions which the new situation requires, new organizations must be effected, new approaches to the new problem have to be made, vast sums of money have to be secured. Religion thus tends to find itself tied up with those who can provide the money. It comes to seem, at least to those who have not, that religion is a class matter, a defender of the rich and the powerful and of the economic system which has given them their wealth and power. As a result, great numbers forsake it in any of its organized forms. If they are to be won back to religion, forces

CHANGE-PRODUCING FACTORS

within the church must make a desperate effort so to re-think and re-mold religion that it will meet the needs of those who labor and are without financial resources as well as those of the more fortunate social groups. It is yet too early to see with certainty just what will be the results of the rapid urbanization of the population on religion, but one has only to note a few of the glaring contrasts between religion as it is found in the rural districts and religion as it is found in the great cities, to make him wonder if there are not developing two widely distinct types of religion, an urban and a rural type.

Again, economic change has given man a degree of leisure that he has never before enjoyed. It has put within the reach of vast numbers of people the means of travel, of buying books, of possessing pictures, of owning a radio, of attending school, thus very greatly raising the general standard of culture of the group. Religion cannot but be affected by such changes. Great mobility has been given the population through the ability of even humble folk to possess a motor car. This promotes acquaintance with a much wider range of persons and things than in an earlier day when it was more difficult to get about. Out of such increased mobility grow enormous social problems with which religion is forced to reckon. Moral problems are raised which react seriously upon religion, particularly at the point where authority is invoked for their settlement. The problem of the observation of the sacred day, the Sabbath, is a case in point. That of diversions in general is another. Religion usually comes to terms

MODERN TENDENCIES

with the changing age, else it is apt to find itself outdistanced and soon forgotten. In a thousand ways economic progress has wrought change in religion. Then, political change is fruitful in producing religious evolution. One has only to glance at the theologies that have appeared within Christian history, and the organization of churches, to observe the very close correlation that exists between political organization and religion. It is necessary only to watch the little city state gods of ancient Egypt grow with the city until, for example, when Thebes becomes the capital, Amon-Re the Theban deity is recognized as chief god, or to watch Marduk in old Babylonia grow as the city grew until he stands at the very head of the pantheon, to see how close is the correlation between political organization and the forms which religion takes. It is no accident that men are today, in a relatively democratic age, beginning to talk about the democracy of God, nor is it accident that the great monarchical forms of religion persist today in the least democratic countries of the world. Is there any correlation, one wonders, between the fact that all the great dictatorships of the world today exist in countries where a monarchical faith has been the dominant form of religion? After the authority of a political power comes under review and men question its right to rule, it is very natural that in the realm of religion questions as to ultimate authority should also arise.

One of the most fruitful sources of religious change is that of inter-cultural contacts. The present age furnishes the best illustration of that fact.

CHANGE-PRODUCING FACTORS

What are some of the phenomena that should be classified here? First of all, probably the one thing that has produced the most radical changes in religions other than Christianity, within recent years, has been the deliberate attempt to propagate Christianity in other lands. The missionary enterprise, then, as an example of cultural interchange provides perhaps the best illustration that can be found. Here is a definite effort on the part of the Christian world to bring to people of other faiths a knowledge of Christianity. Missionaries have always sought after two types of result, one the direct conversion of the members of other faiths to Christianity. This has brought many millions of adherents to the faith; but Christianity's greatest effect has probably not been in direct proselytization, but rather the indirect effect upon the religions with which it has come in contact. Along with that, of course, go the changes that have come upon Christianity by reason of its contact with other religions. This latter phenomenon we are only recently taking largely into account. Illustrations without number might be given. Take two or three. Note the effect, for example, of the emphasis of the social note in Christianity, its philanthropic effort, its cure of the sick, its attempt to educate the people. It has had almost always the effect of stimulating the same type of thing within the religions native to the lands in which it has worked. This has been notably the case both in India and Japan. Buddhism in the latter country has from the standpoint of its social work become almost like Christianity. Thus in a practical way our Chris-

MODERN TENDENCIES

tianity has affected them. Then fundamental beliefs undergo change due to this sort of contact. The idea of God itself seems to have been very markedly affected among certain groups of people in India. The moral emphasis which has been so prominent in connection with Christianity has wakened in many of the great faiths a new or renewed interest in ethics. One finds, for example, Mohammedan teachers whose ethical stress in the present day is scarcely distinguishable from that of the Christian. Indeed, they are attempting in Europe and America to point out the moral lapses of Christianity and where Islam has gone beyond her.

Then again there is the largely increased travel between various countries of the world. While a few years ago it was the exception for others than those whose business required them to do so, to go to the Orient, now great numbers of Europeans and Americans every year travel about the lands of the Orient. Here they acquire new ideas and receive new impressions, at the same time creating impressions and sharing their own ideas with the people whom they visit the world over. Thus they become unconscious missionaries of the peculiar culture to which they belong. Their attitude, whether positive or negative, toward religion is very apt to register itself in the minds of the people of a different faith. Commercial interchange is never limited simply to the exchange of commodities. Along with this exchange goes also an exchange of ideas and the mutual modification of faiths. It is difficult for an American to reside for prolonged periods as a foreign commercial repre-

CHANGE-PRODUCING FACTORS

sentative in lands of another faith, without having his own attitude toward religion and perhaps some of his religious ideas considerably modified. It is a fact familiar to every one that the success of the propaganda of a foreign religion, such as Christianity, is very greatly helped or hindered by the character of the business and commercial residents who come from the same country as the missionary.

Another form of cultural interchange that has been markedly influential in producing change during this present century is the exchange of students, the most notable instance being that of Chinese students studying abroad. Thus the indemnity students who are sent every year to the United States by the Chinese government spend anywhere from three to six years in America, come in contact with its various types of social and religious life and return to their own country to become leaders of the thought of the Chinese people. A large number of them have gone into educational work and have thus been in intimate contact with the student life of China. They have had thus an unusual opportunity to influence Chinese thought. Others have gone to Europe, others to Japan. Out of it all, it is not strange that attitudes toward the old faiths in China have been very greatly modified.

But it is not alone students who have crossed our national and racial frontiers to affect and be affected by contacts with other peoples. Great intellectual and religious leaders are with increasing frequency going, often enough by specific invitation, to lecture in other lands. In American and European universities it is by no means unusual to sit at the feet of a great inter-

MODERN TENDENCIES

preter of an alien faith as he understands it, and there is a steady stream of European and American lecturers who carry the philosophic and religious ideas of the West to the Orient. Here is surely seed of religious change.

Probably no cultural interchange is more influential than that resulting from conflict or war. Many things were blamed on the World War. Few influences, however, have been more productive of changed attitudes toward religion than those growing out of that great conflagration. Thousands of Oriental people were transported to Europe, brought suddenly face to face with the so-called Christian civilization. They had a chance to see the actual everyday functioning of the Christianity which had been proclaimed to them by the emissaries from the West. It is little wonder that they were disillusioned and have raised many serious questions with reference to Christianity. But not only with reference to Christianity were questions raised. Religion itself and the validity of its claims have been very seriously challenged. If religion at its vaunted best had produced no better thing than this, was religion longer to be followed?

Then consider the interchange of literatures, the translation of books and magazines and stories from one language to another. The extensive use of moving pictures from other lands has had a remarkable effect. Who can estimate, for example, the results of the widespread showing before women of Moslem lands pictures depicting the utter freedom of women in the West? Or who can estimate the effect upon,

CHANGE-PRODUCING FACTORS

say the Chinese people, of the widespread circulation of films which carry the attitude of depreciation toward religion or religious organizations so frequently found in current films? It is yet too early to predict what may come out of the radio as a means of cultural interchange. Possibly here the difference of language, until television becomes a fact, will prevent it from being so widely influential as have been the moving pictures. But the ease of communication by means of the telephone and the wireless is to be charged doubtless with very far-reaching effects in the direction of religious change. Thus cultural interchange is a potent factor in a wide variety of religious change that is taking place all over the world.

And finally, changes in the intellectual realm which make for widespread intellectual progress are always accompanied by a religious change. What is meant here has already been foreshadowed in what was said with reference to the change of religion due to the more theoretical aspects of scientific advance. Any serious changes in the philosophical world are apt to produce corresponding changes in religion. Take the whole modern tendency in the direction of a mechanistic philosophy. How it has come as a challenge to the current religious thought of the day and how eagerly religionists have grasped at such new foreshadowings of a spiritual interpretation of the universe by science itself, as evidenced in such books as those of Robert A. Millikan and Professor A. S. Eddington! Or take the whole modern field of psychology, how the behavioristic school has affected the thinking of many religious people! And what a

MODERN TENDENCIES

comfort religious thinkers find when well-known psychologists take a distinct stand on the side of religion, which had been threatened by the new psychology! Any far-reaching modification in our conception of the universe is apt to entail corresponding changes in religion.

Then, one final item. The widespread education of the masses of people throughout the world is having a very marked effect upon religion as conceived of among the masses. Perhaps no more important thing is happening in that land of kaleidoscopic change, China, than the great mass education movement which is almost overnight bringing to numberless Chinese the ability to read. By reason of the simplification of the language and the writing with only a thousand word characters, reading has become a privilege not only for the educated man but for the coolie. China will bear the marks of it in religion as well as socially and politically. Turkey is beginning to experience something of the same thing among its women. Village schools are multiplying in India; throughout the length and breadth of Latin America illiteracy is rapidly passing. Religion already begins to feel the effect of the incoming of new ideas to which these people had been total strangers.

Thus we have seen that religion does change as a result of a great variety of contributing factors, scientific, economic, political, inter-cultural and intellectual. Practically every land in the world which has emerged at all into a civilization is feeling as never before the interplay of these vast forces. Only one who is blind to what is going on in the world at

CHANGE-PRODUCING FACTORS

present or who, in the interest of some ancient doctrine, deliberately declines to believe that religion can change, will be surprised as he follows through the succeeding chapters to see that religion not only in America and Europe but religion all over the world is going through a sometimes violent, sometimes slow, but nevertheless sure process of change.

CHAPTER II

TENDENCIES IN HINDUISM

INDIA, known affectionately to something over three hundred million people as Mother India, has, by common consent, been considered perhaps the most religious of all the lands in the world. Thirty-three million gods, every one of them worshipped by some of the inhabitants of that great subcontinent, make up the pantheon of this remarkable people. Extreme devotion to some god or other or to some religious ideal, the wildest extravagance of ceremony and ritual, the most notable consecration to so-called spiritual matters and the most profound speculation with reference to the world and its meaning, have characterized for centuries this strange mixture of races which is modern India.

How fares religion among Indians? Isolated, to a degree, from the main currents of the world's life, yet inevitably of these later years experiencing the rapid penetration of the forces that have made the West, what changes has religion undergone? Has it been able to remain stable, unmoved, in the face of the changing world?

What Is Hinduism?

To record the degree of change in Hinduism is a very difficult task, made so by the very vagueness of

IN HINDUISM

the meaning of the term "Hinduism." What constitutes Hinduism? Is it some particular belief?—but Hindus hold the most widely divergent beliefs. No one has yet been able to compass the totality of Hinduism in a single definition. Professor Radhakrishnan says:

"There has been no such thing as a uniform, stationary, unalterable Hinduism whether in point of belief or practice. Hinduism is a movement, not a position; a process, not a result; a growing tradition, not a fixed revelation. Its past history encourages us to believe that it will be found equal to any emergency that the future may throw up, whether on the field of thought or of history." [1]

Professor C. R. Das has written of it thus:

"No definition is possible, for the very good reason that Hinduism is absolutely indefinite. It is really an anthropological process to which, by a strange irony of fate, the name of 'religion' has been given. Starting from the Vedas, embodying the customs and ideas of one or a few tribes, it has like a snowball gone on ever getting bigger and bigger in the course of ages, as it has steadily gone on absorbing from the customs and ideas of all peoples with whom it has come into contact, down even to the present day. It rejects nothing. It is all-comprehensive, all-absorbing, all-tolerant, all-complacent, all-compliant. Every type of mind can derive nourishment from it. It has its spiritual and its material, its esoteric and exoteric, its subjective and objective, its rational and irrational, its pure and impure aspects. It may be compared to a huge irregular multilateral figure. One side for the practical, another for the severely moral, another for the devotional and the

[1] *The Hindu View of Life* (London: G. Allen and Unwin, 1927), pp. 129-30.

MODERN TENDENCIES

imaginative, another for the supremely ascetic, another for the sensuous and the sensual—even the downright carnal—and another for the philosopher and the speculative." [2]

A still more recent writer, Professor Sarma, says of it:

"Hinduism is rather a name given to a league of religions. In its comprehensive and tolerant fold we find all types of religion from the highest to the lowest, for it does not force all minds into one groove. It frankly recognizes the various grades of culture that obtain in the community." [3]

Still another writer characterizes it thus:

"Provided a man follows the round of rituals, ceremonies and a number of social functions laid down by the scriptures and traditions, he is a Hindu, no matter whether he is an atheist, a free thinker, an agnostic or skeptic—no matter whether he believes in one God or many gods or no god at all." [4]

How is one to judge change within a religion at once so complex and elastic! The answer seems to be that it will be found chiefly in terms of social change, since the one common element that binds the mass of Hindus together is not belief but practice of certain social customs; in their own phrase, "the Dharma." Religious ideas are unquestionably in a state of flux in India and we shall show some evidence of this change, but the vastly more important changes are

[2] *Hinduism* (Madras: G. A. Natesan, 1924), p. 45.
[3] *Primer of Hinduism*, quoted by *Indian Social Reformer*, Vol. 40, p. 83.
[4] R. C. Adhikary, "Present Religious Situation in India," *Journal of Religion*, Vol. 6, p. 166.

IN HINDUISM

to be found in the realm of social organization and practice. Here the modern age, which is causing such revolution in the religious thinking of other peoples, is having its deepest effect. That thought and practice are bound up together none will seriously question, and that corresponding changes within the thought-life of particular groups in India will come about as a result of accepted change in social organization and practice seems clear.

That there is a good deal of unrest and uncertainty in the minds of, particularly, the educated Indians appears in statements such as the following, which are simply samples of a sort of utterance that is found very commonly in the Indian press. Mr. R. C. Adhikary, writing on the present religious situation in India, declares:

"Hinduism is passing through a period of renaissance. Mohammedanism is in a state of stagnation. Christianity is in a state of stupor. The minor creeds emanating from Hinduism are characterized by a tendency toward reabsorption into the original mother creed." [5]

Or again a writer in the *Indian Social Reformer* asserts:

"In India there is a tremendous revival of religion. There is danger ahead, as well as glory; for revival sometimes breeds fanaticism, sometimes goes to extreme, so that often it is not even in the power of those who start the revival to control it when it has gone beyond a certain length.

"It is better therefore to be forewarned. We have

[5] "Present Religious Situation in India," *Journal of Religion*, Vol. 6, pp. 163-73.

MODERN TENDENCIES

to find our way between the Scylla of old superstitious orthodoxy and the Charybdis of materialism." [6]

Contrary opinions are found which serve only to emphasize the fact that something is happening, even though those actually on the ground are not able to appreciate exactly what is going on. An eminent writer declares at one moment:

"If Hinduism lives to-day, it is due to them (certain principles) but it lives so little. Listlessness reigns now where life was once like a bubbling spring. We are to-day drifting, not advancing, waiting for the future to turn up. There is a lack of vitality, a spiritual flagging. Owing to our political vicissitudes, we ignored the law of growth. In the great days of Hindu civilisation it was quick with life, crossing the seas, planting colonies, teaching the world as well as learning from it. In sciences and arts, in trade and commerce it was not behind the most advanced nations of the world till the middle of this millennium. To-day we seem to be afraid of ourselves, and are therefore clinging to the shell of our religion for self-preservation. The envelope by which we try to protect life checks its expansion. The bark which protects the interior of a tree must be as living as that which it contains. It must not stifle the tree's growth, but must expand in response to the inner compulsion. An institution appropriate and wholesome for one stage of human development becomes inadequate and even dangerous when another stage has been reached." [7]

And two pages later in the same book, in the very closing paragraph:

"After a long winter of some centuries, we are to-day in one of the creative periods of Hinduism. We are be-

[6] *Indian Social Reformer*, Vol. 40 (April 26, 1930), p. 554.
[7] S. Radhakrishnan, *op. cit.*, p. 128.

IN HINDUISM

ginning to look upon our ancient faith with fresh eyes. We feel that our society is in a condition of unstable equilibrium. There is much wood that is dead and diseased that has to be cleared away. Leaders of Hindu thought and practice are convinced that the times require, not a surrender of the basic principles of Hinduism, but a re-statement of them with special reference to the needs of a more complex and mobile social order. Such an attempt will only be the repetition of a process which has occurred a number of times in the history of Hinduism. The work of readjustment is in process. Growth is slow when roots are deep. But those who light a little candle in the darkness will help to make the whole sky aflame." [8]

The Editor of the *Indian Social Reformer*, in an article entitled "The Religious Crisis," writes as follows:

"It is becoming increasingly clear every day that the country is faced with a religious crisis whose consequences may be more far-reaching than those of the political or social upheaval. The demand of the *antyajas* to be admitted to Hindu temples is being pressed all over the country and must be conceded at no distant date. The columns of the Bombay Chronicle are filled day by day by letters from Parsi protestants who inveigh against the sacerdotalism of the fire-temples. Less prominent but not less real is a parallel movement among Mohammedans to question the authority of the priestly heads of the several sects and castes of Islam in India. Among Indian Christians likewise there is an insistent feeling against the isolation from Indian religious tradition which has been imposed upon them by the foreign character of the Christian Churches in India. In every case, however, the protest is not against religion, though there is a small group of anti-religionists

[8] *Ibid.*, p. 130.

MODERN TENDENCIES

also, but against the corruptions of religion. The aim of the protestants is not to demolish religion but to demolish the barriers which have been erected in the name of religion between man and man, and between man and God. This is a healthy sign of the times, and under wise guidance, this movement is likely to do more to promote peace and harmony between our communities than other and more self-conscious attempts to remove differences." [*]

The Tendencies

It seems to the writer that it is possible to discern at the present time the following main tendencies in Hinduism: first, a general tendency toward irreligion—something unusual in the long history of India; second, opposition to priestly influence and to the very existence of that group which has been for centuries the most revered of all India's social groups, the Fakir or Holy Man; third, a rather strong reactionary tendency not unlike the Fundamentalist movement within Christianity; fourth, a rationalizing tendency which seeks to modernize the Hindu faith, making it conform to the modern scientific demands that are made upon it; fifth, a marked syncretic tendency expressing itself in a number of different forms; sixth, and by far the most important of all, a tendency toward social change that is nothing short of revolutionary. The most notable changes here are to be found in the position of women, particularly in matters relating to early marriage, divorce, purdah and widowhood; the breakdown of caste, particularly with reference to the untouch-

[*] "The Religious Crisis," *Indian Social Reformer*, Vol 40 (Oct. 26, 1929), p. 113.

IN HINDUISM

ables; and finally the reform of certain religious practices which have failed to justify themselves to the growing moral sense of the leaders of India, the most notable example here being the attempted abolition of Temple prostitution. How these social changes may be expected to react upon religious ideas will appear as our discussion proceeds.

Before proceeding, however, to the detailed evidence for each of these tendencies it will be worth while to call to mind the forces that have played upon India for the last century or more and which have had as their inevitable result these far-reaching symptoms of change.

While the present study attempts to limit itself rather strictly to the tendencies observable within the present century, it will be readily recognized that the causes underlying these tendencies go much farther back in history. Merely to enumerate the main contributing factors without discussing them in any detail will help toward an understanding of what is now happening in the religious life and thought of India.

Influences Affecting India's Religions

Seven main influences may be noted as contributing to the present situation: first, centuries of foreign domination by European powers, but particularly the influence of Great Britain's rule which has brought about the introduction of many foreign cultural elements into India's life, not the least of which is, second, western education. For this the British régime is not alone responsible, though the govern-

MODERN TENDENCIES

ment support of education has been constant and generous and its general characteristics determined by government. Not a little of the actual educational work, however, has been performed by the missionaries from Christian lands. This is, of course, a part of that much more extensive influence which may be characterized as, third, missionary propaganda from the West with its direct, as well as indirect, introduction of a religion foreign to Hinduism. Fourth, the introduction of machinery from the West. This has not proceeded nearly so far as in some oriental lands, notably Japan, yet the effects of industrialization are very clearly apparent to the student of Indian affairs. Probably no more important factor is to be discovered in the breakdown of established social institutions which entails a change of religious thought, than this mechanization of Indian life. Mr. Gandhi has seen very clearly whither it would lead his people and has thrown his full strength into the struggle to maintain in India those values which are threatened by its incursion. Fifth, the experience of the World War which brought India into a more intimate contact with Europe and gave her a new perspective in which to see the peoples of the West. This experience, confirming as it did certain observations with reference to western powers which had first grown out of the Russo-Japanese War, in which an oriental nation had successfully defeated a great European country in a trial at arms, had not a little to do with the intenser phases of, sixth, the new nationalism in India. This, perhaps more than any other single factor in the immediate present, is determining the

IN HINDUISM

tendencies in religious thought and practice. Seventh, the interchange of ideas between the East and West produced, in the case of India, chiefly through India's ability to read whatever is available in the English language; the exchange of professors between eastern and western universities, and finally the increasing number of Indians who travel and study in the West. Probably the influence of the moving picture, carrying as it does the supposed life of the West, ought to be noted in this connection. It can hardly fail to influence, for example, the outlook of the women of India when they see the liberty which the pictures attribute to their western sisters. Just how these various factors have contributed to the modification of India's religious life and thought we will attempt to indicate as we go forward with the study.

If in a catalogue such as the foregoing the influences seem to be mostly from outside India herself, let it not be supposed that there has been lacking creative thought on the part of Hindus themselves that has led her in the direction of change. Apparently self-generated reforms or advances in her thought as a result of the appearance of great independent Indian thinkers have occurred too frequently in the long course of Indian history for a modern observer to suppose that she must of necessity owe her twentieth-century changes in religion and thought solely to external stimuli. But in the closely interrelated world of today it is not easy to isolate any single responsible factor. And, after all, it is upon the Indian mind that the impulses strike. The re-

MODERN TENDENCIES

sponses, one will expect to find characteristic of the peculiar genius of India.

The Radical Reaction

It is somehow difficult to associate irreligion with India. To be sure there have been small groups from time to time in the long history of her evolution who, from the standpoint of traditional ideas of religion in the West, would have seemed to be irreligious. The Charvakas are perhaps the most notable example, yet even they today are considered a branch of Hinduism. However, with the fierce play upon her of the multiple material forces that have wrought so much havoc to the religious life of other peoples, it is hardly to be expected that India's religion should prove invulnerable. One finds frequent lament for the current irreligion or anti-religious attitude on the part of, particularly, the younger radicals in India. Dr. MacNicol, a long-time missionary of the Anglican Church in India, in an article [10] which was characterized by the editor of the *Modern Review*, a leading Indian magazine, as a "very penetrating study of the religious situation in India" offers convincing evidence of the present situation in this regard. He quotes a recent writer in the periodical of the Rama Krishna Mission under the title "Whither India," as declaring that the greatest danger to religion in the present period is from leaders whose aim is "to banish religion from India." "With this writer's fears and forebodings we must fully sym-

[10] Nicol MacNicol, "A Christian Looks at India," *International Review of Missions*, Vol. 18 (Jan. 1929), pp. 59 ff.

IN HINDUISM

pathize," says Dr. MacNicol. "It will be a disaster not alone for India but for the world if this people should abandon the controlling interest of all her past history and should shift her course now from spirituality to secularism. In seeking to avert the catastrophe the Christian will stand side by side with the adherent of the Rama Krishna sect." The clue to this new development he finds in the shifting of the center of interest from religion to politics. "Religion," he writes, "no longer has a central place in the life of educated India that it once had. It has been degraded to become a means to a secular end. It has been deliberately so used by political leaders . . . and is frankly spoken of by some as though it were little more. As a consequence the central thing in Hinduism has become Sangathan (or disciplined Hindu organization) rather than Sannyasa (the traditional Hindu ideal of abandonment of the world) and everything in religion is made subordinate to . . . 'the toning up of Indian muscles.'" The acceptance of what he calls the creed of secularism is having a fatal influence not alone upon Hinduism but Islam and Christianity as well. When it was advocated that religion be taught in the schools, there was violent protest from many quarters. One wrote, "Of all the people in the world it is we Indians that require more and more materialism. We have had too much of religion. That accounts for our position today as a bankrupt nation." It is doubtless this widespread feeling, thinks Dr. MacNicol, which has caused Pandit Motilal Nehru and his fellow nationals to exclude religion from their concern in the forma-

MODERN TENDENCIES

tion of a new constitution for India and to apply themselves to the task of "establishing a secular state. One group among the young political leaders . . . have definitely set before themselves as one of their aims 'to free India from the grip of religion.' " [11]

As a result of the invasion of secularism he declares that the present generation has lowered the whole moral and religious level in the case of certain circles of the community He quotes Gandhi as saying: "I am inundated with letters from young men who write frankly about their evil habits and about the void that unbelief has made in their lives. No mere medical advice can bring them relief. I can only tell them that there is no way but that of surrender to a trust in God and his Grace." But, continues Dr. MacNicol, even where no such evil spirits have entered and desecrated the empty places "there has been everywhere grievous loss from the loss of faith. . . . Today the barriers are down and secularism especially has come in like a flood." [12] If at the present time such an attitude toward religion is chiefly to be found among the more highly educated classes, it does not require a prophet to foresee that in the course of time, unless some strong counteracting agencies are put at work, the same ideas will filter down into the thinking of the masses of illiterate India. Two or three facts observable seem to point in this direction; first, the growing tendency to discredit the Holy Men or Fakirs and, second, a marked hostility to the priestly class expressed in definite anti-priest movements in some of the great

[11] *Ibid.*, p. 63.   [12] *Ibid.*, p. 64.

IN HINDUISM

cities. The importance particularly of the first of these tendencies can only be appreciated when one understands how highly revered the Holy Men of India have been. One needs but to recall that it is of the very essence of Brahmanism for the faithful Hindu to enter in old age upon the life of poverty and asceticism. Theoretically every twice-born Hindu passes through the stages of student, householder, forest dweller and mendicant. Nothing has been more characteristic of the soul of India than the high regard she has had for those who have followed the Hindu ideal to its logical end. Doubtless there have been many abuses by the mendicants who have found it an easier life than that of sharing the hard work of the world and maintaining not only themselves but dependents. It is common now, according to Dr. MacNicol, to hear "Indians even denouncing this virtue of spirituality as mere sloth and the source of all their woes. It is this newer attitude which stirs Govinda Das in his recent book on Hinduism to exclaim: 'It is the doughty warrior in life's battles who safely crosses the ocean of Samsara (the round of rebirth) and not the cross-legged weakling (the Orthodox attitude of meditation).'"[13]

A prominent Indian leader,[14] discussing the problem of begging in India, wrote not long since:

"We Indians have put a premium on pauperism; we have given the mendicant a place in our religion. We

[13] Quoted by Nicol MacNicol, "A Christian Looks at India," *International Review of Missions*, Vol. 18, p. 68.
[14] The Late Dewan Bohadur, A. K. Pai, *Indian Social Reformer*, Vol. 40 (April 19, 1930), p. 539.

uphold the Sadhus and the so-called religious mendicants as a means to an end . . . we consider the beggar as a means of salvation . . . any stern measures to deal with the religious mendicant raise the wrath of the orthodox Hindu who has a notorious weakness for the Fakir or Sadhu. The Fakir is the prince of beggars . . . carefully considered the Sadhus and Fakirs are a source of nuisance, mischief, and in some cases even crime. . . . The prudent course to take is to teach the people to throw off the thralldom of old-world-ideas, to carry home to them that an idle beggar is a pest, even if he be a Fakir. . . . It has been said to us that we are the slaves of the gods; let it not be said of us that we are the slaves of Sadhus. I therefore urge on my Hindu brethren not to be Sadhu ridden. To encourage Sadhus in their profession is not compassion but superstition.

Evidence of the anti-priest movement is to be found in various articles, typical of which are two, a rather elaborate defense of the priesthood by the editor of the *Indian Social Reformer,* and a writer in the *Journal of Religion* on the present religious situation in India. The direction the attacks upon the priesthood take may be inferred from following statements from the *Indian Social Reformer:*

"It is far easier even to wipe out priesthood from society than to reform it and it is moreover far more spectacular, but that would suggest to the organizers of the movement who are moved by a real need that a more lasting service could be rendered to the community by a serious attempt to improve the type of priests. After all, the priests in an Indian community are not worse than the other members, and the fact that the calling has fallen into disrepute ought to attract men of the very best ideals to raise it."[15]

[15] *Indian Social Reformer,* Vol. 40, p. 454.

IN HINDUISM

"Again, the activities of the priest in modern times have been considerably curtailed. Whilst before he also served as the doctor, the teacher, and in several other capacities, now he is solely concerned with the spiritual side of those who frequent his worship, but with the lessening of his work we are sorry to see that he has not improved. On the contrary the average run of priests in every community has reached so low a level that men of high ideals have not only held aloof from places of worship but have even abstained from joining the profession. This, undoubtedly, is a serious state of things, and Bombay has been hearing much recently of an association for abolishing the priest or, as the organizers of the association call him, 'the middle man in religion.'" [16]

The other article declares:

"Hindus are increasingly discontented to allow the study of ritual practice of religion to be confined to the priestly class, for religion is the common property of all. During the decade ending with the census of March, 1921, the number of Brahmin priests decreased by slightly more than fifty per cent, a striking evidence of the trend of current movements." [17]

Liberal or Reformed Hinduism

The third tendency to be noted is that of a thoroughgoing reforming movement which, while radical in some respects, is nevertheless to be sharply differentiated from the first tendency to irreligion by the fact that it is deeply and consciously religious. The beginning of this reforming movement within Hinduism goes far back of the present century, in-

[16] *Ibid.*, p. 453.
[17] A. C. Woodburne, "Present Religious Situation in India," *Journal of Religion*, Vol. 3, p. 391.

MODERN TENDENCIES

deed well-nigh to the beginning of the nineteenth century, and finds its chief person in the figure of Rajah Ramohan Roy who, in the second quarter of the century, influenced largely by his contacts with Christianity and his study of other religions, founded what has since been known as the Brahma Samaj. The new movement underwent many modifications during the succeeding years of the century and broke up into various branches, but something of the same reforming spirit still characterizes it. To be sure, under the stress of the recent nationalistic urge, there have been concessions to formerly severely condemned practices in individual instances which clearly illustrate the influence of political change on religion. There comes a complaint as voiced in the *Indian Social Reformer:*

"The message that blessed are the poor has not been taught with sufficient emphasis in the Brahma Samaj. We are afraid to be poor. The western dread of poverty has taken possession of us. Things of the world have got precedence over our spiritual blessings in our thought and imagination. Thus we have been seeking the pleasures of life and the riches of this earth too eagerly; and naturally there has grown in our midst an apathy towards religion. The remedy for this state of things lies in the emphasis we put upon the need of spiritual culture. We require amongst us a prophet who can preach by his life—"Seek ye first the kingdom of God and his righteousness and all these things shall be added unto you."[18]

And again in the article by Dr. MacNicol cited above, declaring that the Brahma Samaj had always

[18] *Indian Social Reformer*, Vol. 40 (June 7, 1930), p. 654.

IN HINDUISM

opposed idolatry and forbidden its practice in their institution, the writer says:

"Today Hinduism and idolatry have returned, not as a result of any religious conviction but because they have become a flag of patriotism, and so Saraswati must be worshipped by the students even in the Rajah Ramohan Roy Hostel of the College."[19]

Never very numerous in comparison with the vast population of India, the Samaj and its various branches has proven one of the most influential groups in the whole of India, particularly in the direction of social change, having stood constantly through the years as champions of reform in such practices as child marriage and widow re-marriage. As has been suggested already, the movement was largely influenced by Christian ideas; indeed, the movement might well be discussed under the syncretic tendency. It is distinctly monotheistic and non-idolatrous; it gives a very high place to Jesus and maintains an exalted regard for human values which has been lacking in the general Hindu faith. The growth of the movement has been very slow and it has never attracted the popular masses. Its appeal has rather been to the highly educated, thoughtful portion of the Indian community, numbering among its adherents some of the foremost thinkers and writers that India has produced. Its influence upon Indian life has been wholly out of proportion to its numbers.

But apart from these more definitely organized

[19] Nicol MacNicol, *The International Review of Missions*, Vol. 18, p. 59.

MODERN TENDENCIES

movements of reform, there are individual thinkers and leaders in India who, while conscious of many of the imperfections and disabilities of the historic faith, are seeking nevertheless to find within it, by some kind of rationalization, a faith adequate to meet the demands of Indian life in the present age. No better example of this can be found than that of Professor Radhakrishnan in his *Hindu View of Life,* a series of lectures delivered before a European audience attempting to set forth the values and ideals of his faith. Professor Radhakrishnan is conscious, of course, of many of those elements within Hinduism which seem to the western mind so foreign to what they have regarded as religion, but he goes behind the actual practices of the day and reveals what seem to him the high values that they hold. His discussion, for example, of such phases of Hinduism as caste, karma, rebirth and world abandonment, is most illuminating. He very frankly admits mistakes, excesses, abuses, but these are excrescences to be gotten rid of, while underneath there are solid, universal principles that are to be held to without hesitation. His attitude toward the holiest of all the books of India is significant and betrays the marks of a thoroughly modern mind. He writes:

"The Hindu attitude to the Vedas is one of trust tempered by criticism, trust because the beliefs and forms which helped our fathers are likely to be of use to us also; criticism because, however valuable the testimony of past ages may be, it cannot deprive the present age of its right to inquire and sift the evidence. Precious

IN HINDUISM

as are the echoes of God's voice in the souls of men of long ago, our regard for them must be tempered by the recognition of the truth that God has never finished the revelation of His wisdom and love. Besides, our interpretation of religious experience must be in conformity with the findings of science. As knowledge grows, our theology develops. Only those parts of the tradition which are logically coherent are to be accepted as superior to the evidence of the senses and not the whole tradition." [20]

He recognizes that change in religion is inevitable. Indeed, the whole history of Hinduism reveals a steady movement, and the only thing that a modern need fear is that it become static.

"Religion and philosophy, life and thought, the practical and the theoretical . . . form the eternal rhythm of the spirit. We rise from life to thought and return from thought to life in a progressive enrichment which is the attainment of ever higher levels of reality. Tradition is something which is forever being worked out anew and recreated by the free activity of its followers. What is built forever is forever building. If a tradition does not grow, it only means that its followers have become spiritually dead." [21]

Or, again:

"Leaders of Hindu thought and practice are convinced that the times require not a surrender of the basic principles of Hinduism but a restatement of them with special reference to the needs of a more complex and mobile social order. Such an attempt will only be the repetition of a process which has occurred a number of times in the history of Hinduism." [22]

[20] *The Hindu View of Life*, pp. 18-19.
[21] *Ibid.*, p. 21.
[22] *Ibid.*, p. 130.

MODERN TENDENCIES

Or once more, regarding caste, he says:

"While caste has resulted in much evil, there are some sound principles underlying it. Our attitude to those whom we are pleased to call primitive must be one of sympathy. The task of the civilized is to respect and foster the live impulses of backward communities and not destroy them. Society is an organism of different grades, and human activities differ in kind and significance. But each of them is of value so long as it serves the common end. Every type has its own nature which should be followed. No one can be at the same time a perfect saint, a perfect artist, and a perfect philosopher. Every definite type is limited by boundaries which deprive it of other possibilities. The worker should realise his potentialities through his work, and should perform it in a spirit of service to the common weal. Work is craftsmanship and service. Our class conflicts are due to the fact that a warm living sense of unity does not bind together the different groups." [22]

Completely aware of the implications of modern science for religion, this type of religious thinker has no fear of science. Rather he finds in modern science simply a confirmation, in the realm of the material, of what religion long ago revealed regarding the nature of the universe and its laws. Hinduism, with no such hard and fast dogmatic teaching regarding the creation of the world, has no difficulty with the doctrine of evolution as has Christianity. Each new discovery seems but to reveal anew the truth of the religious teaching regarding the world. An example of this complete recognition of harmony between religious and scientific thought is to be found in the following:

[22] *Ibid.*, pp. 127-28.

IN HINDUISM

"Who could have thought fifteen or twenty years ago that the Vedanta's description of Brahman as having eyes, ears, hands, feet, reception and sensation everywhere, would be satisfied in what science calls ether. You make an etheric stir here and you at once get a response in Australia; you make a commotion in ether here and it immediately causes a similar commotion in the north of Scandinavia. The scientists' experiments, carried out heretically, establish the truths of religion and philosophy." [24]

"Fundamentalist" Hinduism

The fourth tendency is that of a reactionary Fundamentalist attitude toward religion and the attacks made upon it. It is clearly a defense reaction provoked by the tendencies already noted above. This tendency, of course, is not new or peculiar to the twentieth century. Whenever any new movement threatens, there is always a reactionary response in any religion. The nineteenth century reaction to the modern attacks upon the Scriptures, upon supernaturalism, and other phases of their faith brought into being a number of strong movements designed to protect the faith. Farquhar in his *Modern Religious Movements in India* lists more than a dozen such movements that sprang into being between 1875 and 1913, a number of them after 1895, the year which marked the real beginnings of modern nationalism in India, and those movements which did not arise as a direct result of nationalist feeling have been very considerably accentuated by the growth of nationalism. The early years of the nineteenth

[24] *Indian Social Reformer*, Vol. 40, p. 618.

MODERN TENDENCIES

century were years of foreign domination, the introduction of western education and western thought which had as its result a general tendency to undermine the Indian appreciation of the values in their own ancient culture. The end of the nineteenth century saw the beginning of the resurgence of India's pride in her own past, and religion as one of the great cultural features of her past felt distinctly the effects of this reawakening. The most vigorous of all these numerous movements was the Arya Samaj, which was founded in 1875 upon the platform "back to the Vedas" and from that day forward, with almost a fanatical zeal, the members of the Samaj have been preaching their doctrine.

The Arya Samaj represents a very interesting combination of interests. They are exceedingly forward looking in some ways. Their appreciation of human values far outruns that of orthodox Hinduism. Indeed, it may be said that the Samaj accepts many of the highest values of Christianity and western culture but refuses to recognize that these are foreign products. Rather, they declare, all of the best in modern thought and life is to be found in India's ancient scriptures, the Vedas, if one will only read them understandingly. Thus one may find in the literature of more than 1000 B.C. foreshadowings of the latest scientific inventions, such as the aëroplane, the automobile, the radio. It must be confessed that some expert guidance is necessary in order to discover all of these things, but this is provided for by a rendering of the Vedas by their great founder, Dayananda. Unlike the Brahma Samaj,

IN HINDUISM

the movement has grown and expanded until it numbers over half a million as over against some six thousand for the former. It increased over ninety per cent in its membership during the decade from 1911 to 1921. It is very apparent that the strong national feeling is recording itself here. As may well be imagined, this and like movements are by no means hospitable to the missionary enterprise. What need of missions has India when her own sacred books contain all that is needful for modern life? Indeed, the most formidable opposition which the Christian missionary enterprise meets in the present period is from the Arya Samajists.

While the Samaj, together with certain other movements which exalt the values of their own Indian culture, are socially minded and are advocating many needed social reforms there are, unfortunately, among the orthodox group of Hindus those whose devotion to ancient Hinduism is no less, but who have not yet caught the vision of a socially reconstructed India and these have opposed at every turn the efforts of the reforming group to change the age of marriage, the re-marriage of widows, the abolition of Temple prostitution and like reforms. They have held mass meetings, have written articles, and otherwise attempted to convince the public that in the prosecution of such reforms the very basis of Hinduism is being seriously threatened. In a later connection certain of these manifestoes will be quoted.

A comparatively recent movement of this sort is that known as the Mahasabha. While not in sym-

MODERN TENDENCIES

pathy with the extreme obscurantist position of some of the orthodox, it is nevertheless much concerned about the increasing numbers that are forsaking Hinduism for Christianity or Islam. Its major objective seems to be the reconversion of those who have left the faith. This in itself reflects a change in Hinduism, for extreme orthodoxy would have no part in the reclamation of one who had thus broken away. It is not difficult to see here the nationalist influence. What is deprecated is not so much the separation from Hinduism as a religion but as a *national* religion. Other religions are thought of as denationalizing their adherents since they are foreign faiths.

Syncretism

The fifth tendency, that toward syncretism, has already been foreshadowed in the mention of certain movements. It is worth while noting that syncretism takes various forms. There is the unconscious taking over of certain values or practices from one religion by the other; for example, Hinduism from Christianity or Christianity from Hinduism. Then there is the conscious appropriation of the practices or values of one by the other through deliberate choice; and finally there is the purposive blending of elements taken from various religions into what is thought of as a new religion. Theosophy may be taken as an illustration of this latter. All these varieties of syncretism are found in Hinduism.

Hinduism is by its very nature disposed to syncretism. It has been likened by some to a great

IN HINDUISM

sponge which is capable of absorbing into itself many foreign elements. Indeed, it was thus that Hinduism came to its present state. A good example of this capacity to absorb may be noted in the Hindu doctrine of incarnation. Accustomed as the Indian is to the thought of successive appearances by some incarnation of deity, there is no difficulty in considering a new claimant for divine honors as simply another manifestation of the great God Brahman. Gautama, the Buddha, was easily taken into the Hindu system, so when Christianity, with its incarnation of deity in the person of Jesus, approaches India it is very natural that he be considered simply as one more in the long line of incarnations. The offense to Hinduism comes when Christianity maintains the uniqueness of Jesus and refuses to consider him but one of many. The Brahma Samaj is a good illustration of the syncretic tendency though, of course, this does not belong simply to the twentieth century. Here Christianity has furnished a number of the characteristic elements. It is monotheistic like Christianity, though Mohammedanism may also have played its part here as well. It exalts Jesus though it refuses quite to deify him. The modern Samajist in his attitude toward Christ approximates the position held by an orthodox Unitarian Christian. It is non-idolatrous. It is congregational in its worship forms, differing distinctly in this regard from orthodox Hinduism.

The Arya Samaj, while accepting less doctrinally from the Christian faith, has made use of almost every technique of evangelization and social and philan-

MODERN TENDENCIES

thropic work known to Christianity, finding warrant for such practices, however, in their ancient Scriptures as already explained; but obviously the Christian model has been closely followed. However, leaving aside such institutional adoption of Christian thought and practice, there is a great deal of the unconscious penetration of Christian influence in Hinduism. When a Hindu remarks to a prominent missionary in India that he feels it is his *Christian* duty to love his Mohammedan brethren, it is evident that Christianity has made its influence deeply felt. Even an Arya Samajist, in attempting to describe Gandhi, speaks of him as an Indian Christ! Perhaps the most marked illustration that can be found in India at the present time is that offered by Mahatma Gandhi, the well-known Indian leader. Mr. C. F. Andrews, in his valuable book, *Mahatma Gandhi's Ideas*, gives a whole chapter to the place of Jesus in Gandhi's thought, taking his title from an article written by Mr. Gandhi himself in *Young India*. It will suffice here to introduce a few scattered excerpts from this chapter:

"For many years I have regarded Jesus of Nazareth as one among the mighty teachers that the world has had and I say this in all humility. . . . Jesus occupies in my heart the place of one of the great teachers who have had a considerable influence upon my life. I say to the seventy-five per cent of Hindus receiving instruction in this college that your lives also will be incomplete unless you reverently study the teaching of Jesus. . . . If, then, I had to face only the Sermon on the Mount and my own interpretation of it (the message of Jesus as contained in the Sermon on the Mount un-

IN HINDUISM

adulterated and taken as a whole) I should not hesitate to say 'Oh yes, I am a Christian,' but I know that at the present moment if I said any such thing I would lay myself open to the gravest misinterpretation. But negatively I can tell you that to my mind much of that which passes for Christianity is a negation of the Sermon on the Mount. . . . There is one thing which came forcibly to me in my early studies of the Bible. It seized me immediately when I read one passage. The text was this: 'Seek ye first the Kingdom of God and his righteousness and all other things will be added unto you.' I tell you that if you will understand, appreciate, and act up to the spirit of this passage, then you will not even need to know what place Jesus or any other teacher occupies in your heart or my heart. . . . By all means drink deep of the fountains that are given you in the Sermon on the Mount; but then you will have to take up sackcloth and ashes also with regard to failure to perform that which is taught in Christ's Sermon, for the teaching of the Sermon was meant for each and every one of us." [25]

One of Gandhi's favorite Christian hymns, of which he apparently knows and uses a good many, is "When I Survey the Wondrous Cross." As illustrating how various religious currents contribute to the faith of Gandhi, Mr. Andrews' description of the impressive scene at the breaking of his twenty-one days fast is worth noting:

"At about 10 A.M. he called for me and said, 'Can you remember the words of my favorite Christian hymn?' I said, 'Yes, shall I sing it to you now?' 'Not now,' he answered, 'but I have in mind that when I break my fast we might have a little ceremony expressing religious unity. I should like Imam Sahib to recite

[25] From C. F. Andrews, *Mahatma Gandhi's Ideas* (George Allen & Unwin Ltd.), pp. 92-96 *passim*.

MODERN TENDENCIES

the opening verses of the Koran. Then I would like you to sing the Christian hymn; you know the one I mean. It begins:
"When I survey the wondrous cross
On which the Prince of Glory died"—
and it ends:
"Love so amazing, so divine,
Demands my soul, my life my all."
And then last of all I should like Vinoba to recite from the Upanishads, and Balkrishna to sing the Vaishnava Hymn describing the true Vaishnava.' "[26]

But in Gandhi's hospitality to ideas and ideals from other faiths he insists that he is still true to Hinduism and he deprecates exceedingly any attempt at conversion from Hinduism to either Mohammedanism or Christianity, or indeed from any one faith to another. In this opposition to a change of faith he is warmly upheld by the great majority of educated Indians who are under the spell of the nationalist spirit. Loyalty to their own national heritage, they claim, demands that they refuse to be drawn into other and foreign faiths. Gandhi, as is well known, has for one of his main principles that of Swadeshi, which is a compound word meaning "belonging to one's own country." The world is familiar with his insistence upon Swadeshi in its application to social and economic problems. Thus he would have all Indians use only Indian products, in so far as India is able to supply their demands, and he would even go farther and hold that Indians

[26] From C. F. Andrews, *op cit.*, p. 316.

IN HINDUISM

ought to content themselves with that which India can herself provide. But it is the religious meaning of Swadeshi that interests us here. To quote C. F. Andrews:

"With Mahatma Gandhi, Swadeshi represents the principle that one's own surroundings are to be preferred to everything else; that the country of one's birth demands personal homage in preference to that of others. It means still further to him—that to change from one religion to another is an almost inconceivable thing. In Swadeshi he finds a principle which explains his relation to Christianity and other religions. There is to him a religious patriotism as well as a patriotism of national status."[27]

In Gandhi's own words supplied to Mr. Andrews at his request, as the Mahatma's final word on the subject, Swadeshi is thus described:

"Swadeshi is that spirit within us which restricts us to the use and service of our immediate surroundings to the exclusion of the more remote. Thus in the matter of religion I must restrict myself to my ancestral religion—that is, the use of my immediate surroundings in religion. If I find my religion defective, I should serve it by purging it of its defects.... Hinduism has become a conservative religion and therefore a mighty force because of the Swadeshi spirit underlying it. It is the most tolerant creed because it is non-proselytizing, and it is as capable of expansion today as it has been found to be in the past. It has succeeded not in driving out (as I think it has been erroneously held), but in absorbing Buddhism. By reason of the Swadeshi spirit a Hindu refuses to change his religion, not necessarily because he considers it to be the best but because he

[27] From C. F. Andhews, *op. cit.*, p. 118.

MODERN TENDENCIES

knows that he can complement it by introducing reforms."[28]

With this principle deeply fixed in his own thinking, it is very natural that Mr. Gandhi should try to convince the leaders of the Christian missionary enterprise in India, the value of whose contributions to India Gandhi recognizes, that they drop their "goal of proselytizing" while continuing their philanthropic work. Again, in his own words:

"I have endeavored to study the Bible and consider it to be a part of my Scriptures. The spirit of the Sermon on the Mount competes, almost on equal terms, with the Bhagavad Gita for the domination of my heart. I yield to no Christian in the strength of devotion with which I sing 'Lead Kindly Light' and several other inspired hymns of a similar nature. I have come under the influence of noted Christian missionaries belonging to different denominations and I enjoy to this day the privilege of friendship with some of them. Thus I have offered the above suggestion not as a biased Hindu but as a humble and impartial student of religion with great leanings toward Christianity. May it not be that the 'Go ye unto all the world' message has been somewhat narrowly interpreted and the spirit of it missed."[29]

Mr. Andrews' comment upon this position of Mr. Gandhi is worth while, since it throws light upon an attitude of that other great leader of Indian thought, Rabindranath Tagore. Thus, he says, the religious position of Mr. Gandhi

"is not of the type that ever looks forward (if I judge him rightly) to a single world religion and a single

[28] *Ibid.*, pp. 120-21.
[29] C. F. Andrews, *op. cit.*, p. 121.

50

IN HINDUISM

world state, but rather to separate units working out their individual destiny in cordial, harmonized, friendly relations. There will always be impassable barriers between them which appear to him divinely ordained. Herein he differs, as far as I can gather, from Tagore, to whom this limited aspect of patriotism and religion is unthinkable. To Tagore the over-passing of these boundaries is all important; to Gandhi their due observance appears essential in this present stage of human existence." [20]

Under the impulse of strong nationalistic feeling, lesser differences between the various religious groups in India tend to fall into the background. It is readily to be seen that one of the greatest hindrances to the attainment of national independence or a Dominion status within the Empire lies in the hostility between groups, which makes a political union exceedingly difficult. The tension between the Hindu-Moslem communities is held by many to be a sufficient reason for not granting a complete independence to India. National leaders are perfectly aware of this and are making every attempt to bring about a Hindu-Moslem understanding, such that will permit them to work unitedly for their goal. Under the pressure of leaders from both sides there is evidence that a greater spirit of unity is prevailing. The great twenty-one days fast of Mahatma Gandhi in 1924 was an effort to bring the two groups together. Not that Gandhi would have Hinduism and Mohammedanism merge. His principle of Swadeshi, as we have seen, would keep them apart, but he does insistently advocate mutual toleration and mutual in-

[20] *Ibid.*, p. 127.

MODERN TENDENCIES

tercourse which, in the long run, inevitably brings certain modifications in one or the other of the faiths. What he pleads for is that each refrain from attempting to force the other from his own point of view.

"We cannot live in peace," he writes, "if the Hindus will not tolerate the Muhammadan's form of worship of God and his manners and customs, or if the Muhammadans will be impatient of Hindu idolatry or cow worship. It is not necessary for toleration that I must approve what I tolerate." [31]

In the interest of promoting the Hindu-Moslem unity Gandhi threw his own strength into the Moslem Khilafat Movement, which had arisen as a protest against the abolition of the Caliphate. Of course, historically, not a few movements have developed within Hinduism which represent direct attempts to embody elements from Islam. The Sikh Movement is the most noteworthy example of this, but we write of the modern period. A writer in a Bombay paper, the *Subodha Potuka,* believes that political unity of Moslems and Hindus cannot come without religious tolerance. He advocates a conference of leaders of the religious communities which might include other religions as well, the function of the conference to be threefold—"1. To fight unbelief, 2. To bring out the essential unity behind the divergent creeds, 3. and to organize the religious life of both Hindus and Moslems on this liberal basis." It may be a bold idea

[31] From C. F. Andrews, *op. cit.*, pp. 59-60.

IN HINDUISM

to suggest that there ought to be common churches where Hindus, Moslems, and Christians and others could join in worship, but it is the only thing that would bring about inter-communal harmony. . . . We must have a religious basis! Only it must be sufficiently broad and liberal to include every shade of belief. . . ." [32]

Other practical evidences of the syncretizing tendency are to be found in certain Ashrams, a species of community which brings together people of very diverse religious and cultural backgrounds in intimate association and study over prolonged periods of time. Among the most notable of these are Mr. Gandhi's Ashram at Sabarmati, where Hindus, Moslems, Christians, high caste and untouchables live a communal life under a rule formulated largely by Mr. Gandhi. Not a few Christian missionaries have gone to live for varying periods in the Ashram. Perhaps a still better known Ashram is that of the poet Tagore, known as Santiniketan. Here people with different points of view, in intimate personal, almost family relations, study, hear lectures, and engage in discussion of the great issues of the spiritual life. More recently two institutions of somewhat similar character have been founded by Christians. One, called the Christa Seva Sangha, has its headquarters at Poona. The purpose of the newly organized group as stated in their publication, *The Christa Seva Sangha Review*, is quoted at length because it represents a comparatively new trend in the approach of Christianity to Hinduism:

[32] Quoted by the *Modern Review*, March, 1929, p. 400.

MODERN TENDENCIES

"Christa Seva Sangha is a brotherhood of men within which Indians and Europeans live together in a common life of prayer and service. They receive no pay and own no property of their own, sharing a common purse, and seeking no reward for their labor. Each lives under the direction of the Acharya; and all full members of the brotherhood are unmarried, life-membership conferring, after long probation, the honour of the saffron robe.

"The Brotherhood is known as the First Order: a Sisterhood of Indian and English women shortly to be founded will be called the Second Order, and there is a Third Order of married members and others, sharing the ideals and working in association with the Sangha, in India and elsewhere.

"The brothers wear a simple habit of white khaddar as a sign of their desire to be identified with India, their own or their adopted motherland, and in token of the life of *brahmacharya* which they lead.

"Christa Seva Sangha is not a foreign missionary society. India is its birthplace and its home. Moreover, it does not wish to transplant a Western form of culture or religion into this country, but to show that the message of Christ 'is not antagonistic to or destructive of the precious national heritage of India, but sets it forth in its full intrinsic worth and value.'

"Christa Seva Sangha seeks to serve all communities irrespective of creed; it offers its service not as a bribe but as a reflection of the love which Christ himself bears to this land; it would have no one adopt the Christian faith save from an overwhelming and considered conviction of its adequacy for life and thought. At the same time, the Sangha regards Christ as 'the Way, the Truth, and the Life.' Christ is the Sangha's one treasure: poor and humble as it is, he is its sole wealth; the one gift it has to bring to India. And therefore, in no spirit of proselytism but in humble reverence, from no motive of aggression but out of the fullness of de-

IN HINDUISM

voted love, the Sangha would give its Beloved Master to this Beloved Land.

"The brothers live in Indian style, in simple Indian dwellings on the outskirts of Poona. They do their own house-work, cleaning and serving at meals. They work side by side with the coolies in building or on the land. Here animals are loved, and flowers; no meat or fish is eaten in the Ashram; but the Christian virtue of Ahimsa is raised up as an ideal. For all living things are welcomed here, no divisions of class or caste are known; the workman, the scholar and the little child, the 'outcaste' and the man of noble birth are all seen as members of the Eternal Father's family of love.

"Not far from the Ashram there is a Students' Hostel, maintained by the Brothers in the spirit of love, sympathy and service.

"The aims of the Brotherhood are:

"(1) To build up a brotherhood of men, who will try to live as the Lord Christ lived, taking him in all things to be their pattern.

"(2) To enable Indians and Englishmen to live together, on terms of complete fellowship and equality, and thus to be a living demonstration of the truth of Tagore's words: 'Humanity is one at the core. East and West are but alternate beats of the same heart.' "**

Dr. E. Stanley Jones, noted missionary to India, has also founded an Ashram called "The Sat Tal Ashram," which has as its purpose, according to the statement of the founder,

"to yoke the Christian Spirit and the Indian Spirit. We feel very definitely that unless Christianity becomes more truly Indian and more truly Christian it will not make much headway into the soul of India. In the

** *The Christa Seva Sangha Review*, May, 1931.

MODERN TENDENCIES

Ashram we try to produce the Indian Spirit, or rather to let it have full play. Westernism has made so much of our Christianity in the East unnatural and copyist. The Christianity we have produced for the most part is not the flowering of a material genius touched by the spirit of Christ, so much as it is the blossom of an unnatural copying. . . . First of all we try to create an atmosphere that is Indian in the truest sense of that term. If we are to think through our problems in the framework of Indian culture and life it is necessary that the framework should have definite attention. If we are to stand in the stream of Indian thought and life and interpret our gospel from that standpoint it is necessary that the spirit of the Ashram should be truly Indian. . . ."[24]

Here for two and a half months each year a group of men and women, Indian and foreign, wearing Indian clothes, eating Indian food, sitting in Indian fashion on the floor, observing once a week the characteristic Indian "day of silence" made familiar to the West in recent times by Mr. Gandhi, carry out a well-defined program of devotion, study, discussion, recreation and fellowship.

While distinctly Christian in character and purpose the attitude toward the faiths of India is that of an attempt to understand and, where possible, assimilate some elements of it. The spirit is expressed in the words of Stanley Jones:

"With the impact of the Gospel on India's life many things should be destroyed for they have been an in-

[24] *The Message of Sat Tal Ashram 1931* (Calcutta Association Press, 1932), pp. 1-3 *passim*, and p. 285. This publication, containing a number of the papers read and discussed in the Ashram, furnish an excellent indication of its character and purpose.

IN HINDUISM

cubus on the soul of India. But there are many things that are good and beautiful and true in India's culture and religions. The Christian movement will not be indifferent or hostile to these things, but will take them up and embody them in itself."

This is an interesting indication of the fact that the syncretizing tendency is at work within Christianity as well as in Hinduism. Of this tendency numerous other examples could easily be cited. One who wishes to know what the tendencies are might well read the *National Christian Council Review* for July, 1927, in which is included a syllabus used by leaders in considering the Indian background with which Christianity must deal. Here are a few questions which were raised on that occasion:

"Is Hinduism to be gradually transformed into Christianity, to be baptized into Christ, or is Christianity to destroy Hinduism? Or is Christianity to pass into Hinduism and be transformed by it? Again, can ideas like Brahman, Dharma, Karma, be taken over and reinterpreted? Has the Hindu emphasis on unity as the way to salvation any value that can be preserved? Is Yoga practice likely to be of use in the worship of the Christian? Can the Indian ascetic idea—or *Sannyasa*—be utilized more than it has been in Christianity? Can anything in Hinduism take the place of the Old Testament as the Portico to Christianity?"[25]

Other evidences are to be found in the appearance of certain books published by the Christian Literature Society for India. One is *Jesus, the Avatar*. The very title of the book is significant, for Avatar is the Hindu word for "incarnation." Krishna, that great

[25] *National Christian Council Review*, July, 1927, p. 452.

MODERN TENDENCIES

Hindu rival of Christ, is an Avatar, one of ten traditional incarnations of Vishnu. Of course the author does not attempt to effect any identification of these two. He does, however, speak definitely of Jesus as "Avatar of Brahman," the Hindu concept of ultimate reality, although he undertakes to define Brahman. Indeed, the whole book is full of Hindu words with very well defined religious and philosophic connotations which he somewhat re-defines and applies to Christianity. A second book is *Christianity as Bhakti Marga*. "Bhakti" is devotion, faith or love toward deity or some incarnation of deity. A "Bhakta" is the individual who follows "Bhakti Marga," which may be interpreted as the way of devotional faith or salvation by faith. To be sure, both these books may be simply attempts to put Christian thought into distinctive Hindu language, but one who knows the history of Christian doctrine will hardly doubt that such discussions, falling upon the ear of a Hindu, would carry quite a different meaning than that intended by one who is wholly Christian. Charges have been made by certain Christian groups [20] that a recent New Testament translation into the Marathi dialect employs words of purely Vedantic meaning in the rendering of certain Christian ideas, e.g. the union of the believer with Christ is expressed in the language used to express the Vedantic idea of absorption in Brahma with the loss of personal identity; the name of God is rendered by a Hindu word which does not refer to the supreme deity. This, the opponents of the idea declare is not allowable. But it

[20] *Indian Social Reformer*, Vol. 42 (Sept. 12, 1931), p. 27.

IN HINDUISM

is happening, and represents a current trend toward syncretism. All these are distinctly steps on the way to the nationalization of Christianity, which will quite certainly make of it something other than the western world has usually held.

Social Changes Involving Religion

The sixth and last of the tendencies to be noted here is that toward social change and, as we have before indicated, it is in this realm that perhaps the most significant changes are taking place. One may confidently predict that adjustments will be made within the theological and religious aspects of Hinduism to correspond to social change that has already been forced upon it. Space will not allow a detailed discussion of all of the social changes that the present period discloses but significant phases of at least four fundamental social changes will be touched upon; that in the status of women, the breakdown of caste, the admission of the untouchables to participation in Hindu Worship, and the attempted reform in certain institutions connected with the Temple worship, notably Temple prostitution.

1. *Changing Status of Women*

Perhaps no more striking modifications in the Hindu social system are to be found than in the changing status of women. Accorded a relatively high position in the ancient Scriptures of India, numerous restrictions upon her liberty have developed within comparatively recent centuries directly under the sanctions of religion, and it is against these that

MODERN TENDENCIES

modern Indian womanhood is struggling. Early in the nineteenth century, largely due to the influence of one of the great reformers, Rajah Ramohan Roy, the British government outlawed *sati,* or widow burning. According to the most holy of traditions, a widow was supposed to mount the funeral pyre of her deceased husband and accompany him into the after life. It was not, however, without a considerable struggle against the bitterest opposition on the part of orthodox Hinduism that the custom was put under the ban, and even today it is occasionally practiced in the more remote and backward sections of the country. The prohibition against widow re-marriage has never been lifted and the lot of the woman bereft of her husband is, even in this twentieth century, most deplorable, particularly when the widow is a mere child, for she is placed entirely under the control of her mother-in-law and subjected to the most unhappy treatment, her status being little better than that of a servant or slave. Reforming groups are attacking the problem, which is but one phase of the larger problem of marriage, and are practicing and advocating widow re-marriage. A society of young men has for one of its membership requirements that each candidate vow to marry only a widow. As early as 1856 the government had passed a Hindu Widow Re-marriage Act but the legislation has been largely inoperative, first of all since it only legalizes their marriage within British India, leaving entirely out of account the great Indian population living under native rulers. The magnitude of the problem is indicated by the census figures of 1921,

IN HINDUISM

which indicated that forty-eight out of every thousand Hindu girls between fifteen and twenty were widows and that India as a whole had one hundred and ninety-one widows to every thousand population. The total number as given in a debate before the Legislative Assembly in 1927 reaches over 20,200,000. On the introduction of the Widow Re-marriage Bill in the Legislative Assembly, a select committee was appointed to examine it. Twenty-three petitions signed by over five thousand Hindus favored the measure while twenty-eight petitions, signed by over fifty-five thousand Hindus, opposed it. The petitions opposing reforms quoted frequently various Hindu Scriptures to support their position, declaring it the widow's duty to

"emaciate till death, forgiving all injuries, performing harsh duties, to avoid every sensual pleasure, to practice cheerfully the incomparable rules of virtue which have been followed by such women as were devoted to only one husband." [37]

In support of the Bill one of the members is reported by the *Indian Social Reformer* as declaring:

"Every candid Hindu would admit that in the majority of cases young Hindu widows fall into vice; that in comparatively few cases are these severe rules for a life of mortification virtuously observed; that in many cases a licentious and profligate life is entered upon in secret; that in many other cases the wretched widows are impelled to desert their homes and to live a life that brings open disgrace upon their families." [38]

[37] *Indian Social Reformer* (Aug. 11, 1928), p. 782.
[38] *Ibid.*, p. 764.

MODERN TENDENCIES

In addition to these results of the widowhood restrictions, suicide among young widows is very common. Yet despite these clamoring ills, any attempt to bring about widow re-marriage is looked upon by orthodox Hindus as an attack against religion.

The problem of widowhood is enormously complicated by the habit, also sanctioned by religion, of the very early marriage of children. It was in part against the evils of child marriage that Miss Katherine Mayo wrote that well-known book *Mother India* which has been so violently criticized in no less than a dozen books that have appeared since it was first published. That Miss Mayo has not told the whole story of Mother India is perfectly clear. That the one-sided picture of India which she gave the world was in many ways unfair, may be granted. Further, that she has exaggerated certain aspects of the child marriage problem is probable, but any candid comparison between the statements of Miss Mayo and statements made by leading Hindu reformers themselves in debates before the Legislative Assembly will lead one to the conclusion that she was very far from being entirely wrong in her charges with reference to this practice; for almost every evil which Miss Mayo attributes to the system in her book is condemned in even more forceful language by Hindus themselves, some of whom have been very outspoken in their criticism of her book. The net result of Miss Mayo's book, in this regard at least, has been to make the issue a much more living one and has stirred the Indian national pride to oppose violently this and other evils which seem to them to condemn India before the world.

IN HINDUISM

Exact statistics are difficult to secure as to the ages of children at marriage, but on even the most liberal interpretation of the census figures there are very great numbers of mere children who are disposed of in marriage, some of them to men who might well be their grandfathers. The tendency to reform in this regard has been present for a long time in India, and successive steps have been taken which advanced the age of consent or the time of consummation of marriage until, during the year 1930, a legislative act was passed raising the age to fourteen. This is considered a vast step forward in the progress of women to their proper place in the social scale. That this advance has been won against formidable opposition on the part of the orthodox Hindu community is evident from certain pronouncements made in the name of religion when it was up for consideration. Thus the Association of Business Men in Bengal in opposing it, declared:

"In plain language the Bill proposes to prohibit the marriage of Hindu girls before they reach the thirteenth year of age; that is to say before they attain puberty, for Indian girls generally obtain puberty between eleven and twelve years. . . . If anyone had deliberately intended to hurt the feelings of the orthodox Hindu community, to change the face of the Hindu society, and to insult the Hindu religion, he could not have hit upon or devised a more effective means. In the opinion of my Committee, no Hindu having any faith in his religion can agree to such a provision." [20]

Again, a letter from an outstanding Hindu lawyer reads as follows:

[20] Quoted by Harry H. Field, *After Mother India*, p. 99, from a collection of opinions on Hindu Child Marriage Bill, p. 10.

MODERN TENDENCIES

"As a President of the Sanatan Dharm Mahamandal I can voice the opinion of the Sanatan Dharmist Hindu. The Bill is an encroachment on religious sentiments of the people and is an interference with religion. No government or legislature has a right to interfere by legislation with what the Shastras (Hindu sacred writings) enjoin. I therefore desire that this piece of legislation should be opposed."

On the other hand the proponents of the bill insist that no violence is done to Hinduism as a religion, and they charge the opponents of the measure with attempting to arouse the religious fanaticism of the orthodox against the measure by declaring that it is contrary to the traditional faith. It is generally conceded that with the passage of this bill, raising the age of consent to fourteen, a great victory has been won for womankind but that a still higher age of consent must presently be secured.

The third matter in connection with the status of women relates to divorce, which is almost unknown in Hinduism. The conception of marriage as a religious sacrament has been generally held firmly by Hindus down to the present period. In an article on "The Way Out of Wedlock" in the *Indian Social Reformer,* the editor writes:

"Hindu law affords absolutely no remedy for aggrieved Hindu wives. Once they are united in the bonds of matrimony, death alone can release them from the bonds. Ill treatment, cruelty and other acts on the part of husbands, which in any other society constitute grounds for divorce are offences against which there is no redress. A Hindu wife has to grin and bear them all without the hope of a better life. This glaring defect in Hindu law should be remedied if only to save

IN HINDUISM

our women from changing their religion in order to discard wicked husbands. The recent case in the Calcutta Court in which a Hindu lady graduate embraced Islam and thus obtained dissolution of her marriage should serve as a warning to the community. This, in our opinion, is the second case of its kind."[40]

The women of India in general have not concerned themselves with this problem as yet, except in a general way. The Fourth Constituent Conference of Women on Education and Social Reform in Madras in October, 1929, passed the following resolution:

"This conference demands that there should be the same standard of sex morality for men and women: women claim equal rights of legal separation and demand the introduction of an equal divorce law for both men and women."[41]

However, in commenting upon a bill that was introduced into the Provincial Legislative Assembly in Baroda, "The Hindu" writes:

"Peculiar interest attaches to this Bill as it is a pioneer attempt to break through the conception of the inviolability of the marriage tie. In fact, divorce is not quite acceptable to many, even of the social reformers, and it is significant that it is not to be found among the social resolutions passed at the All India Women's Conference."[42]

A divorce bill was introduced into the Legislative Assembly for British India early in 1932, but failed of passage.

The system of Purdah, which has held the woman

[40] *Indian Social Reformer*, "The Way Out of Wedlock," Vol. 40 (June 7, 1929), p. 2.
[41] *Indian Social Reformer*, Vol. 40 (Nov. 30, 1929), p. 198.
[42] *Ibid.*, p. 358.

MODERN TENDENCIES

of India in the seclusion of her own home and cut her off from all contact with other male companions than those of the immediate family, is not considered to have been originally a Hindu custom, but it has succeeded in fastening itself on Indian womanhood. Under the sanction of religion as it now is, any attempt for a woman to unveil herself or to go openly on the streets or enter into society outside her own home is looked upon by orthodox Hinduism as a breach of loyalty to the faith, and any reformer who attacks it is immediately branded as a destroyer of the faith. So long as women were uneducated, as was almost universally the case until quite recently, they apparently accepted this lot without serious question, but the introduction of education among them—pretty largely a missionary project—the opening of their minds to the thought of the world, has led the leaders of Indian womanhood to a wholehearted condemnation of the Purdah system and it is one of the declared purposes of the All India Women's Conference to do away with it. A speaker before the Fourth All India Women's Conference in Bombay, 1930, declared, after having enumerated a number of reasons for the abandonment of the system:

"For all these reasons the abolition of Purdah is essential to woman's progress, and I rejoice to see the noble example set by educated Hindu and Mussulman women of high social position in discarding the Purdah on public occasions." [13]

The fact that it has become a project of the All

[13] *Ibid.*, p. 343.

IN HINDUISM

India Women's Conference is an indication that reform in this particular regard is on the way, regardless of orthodox opposition.

2. *Outcastes and Hindu Temples*

The gradual breakdown of caste is one of the most interesting of the tendencies in modern Hinduism, for while caste is not wholly of a religious origin it has become so thoroughly identified with and supported by religion that probably no more serious blow could be delivered to orthodox Hinduism than the destruction of caste. Even some of the most active opponents of the evils of the caste system look upon it as perhaps the most distinctively Hindu custom of all. The fact that the highest caste, the Brahmin, is related particularly to religion, as the priestly caste, makes any attack upon that particular caste at least an affront to religion.

The whole world is familiar with the major divisions of Hindu society into the Brahmin or priestly class, the Kshatriya or warrior-ruler caste, the Vaisya or farmer-merchant caste, and the Sudra or unskilled labor caste. The first three are known as the twice-born castes and stand on a level very much removed from the Sudra, while below the Sudra even is a vast group known as the untouchables, or depressed classes, made up of the menial servant class and those who perform unclean functions such as scavenger, sweeper, workers in leather and like pursuits. The untouchables, numbering some sixty million, are the most unhappy of all India's population. Particularly in southern India the gulf between the

MODERN TENDENCIES

upper caste and the untouchable is so great that the mere shadow of an untouchable falling upon a high caste man brings pollution. They are denied the use of the wells belonging to the high caste, the public roads, and are, of course, completely cut off from any participation in the worship of the high caste group. For them to enter a high caste temple would be so to pollute it that the high caste man could not enter until it had been purified by an elaborate purification ceremony.

Many factors have conspired to make the persistence of caste distinctions increasingly difficult. Railroad transportation has become an essential part of the common life of all castes, yet for obvious reasons the rigid caste distinctions cannot be maintained while traveling. The introduction of the industrial system with its strange indifference to the social position of those obliged to earn their living at factory work has done much to break down the barriers. The coming of education has—chiefly in mission schools—given tangible evidence that the supposed innate superiority of high over low caste has no basis in fact. All these and many other factors, such as the contact of Christianity with the untouchables, thus bringing to them a new conception of their own worth and offering a hope for advance in the social scale, have awakened in the untouchable group a longing which is beginning to take definite organized form for a larger share of the goods of this life and the respect of their so-called superiors.

One of the most dramatic phases of this untouchable protest, and the one of greatest interest in this

IN HINDUISM

particular study, is on at the present time and takes the form of organized insistence upon their right to worship in Hindu temples. This movement began several years ago, but the first considerable successes have been won in the last three years. Influenced by the example of Mr. Gandhi to use *Satyagraha* or the non-violent method, they have been trying at a number of points to break down Hindu opposition. Announcement appeared in the *Indian Social Reformer* in 1930, that entrance had been won to a certain Kali Temple after an effort extending over a period of more than nine months. The article continues:

"About two hundred high caste women, in order to save the lives of the hungry striking *Satyagrahis*, removed the barriers to the Temple with saws, axes, and hammers, they being helped in this by members of the Young Men's Association and thus threw open the doors of the Temple to all classes of Hindus." [44]

Again, to quote from the *Indian Social Reformer:*

"It was a red letter day in the history of Wardha when the Janmotsava celebration of the Shri Lakshminarayan temple belonging to Seth Jamanlalji was performed. A huge procession of high caste Hindus and so-called untouchables who mixed freely among themselves passed through the main streets of Wardha amidst great enthusiasm and religious fervour. It was followed by a mass meeting of the processionists and others, presided over by Baba Saheb Deshmukh when Acharya Venoba Bhave of Wardha Satyagrahashram delivered a very impressive speech. After the meeting, there was a big feast in which about three hundred

[44] *Indian Social Reformer*, Vol. 40 (May 24, 1930), p. 614.

MODERN TENDENCIES

untouchables were fed in the temple grounds amidst singing. Then followed *harikirtan* in the Lakshminarayn temple. The whole ceremony ended late at night amidst great enthusiasm and ovation." [45]

A bill was introduced into the Legislative Assembly in 1930, providing in effect as follows:

"Notwithstanding any rule or Hindu law or custom prevailing in the country, any custom which declares that any Hindu, by reason of his caste or community, is untouchable or is incapable of exercising the public rights which are open to other communities is invalid and cannot be recognized, notwithstanding any sanction it may have in religion or custom." [46]

The bill has not yet been enacted into law.

Although the entry of untouchables into temples is bitterly opposed by orthodox Hinduism, there are forces which appeal strongly to Hindu national loyalty that favor the movement. For one thing there has been a very marked mass movement among the untouchable classes toward Christianity, whole villages having come deliberately seeking entrance into the Christian faith. This has finally awakened Hinduism to try to do something to detain this movement, but without some concession on their part, the movement is not likely to cease. By becoming Christians many of the social disabilities under which the untouchables live are removed. Shall not Hinduism, if it desires to retain them as Hindus, show some disposition to admit them to its privileges? Then there is the further pressure of Indian nation-

[45] *Indian Social Reformer*, Vol. 40 (Feb. 10, 1930), p. 399.
[46] *Ibid.*, p. 636.

IN HINDUISM

alism. Nothing seems clearer than that a divided India cannot hope to attain independence or self-direction. Roughly one-sixth of the population of India is denied most of the privileges that the other classes enjoy. Can they be brought to support a nationalist movement which promises to offer them fewer advantages than the so-called Christian government from abroad? So it seems inevitable that this movement will expand. An enthusiastic supporter of the reform, Mr. Jamnalal Bajaj, declares:

"Without fear of being contradicted I say that the Hindu's angle of vision in respect of the problem of untouchability and the 'untouchables' has been positively changed and an atmosphere is being created all over the country from day to day which is bringing the community nearer the solution almost hourly. Already a dozen temples have been thrown open in this part of the country to 'all Hindus' without much ado. The doors of many more are being knocked at effectively and without resort to extreme measures. The Ganapati, the Navaratri and the Dusserah festivals all over the country this year have been absolutely unprecedented in the initiative and the warmth with which the class Hindus welcomed and fraternised with their 'untouchable' brethren." [47]

The editor of the *Indian Social Reformer* as long ago as 1929 went so far as to predict that within ten years time most of the disabilities resting upon the outcaste would be things of the past, although this editor himself, while sympathizing with the aspirations of the outcaste group, seriously doubted the expediency of forcing temple entry:

[47] *Indian Social Reformer*, Vol. 40 (Oct. 19, 1929), p. 103.

MODERN TENDENCIES

"We utterly condemn," he says, "the attitude of the temple worshippers who present an uncompromising opposition to the entry of the untouchables. At the same time, however, we cannot think that the movement to force an entry into temples notwithstanding its non-violent character is even the best or most dignified method of vindicating the zeal of the untouchables for the Hindu religion."

He feared that if they should succeed in getting into the temple it would only result in the upper castes leaving them. He concludes:

"It may mean the disappearance of the present form of Temple worship and perhaps it may prove to be the salvation of the Hindu religion." [8]

The latest and most dramatic phase of the fight against untouchability came in the famous "fast unto death" of Mahatma Gandhi in September, 1932. Climaxing many years of effort on behalf of the depressed classes, Mr. Gandhi seized upon the award by the British government of separate communal representation to the "untouchables" as the occasion to protest less against the British who held no special brief for the arrangement, than against the caste groups whose hostility to the claims of the Depressed Classes had obliged Britain to adopt some such method for the protection of a minority group. The fast began at noon, September 20. The British government almost at once announced its willingness to accept some better plan which the classes involved could agree upon. The responsibility for the prolongation of the Mahatma's fast was therefore

[8] *Indian Social Reformer*, Vol. 40, p. 439.

IN HINDUISM

thrown back upon the caste leaders, and enormous pressure was brought to bear upon them to effect an early solution which would satisfy him that the larger interests of the untouchables would be safeguarded. He had insisted that separate electorates for untouchables would only serve to deepen the sense of their separateness from the Hindu group as a whole, and make therefore all efforts to break down caste barriers to them more difficult.

The agreement reached between the opposing parties, known as the Yerravda Pact,[49] which provides for a certain number of reserved seats for the Depressed Classes out of the general electorates to be filled, subject to certain definite conditions by joint electorates, proved acceptable to Mr. Gandhi, who thereupon ended his fast after five days. While the immediate form of the protest was a political one, Mr. Gandhi has made it plain that his purpose was nothing less than the eradication of untouchability root and branch. In a statement from Yerravda prison on November 4, he makes it clear that he considers the Hindu group obligated under the terms of the Pact to do away with the social discrimination against the untouchables. He says:

"Crowds in all parts of India have passed resolutions denouncing untouchability and pledging themselves to remove it from their midst, and they have on innumerable occasions called God as witness to their pledge and asked for his blessings that he may give them strength to carry out their pledge.

"It was against these millions that my fast was under-

[49] The text of the pact is given in *The Indian Social Reformer*, Vol. 43 (Oct. 1, 1932), p. 70.

MODERN TENDENCIES

taken and it was their spontaneous love that brought about a transformation inside of five days and brought into being the Yerravda Pact. And it will be against them that the fast will be resumed if that Pact is not carried out by them in its fullness. The Government are now practically out of it. Their part of the obligation they fulfilled promptly. The major part of the resolutions of the Yerravda Pact has to be fulfilled . . . by the so-called caste-Hindus. . . . It is they who have to embrace the suppressed brethren and sisters as their own whom they have to invite to their temples, to their homes, to their schools.

"The untouchables in the villages should be made to feel that their shackles have been broken, that they are in no way inferior to their fellow villagers, that they are worshippers of the same God as other villagers and are entitled to the same rights and privileges that the latter enjoy. But if these vital conditions of the Pact are not carried out by Caste Hindus, could I possibly live to face God and man?"[50]

In later statements he intimated that he did not consider the matter of inter-dining as of paramount importance, but to those who held that temple entry also was a matter of little consequence, Mr. Gandhi replied: "Nothing in my opinion will strike the imagination of the Hindu mass mind . . . as the throwing open of all public temples to them, precisely on the same terms as the caste Hindus. . . . Hindu temples play a most important part in the life of the masses and I, who have been trying all my life to identify myself with the most illiterate and downtrodden cannot rest satisfied until all temples are open to the outcastes of Hindu humanity."[51]

[50] *Indian Social Reformer*, Vol. 43 (Nov. 12, 1932), p. 164.
[51] *Ibid.*, Vol. 43 (Nov. 12, 1932), p. 162.

IN HINDUISM

Nothing has done so much to stir the mind of India on this question as Mr. Gandhi's fast. The advantage gained by the Depressed Classes has done much to increase their own sense of worth and power. The friends of the outcastes have been stimulated to new efforts in their behalf. One of the practical results has been the formation of an "All-India Untouchability League" designed to give "shape and permanence to the awakening caused in the country by Mahatma Gandhi's historic fast. The organization is to be carried to every part of India, including the Indian States. It will be non-political in character, its main emphasis being on education and social improvement of the Depressed Classes. Numerous manifestoes have been issued calling especially for temple entry, and in Madras where the untouchables have fared worse probably than any other, the Legislative Council without a dissenting vote passed a resolution recommending to Government that it be pleased "to recognize the strong and growing public feeling in the Hindu community that the disabilities hitherto imposed by usage on certain classes of the community in regard to social intercourse and common worship at temples should be removed and justice rendered them. . . ." [52]

Altogether seven "All-India Depressed Class Conferences" have been held, but the untouchable is not alone in his agitation for a new status. There is beginning a movement among the other castes as well against the highest caste, or Brahmin group. The organized movement has already held various

[52] *Indian Social Reformer*, Vol. 43 (Nov. 5, 1932), p. 146.

MODERN TENDENCIES

assemblies under the general name, "The Self Respect Conference." It is "a movement of non-Brahmin caste Hindus against the social and religious superiority of the Brahmins," while the Depressed Classes Conference voices the revolt of these classes against Brahmins as well as non-Brahmin caste Hindus. The effort in both cases is to remove the disabilities, social and religious, that rest upon the so-called lower groups in their relation to the upper. Both these movements are being vigorously attacked as anti-religious, and fanatical religious zeal is being invoked in opposition to them. On being invited to speak before "The Self Respect Conference," one of the speakers declared that he had received an anonymous letter warning him that he would be lending support "to an atheist movement, a godless movement, and an anti-Brahmin movement." He replied in part as follows:

"I am not frightened by the charge brought against you of atheism—atheism indicates a spirit of inquiry and challenge—and if the habit is established among young minds that in matters of religion, and, may I go further and say, in matters of politics, too, no doctrine is to be accepted except after close scrutiny and careful inquiry, you would have done great good to the country. . . . It may be that in the course of the exercise of the habit of such inquiry and challenge you attack religious observances. . . . I want the truth to be realized by you all that it is only a false religion that cannot stand close inquiry, research, or challenge [Hear, hear]. . . . The wonder is that the men who are doing their best to give a scientific foundation to religion are the very men who are labelled as irreligious heretics."[53]

[53] *Indian Social Reformer*, Vol. 40 (May 24, 1930), p. 618.

IN HINDUISM

The significance of this general movement toward the reform in caste can hardly be overestimated from a religious point of view, for bound up with it are two of the very cardinal doctrines of the Hindu faith, namely transmigration and the law of Karma. The thing that has made it possible, more than any other one reason, for the Hindu to look complacently upon the inequalities and disabilities involved in the rigid caste system has been his belief in the principles of Karma and rebirth. To explain, the law of Karma is simply this; "whatsoever a man soweth that shall he also reap," but the reaping is not limited to the span of a single mortal life. Rather, life is thought of as a revolving wheel, the law of Karma carrying one from one rebirth to another, conditioning absolutely the form that the next life is to take. Born in a certain place in the social scale, Hinduism has taught that the individual had his condition to blame only upon what he had done in a previous life. If born as an outcaste to suffer hardship, poverty, disease, filth, and the contempt of his fellow humans, one must accept it as clear proof that in a former life he had so lived and wrought as to deserve no better. And further, he was taught that his only chance at ascending in the social scale in another birth was the faithful performance of the duties placed upon those of his station. This made it possible for the privileged classes to look upon those of the lower scale as condemned by moral law to that station, and to the orthodox Hindu it might even seem an impiety on his part, indeed an attempt to undo the working of the moral law of the universe—if he should even try to

MODERN TENDENCIES

ameliorate the lot of the outcaste. It is easy to see how fundamental a re-working these peculiar theories must undergo as the new sense of personal dignity and worth, consciousness of power and ability to rise, is awakened among the depressed millions of India.

Indeed, some modern Hindus are already beginning to interpret Karma in a different way and find in it even a stimulus to human helpfulness.

In *An Advanced Textbook of Hindu Religion and Ethics* (p. 117), published by the Central Hindu College, Benares, one reads:

"It is a mistake to say respecting a sufferer, 'He is suffering his Karma; if I help him, I may be interfering with his Karma.' Those who speak thus, forget that each man is an agent of the karma of others as well as an experience of his own. If we are able to help a man, it is the proof that the karma under which he was suffering is exhausted and that we are the agent of his karma bringing him relief. If we refuse to carry the karmic relief, we make bad karma for ourselves, shutting ourselves out from future help and some one else will have the good karma of carrying relief and so assuring for himself aid in a future difficulty."

The Passing of the Devadasi

One of the most anomalous of the religious phenomena to be found in India in this twentieth century is the institution of Devadasis or Temple prostitutes. It is this feature of Hinduism which, perhaps more than any other, shocks the moral sensibilities of the Westerner. Conscious as he is of the existence of prostitution, particularly in the great cities of the

IN HINDUISM

West, he has known it usually as an outlaw existing in spite of religion and law. Coming upon the institution of prostitution not as an outlaw of society and condemned by religion but upheld by it and indeed associated with its very temples, it is not to be wondered at that he feels a sense of shock. It may in part be the result of this feeling on the part of the West, expressed recently in books like that of Katherine Mayo, that lies behind the present-day Hindu attempt to do away with the custom. One catches statements such as the following:

"It is the existence of customs like the one referred to in this resolution (that against the custom) that gives a handle to the enemies of India like Miss Mayo to write books like *Mother India*. The abolition of this custom will prevent the existence of at least one source of adverse comment from persons like Miss Mayo. I have no desire to say more than this; indeed, no further words in support of the resolution seem necessary." [54]

Or again:

"Why should we sanctify vice by giving it a cloak of religious custom and allow persons like Miss Mayo to hold us up to ridicule for tolerating such a sinful practice in the Temples." [55]

However, while such criticisms have undoubtedly intensified the opposition to such evils, the developing moral sense among leaders of Hinduism has

[54] From a statement by Mr. A. B. Shetty taken from the *Legislative Council Debates of Madras* (Nov. 5, 1927), p. 522.
[55] *Ibid.*, p. 519.

MODERN TENDENCIES

for more than a generation led them to condemn so vicious a system. Over twenty years ago one of the native states, Mysore, outlawed the institution within its borders.

The tendency among modern writers is to minimize the extent of the practice, and it seems quite certain that it has grown less important in recent years, but it is still sufficiently prevalent when one of the main champions of its overthrow can declare that every year thousands of young innocent children are condemned to a life of

"immorality and vice, disease, suffering, and finally of death, resulting from infectious and venereal diseases contracted in the pursuit of their profession as Hindu religious prostitutes." [56]

Certain castes uniformly dedicate their girls to the Temple service by a ceremony known as "marriage to the gods." While having various cult functions to perform, the outcome of Temple dedication is inevitably the practice of prostitution. Thus the editor of the *Modern Review of India* writes:

"The castes which dedicate their girls to gods invariably carry on the most nefarious trade of prostitution. . . . The sham ceremony of dedication does not at all deter either the Elders or their girls from beginning their ancestral trade of prostitution as soon as the girls reach the age of puberty. . . . Such dedication has come to mean initiation into prostitution. None, therefore, need associate even the slightest idea of sacredness with such a dedication." [57]

[56] Quoted by Harry H. Field, *After Mother India* (London: Jonathan Cape, 1929), p. 152.
[57] *Modern Review of India* (March, 1929), p. 307.

IN HINDUISM

When defenders of the practice attempt to show that in its origin the dedication ceremony had nothing to do with prostitution, Dr. Muthulakshmi Reddy (Mrs.) declares:

"Whatever the origin of the practice in ancient days of the dedication of women as Devadasis in Hindu Temples, it is unfortunately the case that the practice has now degenerated mainly into a method of initiation of young women to a life of immorality and prostitution. The existence or otherwise of Shastric sanction of the practice of dedication as Devadasis is therefore immaterial. The Shastras are against vice and impurity of all kinds, and enlightened public opinion is against tolerating the continuance of a practice which in the name of service to God has condemned a certain class of women to a life either of concubinage or prostitution." [58]

As indicated, vigorous opposition has arisen among orthodox Hindus. They have resorted again to the charge that religion is in danger and have succeeded in stirring up much popular opinion against it. They invoke the sacred books for its continuance. When legislation was proposed in the presidency of Madras a manifesto was issued by members of the Devadasis Association of Madras, which claimed to represent over 200,000 members. In part, they declared:

"We have to our credit the support of the entire Devadasis class, with very few honorable exceptions, who are our enemies; the support of the Sastras, such as Pancharatra, Vaikhanasa, Puranas, Upanishads. Customs and Traditions; the support of the Pandits and the Hindu society in general, drawn from all classes

[58] *India Social Reformer,* Vol. 40, p. 380.

and castes; the support of the public as may be known from several protest meetings held all over the presidency, and the volume of opinion gathering every day from the Press."

They conclude their manifesto with an "Appeal to the Public":

"The Devadasis are today proposed to be destroyed; Hindu girls may follow next; widows may take their chance later; Temples may be demolished; worship desecrated; and we shall be torn asunder from all traditions. Our Hindu brethren who love Hindu gods, who worship in the Hindu Temples, come to our rescue and save us from peril." [59]

Nevertheless, various writers assert that for the most part the leaders of the Devadasis are interested in its abolition as a system.

It has been asserted by some defenders of the system that the Devadasis are recruited from a single prostitute caste. Indeed, one defender who wrote in reply to *Mother India* rationalizes the support of the Devadasis system in this fashion:

"In India the prostitutes form a class by themselves. It is untrue to say that they belong to respectable families of rank and position. The mother of a prostitute was a prostitute once. The daughter becomes a prostitute. . . . The idea of allowing the young girls of the prostitute class to grow in the atmosphere of the Temples is to instill into them some religion, some fear of God, so that when they become of age they may not indulge in promiscuity but be the mistress of one man. The prostitutes of India are, therefore, one of the most

[59] "Manifesto to the Madras Government" by the members of the Devadasis Association, December, 1927, quoted by Harry H. Field, *op cit.*, p. 156.

IN HINDUISM

god-fearing and loyal class of mistresses known to that unfortunate profession." [60]

However, Dr. Reddy directly refutes this in the following statement:

"It is a well-known fact that the Devadasis are recruited from various castes among the Hindus, having different names in different districts, and that their strength is kept up by adoption from other Hindu communities, because when the old Devadasis become sterile, which they very often are by the nature of their profession, they buy girls from other caste-Hindus, and so every Hindu community at one time or other shares in the degradation and misery of such a life." [61]

And the same champion of reform clearly distinguishes the Temple prostitues from the brothel class, declaring that the former

"are only the victims of tradition, custom, or mistaken religious fervor. . . . The Temple and the illiterate Hindu public are responsible for developing a kind of mentality in those children which makes them, when they grow to be women, view a criminal, unholy, and anti-social act . . . as a hereditary right and a caste Dharma." [62]

As already indicated, Madras was the first of the British states to pass legislation designed to outlaw the practice, but a bill was introduced into the Legislative Assembly for all of British India in 1930 which, it was hoped, would have the result of de-

[60] C. S. Ranga Iyer, *Father India* (London: Selwyn and Blount, 1927), pp. 51-52.
[61] Dr. S. M. Reddy, in *Official Report Legislative Council of Madras* (Nov. 4, 1927), p. 416.
[62] *Ibid.* (Nov. 5, 1927), p. 514.

MODERN TENDENCIES

stroying the institution. The proposed bill provided for "the enfranchisement of lands held by such women on condition of service in temples"; the recognition of the validity of a marriage contract entered into by a Devadasi "notwithstanding any law or custom declaring such marriage to be invalid by reason of her subjection to the ceremony of dedication to service in a temple," and the fixing of severe penalties for those who "perform, permit, take part in or abet the performance of such ceremony." [63]

The bill failed to pass but its proponents refused to accept the defeat as final. In 1932 another bill was introduced,[64] the fate of which it is too early to predict. But the All-India Women's Conference includes among its reform projects the abolition of the system and are actively engaged in creating public sentiment favorable to the reform. Many liberal and reform periodicals are stressing it frequently. The growing list of states, native and British, which have outlawed or greatly restricted the practice—a list which includes, according to a recent check, Mysore, Travancore, Cochin, Pudukottah, Madras, and the United Provinces of Agra and Oudh, clearly indicates that the movement is gathering momentum. It would seem probable therefore that within a comparatively short time this reproach upon Hinduism will be removed.

We have discussed thus far the main tendencies which are to be observed in India at the present time;

[63] *Indian Social Reformer,* Vol. 40 (Feb. 1, 1930), p. 364.
[64] *Ibid.,* Vol. 42 (March 12, 1932), p. 435. See also Vol. 43 (Sept. 10, 1932), pp. 20-21.

IN HINDUISM

a general tendency in the direction of irreligion among a growing group; increasing opposition to priestly influence and to an extent to the Holy Man; a strong reactionary, "fundamentalist" tendency; a definite rationalizing tendency which seeks to "modernize" Hindu faith; a marked syncretic movement; and finally a well-nigh revolutionary tendency in the direction of social change. But even this is not the whole story. Nothing has been said of the increasing emphasis upon education, with an attempt to fit the education to the peculiar type of life to which the majority of Indian people are destined, with its stress upon the education of women which is a marked step forward and is apt to be productive of far-reaching changes in the mental, moral and religious outlook of women. Nor have we done more than mention briefly in connection with the Brahma Samaj one other tendency which, while somewhat indefinite, is observable even in the ranks of the most orthodox to some degree, namely the increasing tendency to express religion through some sort of social service. This represents real change in Hinduism. Early Buddhism gave an impulse in this direction, but the predominant ideal of Hinduism has been that of seeking individual release from the round of rebirths. Karma and the doctrine of reincarnation have cut effectively the impulse to self-giving for the sake of others. But a new day dawns—slowly, to be sure, and perhaps chiefly as a result of the Christian teaching regarding social service. Organizations such as the Servants of India Society and the Ramakrishna mission, with their well-defined programs of social

MODERN TENDENCIES

uplift, are multiplying, and by the Arya Samajists at least definite sanction for this emphasis is being found in the Vedas themselves. In all this lies promise of almost unlimited change in the religious and social life of India.

CHAPTER III

MODERN TENDENCIES IN CHINA

No country in the world has undergone greater change since the dawn of the twentieth century than China. In the opening chapter of the book an attempt was made to list the major factors which produce change in religion. If the reader will recall these and think through the last thirty years of China's history he will see that not one of them is lacking in China. Scientific discovery! Everything that the scientists of the world have brought to light has suddenly become the property of the leaders of China. With bewildering rapidity the most advanced concepts of the thinkers of the world have been taken up by the eager students of Cathay, and projected into the schools. There is no other word with such magic as Science. It is invoked as the solution of every problem. The reverence toward it approximates religious reverence. Its authority is as near absolute as any authority is permitted to be in this new day of freedom. Slowly, but surely too, the practical applications of science are penetrating the one-time China of the closed door. Machines are making their way in to displace old ways of doing things. The tempo of life is gradually being speeded up, especially along the coast and great waterways.

MODERN TENDENCIES

Economic change! Not yet so marked as in some parts of the world, yet here, too, the beginnings of industrialization are to be observed with its attendant social changes, such as city crowding, the breakdown of the family system, the overthrow of ancient guilds, the growth of modern labor organizations.

Political change! For about thirty years China has been in the process of making over her political structure, passing from an absolute monarchy to a republican democracy, at least in form, and is now in the midst of a struggle between republican forces and those of communism for control. At the same time she is involved in an effort to secure a new level for herself in the international sisterhood of nations, by throwing off the external limitations upon her sovereignty in the form of the unequal treaties, extraterritoriality and foreign concessions.

Inter-cultural contact with other peoples! The interchange of cultures! Surely China has experienced this in large measure. Christian missions, active for over a century, but greatly intensified in recent decades—exchange of students, literally thousands studying in the universities of the West—extensive travel of occidentals in the Orient—the exchange of college lectures, the translation of books, the movies!

Intellectual change! The acquaintance of Chinese thinkers with all that the West has had to offer in the way of philosophy, the application of the scientific methods of inquiry to their own classic thought has wrought enormous changes in their outlook. General education, lifting of the general level of educa-

RELIGION IN CHINA

tion by a new modern school system, mass education, an entire literary renaissance! All these China has undergone in less than a single generation. It has been aptly said that what Europe and America passed through in a period of centuries, China is experiencing in less than a generation, namely political revolution, intellectual renaissance, industrial revolution, as well as a thoroughgoing social revolution. Could religion escape change in so kaleidoscopic a shifting of the very bases of Chinese life? Of course it could not and has not. As a better background against which to estimate the religious change let us survey with rapid strokes what has taken place since the beginning of the twentieth century.

Political Revolution

As the nineteenth century came to an end the old Manchu Dynasty of China was seen to be tottering to its fall. Quiet forces had been at work beneath the surface for a long time to bring it about. The royal house had resisted stubbornly any attempt at reform. In the early years of the twentieth century, as a concession to the insistent demands upon them, they abolished the old classic examination system and made some beginning at the introduction of the newer western education. Pressed by the forces of reform, the dowager empress made vague promises of a constitution, but ten years or more must pass before the constitution would become a reality. The people were too eager for change, however, and in 1911 the political revolution occurred which banished the Manchu Dynasty forever and set up the

MODERN TENDENCIES

Republic of China. This is not the place to recount the successive struggles for supremacy of various republican groups nor the long drawn-out guerrilla warfare waged by the war lords of various sections, making impossible the ordered, peaceful development of the country. The attempt of the Yuan Shih Kai to reëstablish the empire with himself as emperor came to naught. Nor has the president of the republic at any given time ever held effective rule over the vast reaches of the eighteen provinces. The rise of the people's party, Kuomintang, in the south and its spectacular march upon the northern capital, opened a new era in the development of modern China. For a time it appeared that at last the nation had been unified, but the subsequent revolt of the communist group and other disaffected portions of the country has kept the government in continuous warfare, and effectually prevented it from carrying out its very excellent program of national development. Thus for a period of twenty years it may be said that China has been in the throes of a political revolution, the end of which is not yet apparent. The overthrow of political authority, the breakdown of government in general, and particularly the rise of the militarist to control over the scholar, could not fail to produce far-reaching effects upon the religion and thought of China. Particularly has the growth of nationalism, with its keen criticism of and hostility to foreign peoples and cultures, affected profoundly the attitude of the Chinese people, especially toward Christianity which, as a foreign religion, was rapidly gaining in prestige and numbers.

RELIGION IN CHINA

The Intellectual and Social Revolution

But if China has undergone prolonged and painful political revolution, her intellectual and social revolution has been no less marked. The educational system has been completely overhauled within our period. On the discontinuance of the old classical system a total reorganization of the schools took place. In organization, in curriculum, indeed in fundamental aim, China struck out on a new path. As might have been expected, she borrowed heavily from the West—perhaps much too heavily for her own good. Many of her leaders now think so. But to build suddenly an educational plan adequate for a land as vast and populous as China is no mean task. Especially is this true where there is almost continuous revolutionary activity going on and the resources that might be counted upon for educational purposes are being exhausted in futile sectional rivalries. Even so, China has made very rapid progress. From 1915 to 1923 the number of schools increased from 86,799 to 178,972, the number of students from 2,905,152 to 6,617,792, or, over one hundred per cent gain. The years since 1925 have been years of great unrest. The schools have been seriously affected by the recurring military campaigns, and it is possible that the number of schools and pupils is less today. Unfortunately no later statistics for the entire school system are available.[1] Probably no more far-reaching movement has occurred in the modern world than

[1] The 1932 *Statesman's Yearbook* gives the 1923 statistics as the latest.

MODERN TENDENCIES

what it is now customary to call the literary renaissance of China, the so-called founder of which is still at this writing under forty-five years of age, for it has resulted in the unification of the Chinese people by means of the creation of a literature in the common tongue. For centuries only cultured men, scholars, could read the literature of China. Since the literary medium was different from that commonly spoken, the decision of the younger group of writers to forsake the classic literary language and express themselves in the vernacular has suddenly opened to millions of Chinese a new world of thought. Simplification of the writing of the language, the adoption of a limited number of word-signs, approximately one thousand, which even an illiterate adult could learn in a comparatively short time under the instruction of student-teachers, who gave themselves to the great mass education movement, made it possible within a comparatively few years for a new set of ideas to penetrate the masses of Chinese people.

The social revolution resulting from these multiple new forces has been startling. Old traditional ways of thinking and acting have been broken down. Age-old authorities have lost their power to command. The family, that most important of all the social institutions of China, has been profoundly affected. The attitude of youth toward its elders, a principle so deeply imbedded in the tradition of China, has lost its force. The relationship between the sexes has been modified almost beyond recognition, and along with this have gone corresponding changes in the attitude toward the religious institutions. It would be un-

RELIGION IN CHINA

natural to suppose that these alone should be exempt from the whirl of change that is touching every other phase of human life. Surely one would, on the basis of such facts as these, expect to find in China more profound and far-reaching changes in the religious outlook than in almost any other land in the world.

An indication of the ferment in the mind of China and its eagerness for change from the old may be found in the following list of publications that have appeared in recent years in China. Most of them are, of course, products of the younger group of intellectuals, but it is precisely this group that will give direction to Chinese evolution in the next few years. Note the emphasis on the *Young,* the *New.* There is the New China, New Life, New Woman, New Man, New Individual, New Group, New Society, New Spirit, New Voice, New Culture, New Light, New Education, New Student, New Learning, New Voice of Society, New World and the New Air. There is Young China, The Young World, The Youth, The Progress of Youth. There is The Dawn, The Morning Bell, The Morning Star. There is also Freedom, Truth, Women, Struggle, Science, The Citizen, Self-Consciousness, Labor and Learning, Reconstruction, Emancipation, Renaissance. What a yeasty condition is clearly indicated merely by this list of magazine titles. How could religion or any other phase of culture expect to remain static in an age which could give birth to such a group of periodicals all in the language of the people?

Down to the opening of the twentieth century there were three religions of China, known to the

MODERN TENDENCIES

West as Confucianism, a term unused in China, but which usually gathers up in itself what was known as the old state religion, the ancestral rites and the worship of the numerous tutelary deities charged with the oversight of the whole round of home and community life; Taoism, which in recent centuries has meant little more than a system of necromancy, dealing largely with the control of the world of spirits, a far remove from the noble philosophy of the traditional founder Lao-tze; and Buddhism, which has since the fourth century A.D. been practically a native religion. Largely monastic and dealing much with the life after death, it has for centuries led a placid existence, exerting a gentle moral influence upon the life of China. But for a long time it has been in a state of decadence.

Mohammedanism has been many centuries in China, where it numbers between fifteen and twenty million followers, but it has never really made itself indigenous. Christianity, commanding only a very small following, perhaps five million all told, has been in the present period the one vigorous aggressive religious force in China, but always held to be a foreign faith. Its activity has been chiefly the product of the restless missionary urge of occidental Christianity. How have these religions fared, and what may be said to be the general religious situation today?

As a result of these numerous change-producing factors in China, it is possible to distinguish the following chief trends within our period:

1. A radical anti-religion movement which opposes religion in any form.

RELIGION IN CHINA

2. A marked anti-Christian movement based on various motives, but perhaps most of all on

3. A strong sense of nationalism which, like vigorous nationalism anywhere, opposes any rival claimant for allegiance and amounts almost to a religion. The near-cult of Sun Yat Sen is one of its phases. The rapid growth of the demand for national versus foreign control of the Christian church in China is another phase.

4. A liberal but not anti-religious attitude expressing itself in three ways. It includes those who say:

(1) Not to destroy religion but to subject it to searching inquiry and preserve only that which will stand testing.

(2) Not all religion but religion as it is now must be gotten rid of and an adequate religion found.

(3) Religion has performed a very useful function in the past, but it is not indispensable. Seek a substitute for it, e.g. esthetics, which will not be subject to the handicaps under which religion operates.

5. The reform or revival of the older religions, especially Confucianism and Buddhism.

6. The rise of various syncretic religions which attempt to find in the fusion of disparate elements of various faiths the satisfaction of needs, which apparently the old faiths had failed to supply.

The Anti-Religion Movement

That there has developed a group of radicals in China, who repudiate religion as they have usually

MODERN TENDENCIES

understood it, should occasion no surprise. There has always been a considerable group of the literati who made little place in their thinking for the supernatural, and that has been at the center of most religion as they have known it. Indeed, one might be a very loyal follower of the great sage and be at least agnostic concerning the gods. He might follow the great philosopher Chucius and positively deny the existence of God. Many of these men do not think of Confucianism, in the sense of faithfulness to the fundamental teaching of Confucius regarding the five relations or the superior man, as a religion at all. But men of this sort, while non-religious, are not usually anti-religious. They are quite content to allow others to be either religious or non-religious, as they choose.

The anti-religion movement is, or has been, at various periods definitely and aggressively opposed to religion in any form, and has sought in various ways to propagate unbelief, and make converts to that point of view. That is, it has gone beyond the stage of individual unbelief and has organized itself into a movement with a fixed purpose to destroy religion.

Various causes have contributed to the formation of the movement. For one thing, the incoming of Science, spelled with a capital letter, with its supposed destruction of the basis for rational belief in the supernatural. A materialistic philosophy, partly a product of the West, has seemed to negative the possibility of a universe in which the spiritual has primacy. Not a few of China's returned students

RELIGION IN CHINA

from America or Europe have brought back with them a practical, if not a theoretical, atheism. R. Y. Lo says:

"Many of the students educated abroad have returned as free thinkers. These returned students from American and European universities have no use for religion. They take pride in ridiculing and exploding the faith of the ages in Voltarian fashion. The Young China Association, made up of these students, furnishes a good illustration. Its membership is limited to those who hold no religious beliefs." [2]

It is doubtful, however, if without the stimulus given by Communism which, coming as it did from Russia, had an avowedly anti-religious bent, would have assumed the character that it has. Communism in Russia is committed definitely to the complete destruction of religion, because in religion Communists believe they see an impossible barrier to their goal. Religion is believed to be the opium of the people. In their evangelistic zeal they have attempted to lead the Chinese to the same attitude they themselves have. Their task was made much easier by two considerations: first, the crudity and superstitious character of much of the religion as practiced—doubly crude and superstitious from the standpoint of the emancipated younger group of students and intellectuals; second, from the fact that the most aggressive form of religion, Christianity, was a foreign product, and suspected of being a tool of imperialism. Much of the strong anti-religious feeling derives from anti-Christian feeling.

[2] R. Y. Lo, *China's Revolution from the Inside*, p. 97. Copyright, 1930, by permission of the Abingdon Press.

MODERN TENDENCIES

The grounds of hostility to religion itself are summarized by R. Y. Lo as follows:

"1. Religion is hostile to progress. It is biased, dogmatic, and intolerant toward those who dare to disagree. Directly, it hampers the development of individual thought and expression; indirectly, it hinders human progress.

"2. Religion is unnatural and the mother of superstition. It was created for the consumption of primitive people and has outlived its usefulness. Moreover, religion sets up its belief in supernatural beings; hence it develops superstition.

"3. Religion is divisive in influence. Religious bias and exclusiveness foster jealousy and hatred. It does not make for unity and harmony within the human race.

"4. Religion is other-worldly and ignores the material welfare of human beings. It teaches sacrifice of the known for the unknown and undervalues the importance of physical existence." [3]

The anti-religion movement has centered in the universities and student groups, precisely among those who are most apt to raise questions and demand demonstrations or proof of its truth and worth. Dr. Lo quotes a writer, whom he evidently regards as typical of a large number of people:

"Everything is being questioned, even the holiest sanctions of the old faiths are now sneered at as foolish superstitions. Science is overthrowing geomancy. The idols of the temple and of the mind, shaken and undermined by the New Thought, are tottering to their fall. The cake of custom is being hopelessly smashed. The process once begun cannot be stopped until every doc-

[3] R. L. Lo, *op. cit.*, pp. 95-96. Copyright, 1930, by permission of the Abingdon Press.

RELIGION IN CHINA

trine and every institution is thrown into the crucible out of which most will never emerge at all, and only a few will stand the ordeal by fire."[4]

While the Kuomingtang, or the People's party, which is in nominal control now in China, as a whole is not hostile to religion—it will be recalled that President Kiang Kai Shek was recently baptized as a Christian,—there is a vigorous minority group which is aggressively anti-religious in its outlook. A. R. Kepler, writing of the "Kuomingtang and Religion," says that the majority of Chinese educationalists would declare:

"Each individual should be enabled to make choice for himself what religion, if any, he wishes to embrace, which makes it necessary to safeguard the child's mind against religious teaching until maturity is reached."[5]

The Ministry of Education, he says, has a "fixed policy" of "denying passports to any students who wish to study abroad, unless they first give assurance that they will not include any religious subjects among their post-graduate studies abroad."[6]

Resolutions have been passed by certain groups related to the educational program asking that the government prohibit all children under thirteen from attending any religious service at all, on the ground that it would violate the principle of religious free-

[4] R. Y. Lo, *op. cit.*, p. 52. Copyright, 1930, by permission of the Abingdon Press.
[5] A. R. Kepler, "Kuomingtang and Religion," *Chinese Recorder*, Vol. 61, p. 616 ff.
[6] *Ibid.*, p. 620. The writer has been informed by persons recently come from China that in recent months this policy has been somewhat relaxed.

MODERN TENDENCIES

dom. While it is religious freedom that is invoked in these statements, the last would lead logically to the disappearance of religion eventually, which is exactly the aim of the anti-religious group. The government, however, failed to act on the resolutions.

The anti-religion movement, as such, came into being in 1922 as a reaction to the World's Christian Student Federation, which was meeting in Shanghai. At first primarily anti-Christian, it grew into an anti-religious movement directed against all religion. It has not been uniformly aggressive since that time, tending to flame up especially in times of some sort of crisis. Writers in recent periodicals indicate that for the present it is comparatively quiescent, but that it has by no means disappeared. They are sure that, given a sufficient stimulus, a resurgence of the movement may be expected.

The Anti-Christian Movement

The anti-Christian phase of the more general movement was, as already stated, the first to appear, openly asserting itself on the occasion of the World Christian Student Federation convention. It took just such an event to focus the attention of the younger Chinese on the growing importance of Christianity, a foreign religion in China. There have appeared many counts against Christianity, but it stands first and foremost as a foreign faith, the growth of which in China they consider a distinct threat to China's sovereignty. In a day of heightened nationalism such a suspicion even is a sufficient basis for

RELIGION IN CHINA

hostility. We let Dr. Lo summarize for us their complaints against Christianity:

"In particular:
"1. Christianity is contrary to reason and logic. Its doctrines of creation, virgin birth, and resurrection are beyond reason and contrary to facts.
"2. Christianity is passive and counter-revolutionary. It believes in individual redemption from sin but says little about social salvation. It exhorts contentment, hence it is hostile to change and revolution.
"3. Christianity is hypocritical. It preaches fraternity, equality, and sacrifice but does not practice them in life.
"4. Christianity is the vanguard of imperialism and in alliance with the capitalistic class. It has been imposed upon China by treaty and gunboats." [7]

Communists are, of course, strenuously antagonistic to Christianity. They look upon it as a means used by the capitalist classes for the oppression of the workers. Dr. Lo quotes a Communist declaration as follows:

"Christianity is the instrument in the hands of the oppressors. In mission schools the pupils are denied both freedom of thought and action. They are forced to read exclusively the hypocritical and idle creed of love for humanity and service to Jesus. At the same time the streets of Shanghai and Hankow flow with the blood of Chinese in consequence of measures adopted by the Christian Municipal Council, Christian British naval infantry, and sailors." [8]

[7] R. Y. Lo, *op. cit.*, p. 96. Copyright, 1930, by permission of the Abingdon Press.
[8] *Ibid.*, p. 105.

101

MODERN TENDENCIES

Inflamed by such charges, lawless mobs have destroyed not a little mission property and some lives have been sacrificed. Native Christians known as "the running dogs" of the foreigners have been subjected to bitter persecution, even to martyrdom. The work of the churches has been seriously handicapped. The lawless phases of the movement seem to have passed for the present. However, heavy limitations are being placed upon the freedom of missionary work, particularly in the educational field. Mission schools have not been closed but they have been required to undergo many changes in organization and in their teaching. A long struggle has been waged to maintain freedom to teach religion in the schools. The present status of the problem seems to be that, while religion may be taught, no courses in religion may be required of any student, nor may he be compelled to attend any kind of religious services in secondary and higher schools. Not even elective religion courses, nor voluntary religious services may be held in primary schools. All missions' schools have been required to register with the government, which implies acceptance of govermental oversight. Many have declined to do so and have closed their doors. Others are postponing it as long as possible and the government has been reasonably patient. But it seems certain that eventually those refusing to register themselves will be closed. Many missionaries are quite content to have religion courses and meetings elective, but their supporting boards and constituencies have preferred to close them rather than surrender the right to require religion in the schools.

RELIGION IN CHINA

Dr. Lo says, regarding the movement:

"But with the gradual restoration of law and order throughout the provinces, the activities of the lawless elements of the Anti-Christian Movement have practically subsided or have been altogether suppressed. At present we seldom hear of molestation of missionaries or interference with the missionary work. The churches are recovering slowly but steadily, and missionaries are returning in large numbers. Nevertheless, the forces which called the Anti-Religion or Anti-Christian Movement into being, are still there. Unless and until the causes for attack against Christianity are removed, no real peace and understanding between the Christians and non-Christians in China can be expected." [9]

Nationalism and Religion

One frequently hears today the saying that nationalism is the real religion of the modern world. It is said even of Americans, who in their zeal and patriotism lift the nation in their thought to a place of supremacy above any claims of religion. It may be said at once that the use of the term religion in that sense is a loose usage, particularly as applied to countries like the United States. It may not be wholly out of place so to use it, however, in China or, as will later appear, in Russia. Here there are real evidences that nationalism at least approximates religion, not only in the fact of dependence upon it, for what in other places religion has usually supplied, not alone in the utter devotion which it claims on the part of its followers, even to sacrifice of life, but in

[9] R. Y. Lo, *op. cit.*, p. 107. Copyright, 1930, by permission of the Abingdon Press.

something resembling a cult. In China the nationalist ideal is epitomized in the three great principles of the people's party, namely the principle of nationality, the principle of the people's living, and the principle of the people's rights. It is no part of our task here to explain in detail the full content of these terms; but, briefly, the people's nationality or people's race has to do with the relations of China to other nations; she must recover her full independent sovereignty, unconditioned by the interference of foreign powers in such matters as "concessions," "extra-territoriality" or control of customs. It demands the speedy abrogation of "unequal treaties."

The people's rights have to do chiefly with the right of the people in relation to government—the right of democracy. It is summed up in the four rights of election; veto, originating of laws, and repealing and altering laws; and the five functions of government, which do not so much concern us here.

The principle of the people's living has to do with the economic and social rights of the people, and looks toward a reconstruction of the social and economic structure of China with a view to securing an equitable distribution of goods among all classes of people. It is sometimes translated the people's socialism.

These principles, set forth in the will of the great revolutionary leader, Sun Yat Sen, find something like a concrete embodiment in the person of that leader himself, who died in 1925, and thus provided a center about which might develop a near cult. In another country and among other people such a cult

RELIGION IN CHINA

might be readily disposed of as a patriotic veneration, but in China, where the worship of ancestors has been called religious by Western observers, it is easy to classify the ceremony that has already grown up about Dr. Sen, as religious. If the veneration of Confucius is religious to a Chinese, then it is difficult to escape calling the Sun ceremonies other than religious. A writer in *Asia* describes the ceremony:

"The cult of Sun Yat Sen in South China, like that of Lenin in Russia, probably has more followers than any other single 'religion.' Every home in Canton has its picture of the great revolutionary leader, reminding one strongly of the 'Lenin Corners' in workers' dwellings throughout the Soviet union. On Monday mornings, in every office under the wing of the Nationalist government there is a fifteen-minute service in memory of Sun Yat Sen. I attended two such meetings in the assembly room of the Kuomingtang National Headquarters. After a revolutionary hymn, everybody bowed three times before the giant portrait of Dr. Sun, whose last will was then read aloud in staccato monosyllables. In conclusion there were three minutes of silence, while the gathering stood with heads bowed in meditation." [10]

But not only is this ceremony carried on in party headquarters. Something similar is required in all schools, including, of course, mission schools. The children stand and repeat the three principles as found in his will, bow before the picture of Sun, and remain in silence for a brief period. Formerly this was required at the opening of all public gatherings such as the theater, weddings, funerals, etc.

[10] J. M. Roots, "Sun Yat Sen—the Washington of China's Revolution," *Asia*, Vol. 27, p. 363.

MODERN TENDENCIES

In 1929 it was decreed that it should be omitted at theaters, weddings and funerals on the ground that performance under such circumstances tended to cheapen the cult.

Will such observances continue permanently? With a change of government may it not disappear completely? Possibly so. In an earlier day, before the rise of the modern spirit in China and the new emphasis on education, it would have been much easier for a permanent cult to develop. The modern age is not so well calculated to produce gods as previous ages. But we are recording trends here, and it is impossible to neglect the possibility, at least, that here is the beginning of a potentially new religion.

We have already indicated, as partly a result of nationalistic feeling, the rise of the anti-Christian movement. Still another manifestation of that nationalism working within rather than outside of Christianity is the tendency to nationalize organized Christianity in China. Two factors have promoted this tendency. First, entirely apart from organized nationalism as a political system, the native Christian church has developed far beyond the early stage of dependence upon foreign direction, and has produced a leadership which is capable of assuming responsibility for its own direction. It was growing up and, as natural, began to feel its own strength and capacity for self-direction. Had there been no nationalist uprising, the process would probably have been slower, but it would have occurred inevitably though gradually. Given the raw material with which Christianity worked, no other outcome could have been expected.

RELIGION IN CHINA

But the revolution and the rise of nationalism has greatly accelerated the movement. Christianity was a foreign religion—it was held to be a tool of imperialism. It became necessary if it were to persist in China that it be freed from the onus of such charges. The indigenization of the church, the elimination of foreign control would help to remove the stigma which it bore. National Christian leaders have comprehended this and as a result the whole nationalizing process has been hastened.

In the beginnings of the missionary enterprise the foreigners did everything; they were the preachers, the teachers, the directors, the superintendents, the bishops, the heads of institutions. Little by little, national workers were raised up and trained. Gradually they became more numerous than the missionary force. They became the preachers and the teachers; the work of the missionary became largely that of superintendence and direction. It is theoretically the business of the missionary to train others who can assume his work. In practice, missionaries have not always recognized that the time has arrived to yield place to the national. But gradually, as able men have appeared, capable of serving as leaders, they have been given greater responsibility—not usually as soon as the national has wanted it, however, or thought himself capable of assuming it. It has now come about, however, that even churches which have an episcopal form of government have admitted nationals to the episcopacy. National church organizations have been gradually acquiring a large measure of autonomy. Some of them are now wholly

MODERN TENDENCIES

independent of the organization in Europe or America, to which they owe their founding.

National feeling has led to an impatience with nonessential sectarian divisions within Protestantism, based on doctrinal or political differences which can have little or no meaning for an Oriental. The result has been a tendency toward coöperation and even organic union of various denominations. The National Christian Council is in part an outgrowth of this impatience. An even more marked example, however, was the formation in 1927 of a national church called the United Christian Church in China, in which a number of denominations have fused. Doctrinally, there has been little tendency thus far to depart from the historic creeds of western Christianity, but even here there is a growing disposition to define for themselves the meaning of the religion of Jesus to the Chinese people. "Why," some are saying, "should China accept a Nicene Creed, essentially a foreign formulation of belief? Why should she not on the basis of a careful study of the sources of Christian teaching reformulate her belief in terms that will have real meaning for her own people?" In Korea there occurred recently a fusion of the two Methodisms, North and South, in a Korean Methodist Church. The formulation of their articles of faith in their simplicity and directness offers a model that might well be followed in the West. It is essentially an untheological statement upon which a practical working Christian organization can well base itself. China will in the future produce her own creeds, and they

RELIGION IN CHINA

will be true to the genius of Christianity as China understands it. An illuminating book appeared recently containing the thought of a considerable number of representative Chinese Christian leaders on a common theme, *The Jesus I Know.*—In the final writing of such a basis of belief there will be a sure recognition of the values in their own historic culture.

Liberalism in Religion

A fourth tendency may be distinguished which, while radical in its attitude toward religion, is not anti-religious. It would not destroy religion necessarily, but it would subject it to every possible rigorous test and reject that which does not justify itself. It is really an attitude of questioning rather than hostility, and it is a part of the whole tendency manifested in the New Thought Movement. It cannot be better illustrated than in the words of Dr. Hu Shih, one of the prominent leaders of that movement, who writes:

"(1) In regard to traditional customs we must ask whether or not they have any value today.

"(2) In regard to the traditionally handed-down teachings of our saints, we must inquire whether or not they are adequate for us now.

"(3) Toward conventional forms of belief and action we must ask, 'Is it necessary to accept them as right because they are accepted by the majority?' " [11]

That such an attitude taken over by the younger student groups should lead to the repudiation of all

[11] R. Y. Lo, *China's Revolution from the Inside*, pp. 51-52. Copyright, 1930, by permission of the Abingdon Press.

MODERN TENDENCIES

religion and send some of them into the anti-religious movement, especially in view of the difficulty of impartial inquiry in an atmosphere surcharged with prejudice and hate, is not at all surprising. But by no means all who adopt it come out with a negative attitude toward religion. Mr. H. C. Hu points out two divergent groups, one of which declares that "while religion has external value, present-day religion has no value. All existing religions need radical revision," [12] the other that in view of the vast influence of religion on mankind "it is now necessary to apply the scientific method to the study of the history of religion, in order to discover what results have been good and what bad. . . . This party believes that religion should be given a chance to prove its own worth." [13] That this would mean to undergo revision seems to be implied in the latter statement, so that these two groups have that element in common. Still another liberal group recognizes that religion has performed a useful function in the past, but they hold that the real needs thus served can quite as well be served otherwise than by religion. They would substitute for religion, therefore, such means of satisfaction, and thus escape the serious handicaps which religion has imposed, for example, superstition and a futile, expensive ritual. Mr. Hunter Yen, writing on "Some Modern Chinese Scholars and Religion," cites a work of Dr. Tsai on *Æsthetics and Religion* as typical of this attitude. On the assumption that science has completely changed our

[12] *Chinese Recorder*, Vol. 54, p. 447.
[13] *Ibid.*

RELIGION IN CHINA

modes of thinking and that experience has taught us that moral laws are not unchangeable, Dr. Tsai thinks that the activities of the mind and will are no longer in close relation to religion. Religion is therefore no longer needed. The only aspect of life which still has a semblance of connection with religion is our emotional activities, which he understands to be the æsthetic feelings. In order to refine such feelings he suggests the cultivation of the fine arts as a substitute for religion.

R. Y. Lo thinks that this is an admission that "science cannot supply inspiration, consolation and the sweetening of life which one finds in religion," but claims that, according to Dr. Tsai Yuan Pei, "while the very means through which religion gives comfort and inspiration are made up of the same materials which æsthetics can offer, yet æsthetics can supply all these at smaller cost and minus all its troubles." [14]

While recognizing the prevalence of the antireligious sentiment and the radical attitude of questioning its value, R. Y. Lo thinks that "with the exception of a few who find religion so irreconcilable with science that they denounce it as a retarding force in human progress and an enemy to civilization, the majority of the thinkers are open-minded, believing that religion should be given a chance to prove its worth." He quotes a writer of renown as declaring: "As I am not a member of any church, I am not interested in defending any organization or ad-

[14] R. Y. Lo, *op. cit.*, p. 60. Copyright, 1930, by permission of the Abingdon Press.

vocating the excellence of any particular faith. But I have often felt that religion contains within it the highest ethics, and so I think that if we want imperfect mankind to make progress toward perfection, we cannot lightly set religion aside." [15]

It will be noted that the phases of religion which occasion most hostility and criticism are its supernaturalism and its institutionalism. There is a very high regard usually for those humanistic values which are a part of religion at its best, and, indeed, constitute perhaps its main strength in the minds of modern-minded religious persons. Many of these might well be classed as naturalistic humanists, and under the broader definitions of religion as held by modern humanist leaders, so far from being antireligious or non-religious, they would be most deeply religious.

It would have been quite unnatural if in the face of the radical attitude toward religion there had appeared no reaction on the part of the organized religions of China. The notable thing is that it was so comparatively mild. China has known no such militant, aggressive, conservative, defense reaction as has appeared in some other religions. Perhaps the very nature of Confucianism made such a reaction less natural than in other faiths, where fixed creeds play a much more important part. Its relative looseness of organization, and its elasticity admit of a degree of variation within the whole that is unknown in such a religion as Islam.

[15] R. Y. Lo, *op. cit.*, p. 60. Copyright, 1930, by permission of the Abingdon Press.

RELIGION IN CHINA

Confucianism from the very first suffered heavily from the revolution. It had been the religion of the state. The Worship of Heaven at the great altar in Peking by the Emperor of China was the climax of an ascending scale of state festivals and sacrifices in which officers of the state from the lower to the very highest rank, were the very ministers of religion. With the coming of the republic most of this disappeared. State temples fell into disuse. It is said that the very Altar of Heaven is now partly grass-grown, and is used as a picnic ground for the people. A picture of the situation in one great center in China could be duplicated in almost every other great city.

A study of one hundred and seventy-five temples in Chengtu, China, not including tutelary deity temples most of which have disappeared from the streets, shows that only one temple has been built in the last three years. Only three, and these outside the wall, are being used exclusively for worship. Fifty-eight per cent of the temples are being used for more or less public projects, including schools, barracks and apartments. Some have been turned into markets, rickshaw stands and garages. In some places the images remain and a priest is in attendance and incense may be burned.[16]

Very soon after the revolution of 1911 an attempt was made by Confucian leaders to restore the teachings of the sage. A Confucian Society was formed, though it was not a reactionary but reformed Confucianism that was proposed, as will appear later.

[16] *Chinese Recorder*, Vol. 62, p. 465.

MODERN TENDENCIES

One of their projects was the attempt to make Confucianism the state religion of the Republic. But religious freedom had been granted in the new constitution and it would be contrary to this principle to admit any religion to a preferred position, argued its opponents. A movement in opposition was started by Protestant Christians in Peking which later, under the name of the "Society for Religious Liberty," came to include not only Protestants but Greek and Roman Catholics, Mohammedans, Taoists and Buddhists.

Yuan Shih Kai, the president, at first favored the Confucian proposal. It will be recalled that he himself tried unsuccessfully to restore the Worship of Heaven as carried on previously only by the Emperor. Later he reversed his position and declared that all religions should be on the same footing, and that none should be discriminated against. However, after the death of Yuan, in the autumn of 1916, when the provisional constitution under which China had operated for several years came up for permanent adoption, a compromise statement was proposed providing still for religious liberty but "that Confucian teachings be made the basis of moral instruction in all public elementary schools."[17] This was vigorously opposed by the Society for Religious Liberty on the ground that it was inconsistent with religious liberty. For, they declared, "If Confucianism is made the basis of moral instruction in the elementary schools, it will necessarily mean that the

[17] C. Y. Cheng, "The Struggle for Constitutional Religious Liberty," *Chinese Recorder*, Vol. 48, p. 266.

RELIGION IN CHINA

moral instruction of the children will be limited. All good teachings which are in other religions will be made secondary, if not left out entirely." The Society sent numerous petitions from all over China to Parliament, besides numberless telegrams. The final result was that the proposed clause was dropped and but a slight addition made to the religious freedom article, which was adopted to read as follows: "The people of the Republic of China shall have liberty to honor Confucius, and liberty of religious worship, which shall be unrestricted except in accordance with the law." [18]

This remains the official status of Confucianism in China.

A marked tendency, not only in Confucianism but in Buddhism as well, was that toward some kind of a reform which would better fit the respective religions to persist and exercise an influence on the China of the modern age. Within Confucianism the most notable effort at reform was the formation in 1911 of the Confucian Society, or as it has sometimes been called, the Confucian Church, with headquarters in Peking. The founder was Dr. Chien Huen Chang, a classic scholar holding the highest degree given under the old system, and also the degree of doctor of philosophy from Columbia University. He was at the time editor of an influential periodical in Peking. While centering in the capital, then Peking, it had branches in most of the provincial capitals and *"hsien"* cities in China. The Peking headquarters were in a modern building providing social, recre-

[18] *China Mission Yearbook* 1917, p. 37.

ational and educational facilities, including a gymnasium and kindergarten.

The credal basis of the Society, as stated by Dr. Chen, was as follows:

"First, By sacrifice to Heaven, the Sages and Ancestors, to do reverence to the three roots of life.

"Second, To gather the five blessings by meditation upon the Sages and classics.

"Third, To establish a harmonious social order by the cultivation of the moon and harmony.

"Fourth, To establish universal brotherhood by the use of property and personal influence.

"Fifth, To attain the highest longevity by nourishing the person and the soul." [19]

The function of the local societies was to "keep the local Confucian temples in repair, and look after the spring and autumn sacrifices. . . . The members are the old scholars and the gentry. In some places this local society has carried on propaganda work by lectures. Outside of these routine activities the societies are not very active." [20]

Other societies were organized with somewhat similar bases. In Shansi province the governor established "The Heart Cleansing Society" meeting for lectures on Sunday, at which attendance was compulsory. It was tolerant of other religions, sometimes Christians were invited to address its meetings, but its basis was Confucian and its emphasis on the "five relations," worship of Shang Ti, thrift, and

[19] Lewis Hodous, "Non-Christian Religious Movement in China," in *The Christian Occupation of China* (Shanghai, 1922), p. 28.
[20] *Loc. cit.*

morality.[21] By 1926 the Society seems to have failed.

Neo-Confucianism

There is great need, according to President Lin Boom Keng of Amoy University, for a revival of a reformed Confucianism—or as it is sometimes spoken of, a Neo-Confucianism. He expresses his convictions in no uncertain language. He says:

"The Mandarin Confucianism is dead. It deserves nothing better than to die. But alas! the age-old theism of the classics, with all the ethics of social life and international goodwill, is also being neglected. The literati of the younger generation are abandoning the true gems of the classics, because, forsooth, religion is only a superstition! . . . There is great danger that the ignorant masses will throw off all respect for the gods and all fear of the unknown, and jettison with these all the ethical practices inherited from the past. Without these practices they would be like ships without charts and rudders, and would be mere derelicts at the mercy of every wind and wave, in the midst of the greatest intellectual typhoon mankind has ever experienced. Disorder, desolation and red ruin are parading through the land, despoiling temples, breaking up schools, disillusioning the chastest women of mankind, and driving the most industrious people on earth to the verge of despair and desperation. We look around and have failed to see how salvation is forthcoming except through a restatement of the old *Ju Chiao*, or Confucianism, minus the official ceremonialism and dogmas."[22]

Dr. Keng states the Neo-Confucianist case thus:

[21] *Loc. cit.* [22] *Chinese Recorder,* Vol. 59, p. 83.

MODERN TENDENCIES

"The Confucians are endeavoring to restate the case for Confucianism in the light of modern knowledge. In this renaissance, Confucianism finds itself happily in a much sounder position than that of any other religion. (1) Its theology is purely rationalistic and is not vitiated by any obsolete creed based on alleged revelation. (2) Its system of ethics is founded primarily upon the fundamental relations of mankind, and is wholly deduced from the principles of filial piety and altruism, subject to revision at any time by altered political or intellectual conditions. (3) It recognizes the need of science in the furtherance of knowledge. (4) It bases its philosophy wholly upon reason and logic. (5) Its politics are the application of the law of love for the government of mankind, and are not inconsistent with the demands of the new democracy. Thus neo-Confucianism, despite its temporary setback through the fall of Mandarin classicism, is a clear advance and may claim to be the kind of religion most suitable to our age, not only in China, but throughout the world. It is socialistic and democratic without being too idealistic, and yet it combines a sane pragmatism with an absolute conviction of the truth of the immanence of the divine spirit in the world."

He states that the approach of the Neo-Confucianists to the teachings of the classics is with a threefold aim, namely:

"(1) Conservation of whatever is excellent.
"(2) Reformation of what is deficient and obsolete.
"(3) Innovation for the sake of progress." [22]

Dr. Y. Y. Tsu quotes another distinguished Neo-Confucian writer who, in discussing the decline of Confucianism and the other religions, says: "Our

[22] Lin Boom Keng, "What Can Chinese Civilization Contribute to Western Culture?" *Chinese Recorder*, Vol. 62, p. 349.

RELIGION IN CHINA

object is to rescue and preserve the moral and spiritual truths from the wrecked or declined religions and beliefs and offer them to the people of today as reliable standards and guides of life that will ensure them against two possible dangers. One is the monistic determinism of science, whose tyranny will drive men into despair. The other is the emotional intoxication of Romanticism, whose allurements will decompose man's spirit and destroy his power of reason and will." In giving his view of the function of religion, the same writer says: "Religion creates a right spirit, a right attitude of mind in man; it provides the basis of morality; its function is to give happiness to men and peace to the world. . . . Religion is not anti-intellectual. On the contrary it is an attempt to give a synoptic or total view of the universe and of life; it tries to explain everything by constructing a harmonious and coherent system." [14]

Even where Confucianism as such may not seem to be the answer to the present need, there is a tendency to fall back upon the ancient culture of China and to find there what the age requires. One very interesting suggestion is that in Mo-Ti may be found much that is worth while for the present situation. Dr. Hu Shih, father of the Literary Renaissance, has devoted not a little attention to him. "Held up for over two thousand years, as an enemy of the orthodox teaching," writes Lewis Hodous, "today his works are being published. Commentaries upon them are mul-

[14] Y. Y. Tsu, "Religion in China," *Chinese Recorder*, Vol. 59, p. 625.

MODERN TENDENCIES

tiplying. His teachings are being discussed and approved by an increasing number of people."[25]

The influence of the American humanist leaders, Babbitt and More, upon Chinese students has been noted in an article by Mr. Mei, who points out that they are reacting critically to the excesses of the Chinese Renaissance movement which, says Mr. Mei, may prove to be rather "Chinese suicide," and attempting to preserve the values in the inherited culture of China. He writes:

"Furthermore, they [the humanists of the Critical Review group] must go much beyond the cold analytical process. A large measure of the driving power of passion and conviction behind those issues is imperatively needed to convert a recalcitrant world. For the question of life and death of Chinese culture is hanging in the balance at this critical moment. And certainly to the modern Chinese there is no higher duty than the preservation and honor of their inherited culture, which is the consecrated fruit of the genius and devotion of the noblest Chinese, and through which their very voice is still audible. It may be treated like Babylonian or Egyptian culture in some Western universities for the gratification of mere intellectual curiosity, it may be scorned as 'relics of medievalism and feudalism,' by revolutionary Chinese, but it should be a religion, with all the ecstasy and pathos of a religion, to those who have started a movement in its behalf."[26]

How far that would include Confucianism may be open to question, but it is in this falling back onto the culture of the past in a critical but at the same

[25] Lewis Hodous, "Mo-Ti and Christianity," *International Review of Missions*, Vol. 13, p. 258.
[26] K. T. Mei, "Humanism and Modern China," *Bookman* (June, 1931), p. 373.

RELIGION IN CHINA

time a conserving attitude that Confucianism's chance to persist and influence Chinese life probably lies.

Dr. D. Willard Lyon makes the interesting suggestion that the conservation of Confucian values may rest yet with Christianity. To quote him:

"On the whole it would appear that, with a few exceptions, modern Confucianists, whose minds are not at the same time suffused with Christian thought, are not expecting to see the Confucianism of the future develop along religious lines. The present movement to conserve the religious values in Confucianism, so far as it exists, would seem to emanate largely from Christian minds. Generally speaking, Chinese Christians welcome a restudy of the old culture, for in such a study they see the possibility of discovering ways whereby Christianity may be made more indigenous in China."[27]

A wise summary of the whole matter referring to Confucianism as well as to other of China's problems is that of Mr. Lyon, who writes:

"To summarize the situation, small indeed is the number of those who still maintain an attitude of uncompromising resistance to the onward march of science and commerce; ultra-conservatives of this type have not been much in evidence since the fall of the Manchus in 1911. It may be assumed that practically all thinking Chinese acknowledge that Confucianism lacks a number of important elements required in a system that is to serve the needs of the new day. Those who are particularly interested in national issues see the necessity for revision in political theory; those whose minds are absorbed with a passion for the western

[27] D. Willard Lyon, "Confucianism in Coming Days in China," *Chinese Recorder*, Vol. 59, p. 84.

MODERN TENDENCIES

sciences see that it is important to harness the Chinese capacity for endurance in mental effort to scientific methods of study; those who feel convinced that the best psychology must be applied to the making of new text-books and other teaching materials; those who are chiefly concerned with China's moral and social problems see from another angle how essential it is that there shall be revision and adaptation in China's ethical practices; but all are feeling that such radical changes cannot be suddenly brought about without disaster." [28]

The Rivival of Buddhism

There are evidences that Buddhism, which has so often been described in recent years as moribund, is awakening to new life. The revival is by no means as vigorous and far-reaching as the Japanese Buddhist revival, but it demonstrates that there is still not a little vitality in it. A prominent indication of the revival is to be found in a number of societies and associations recently formed for the purpose of "propagating the Dharma and benefiting humanity." It is noteworthy that they are made up largely of laymen and women instead of monks, and that they are mostly led by lay scholars. To name only a few of them, they are "The Buddhist Church," "The Enlightening Association," "Society for Enlightening the People," and the "House of the Enlightened." We may note the aims and requirements of membership in but one of these, "The Enlightenment Society":

"First, To propound the essence of Mahayana Buddhism so that opposition may be dissolved, doubts re-

[28] *Ibid.*, p. 77.

RELIGION IN CHINA

moved, faith strengthened, religion energized, and mankind transformed into saintly and heavenly beings.

"Second, To propagate the essence of Mahayana Buddhism so that the wicked may be led into loving kindness, the selfish persons to righteousness, the wise to thirst for the doctrine, the strong to love of virtue and the struggling, misery filled world transformed into a place of peace and happiness.

"Requirements for membership are high . . . faith in the three Treasures (Buddha, Law and Order); the *four great vows* (to love all beings, destroy all passions, to know and teach others to know the law and lead others to understand the teachings of Buddha); observance of ten commandments (Not to kill, steal, commit adultery, lie, exaggerate, slander, be double tongued, covet, be angry or heretical). In addition, one must be diligent in studying the sutras, and faithful in fasting and charity. The Society was founded in 1915. They publish a magazine, 'The Voice of the Sea Waves,' as a medium of propaganda. Membership includes both monks and laymen."[20]

Some of these societies represent an effort to defend the old, but others frankly admit the need of reforms that will adapt their faith to modern conditions in China. This reform takes two directions, first, a willingness to restate in modern terms old Buddhist beliefs; second, there is a tendency to the socialization of religion.

The *Buddhist Monthly* declares:

"This magazine is willing to take in all currents of thought, both expressed and practiced by the human race . . . and to compare them with Buddhism from an unbiased viewpoint. It welcomes any criticism from people of any religion and any branch of knowledge."

[20] T. T. Lew, *China Today Through Chinese Eyes*, New York: Geo. H. Doran, p. 83.

MODERN TENDENCIES

The most notable Buddhist reformer in present-day China is a monk, Tai Hsu, founder of the Chinese Buddhist Association, with headquarters in Nanking and branches in many big cities, some time director of the Research Union of Buddhism, and editor of the influential review, *The Voice of the Surge*. In 1925 he was Chief Delegate to the East Asiatic Buddhist Conference in Japan and in 1929 made a tour of the world, lecturing in many important centers on the new Buddhism. In a little book, *Lectures on Buddhism*, translated into English, he points out certain new tendencies in Buddhism, the most interesting for our purposes being what he calls Scientific Buddhism and Universal Buddhism, the first being an attempt to integrate science and Buddhism, which are shown to be complementary in the total attempt to understand truth. "Science, however," he declares, "has never been able to perfectly understand the universe and has always lived on hypotheses. As can be shown, Buddhism is the only religion which does not contradict scientific truth, but rather confirms it and on more than one subject can furnish a point of departure. In this way the incomplete character of science is overcome and its progress guaranteed. Therefore we have to constitute a Scientific Buddhism which will be the highest expression of belief of which the intellectual world is capable. . . . Buddhism being a complete conception of the world, it is possible for science and philosophy to be brought into harmony with its different doctrines." He conceives of Buddhism as universal, "the crucible in which we can realize the function of

RELIGION IN CHINA

these two main tendencies of civilization, philosophy and science, and the result will be a universal civilization and a universal philosophy."[20] He projects far beyond the limits of China an "International Buddhist Institute" through which he hopes to make Buddhism known in other lands.

Karl L. Reichelt, writing on Present-Day Buddhism in China, says:

"Recently an atmosphere of hope and relief has been evident among the leading Buddhist monks and lay devotees. The reason is that they have succeeded in reviving and reshaping the defunct Buddhist Association for all China, the same which during the régime of Yuan-Shai-Kai played a certain rôle when Yuan's supporters tried to install Confucianism as the State religion. A group of representatives have been to Nanking and pled for religious liberty and a right to maintain their external apparatus—and a favorable answer has been given them, on condition that they live and act according to Mahayana principle and use their time and means for the uplift and spiritual progress of the people."[21]

Evidence of the increasing socialization of Buddhism is to be noted in the avowed aim of a Buddhist seminary at Nanking, which "trains men to benefit the world not self." This it will be recognized is a departure from older Buddhism. The monkish life, they declare, is a life of uselessness and a thing of the past. Special meetings closely resembling revival meetings are held where scripture reading and discussion takes place instead of the

[20] Tai Hsu, *Lectures on Buddhism*, Paris, 1928.
[21] *Chinese Recorder*, Vol. 60, p. 647.

MODERN TENDENCIES

mere reciting of the formal ritual. Educational schemes have been undertaken, including both elementary schools and colleges, which stand on a level with government schools, with the exception that they offer special courses in Buddhism. Some of these are for educating monks who, as a class, have in recent times been noted for their ignorance. In the last three or four years Buddhists have been under not a little persecution at the hands of the nationalists.

Still other evidences of socialization appear in the founding of such charitable institutions as the "Buddhist Mercy Association" and the "Yellow Swastika Society," which corresponds to the Red Cross. Homes for orphans have been opened, preaching missions have been carried on in the prisons, public lectures have been given, preaching bands have gone through the country, libraries have been established and Buddhist literature and Buddhist scriptures have been more widely circulated.

To be sure, the revival movement is not very widespread. Most of the activity is carried on among the more enlightened Buddhists, but it can hardly fail to have far-reaching effects upon the rest of the Buddhist group in China. One of the reasons assigned for the Renaissance in Buddhism is the disillusionment and negative influence of Western philosophy—the more dissatisfied students become with it the more they turn to Buddhism. Still another explanation of the renewed activity in Buddhism is given by Dr. Reichelt, writing on "Some Aspects of Buddhism in China":

RELIGION IN CHINA

"The best aspect of Buddhism of today in China is found among the lay-devotees, of whom many wealthy ones from the interior have fled to Shanghai or other treaty ports. Their number has increased considerably as a large number of scholars, merchants, officials and students, gathered in the treaty-ports, have joined the Brotherhoods. Their sorrow and disillusionment have caused them to turn to Buddhism. Daily meetings are held for these newcomers in the many *chu-si-lin* or in the bigger private homes. It is quite astonishing to see, at the present time, how many of the richer homes try to arrange a special hall (Fo-tang) set apart for worship and meditation."[33]

Not only in Confucianism and Buddhism is reform evident, but we are told there are stirrings of a new life even in Islam:

"Mohammedanism which has long since ceased to be a missionary religion in China is making new efforts to present its teachings to the nation by means of the printed page, and progressive leaders even advocate the translation of the Koran into Chinese. To the more conservative members this sounds like unmitigated heresy. The Koran has always been accepted in archaic Arabic and the ancient text is as much revered as the book itself, if not more so. For its very novelty therefore they cannot bear the mental vision of the sacred text discarded, and the book clothed in common vernacular open to the gaze of the profane. But the translation is going on. This event is as epoch-making and significant to Chinese Mohammedanism as was the translation of the Bible from Vulgate to vernacular to European Christianity. When we consider the tenacious tradition and inertia that has to be overcome before its accomplishment we can realize the tremendous

[33] Karl L. Reichelt, "Some Aspects of Buddhism in China," *Chinese Recorder*, Vol. 59, p. 174.

MODERN TENDENCIES

dynamic of the reform movement in Chinese Mohammedanism." [33]

Syncretism

The last tendency to be mentioned, that of syncretism, is one of the most interesting phases of the religious life of China in this modern age. The main movements have been admirably discussed by Mr. Paul D. Twinem in the *Journal of Religion*. For our present purpose it must suffice to indicate merely the names of the more important ones and to describe one of them in some little detail. It should be said that these were most of them the products of a comparatively brief period from 1914-1922. Out of ten such societies known to exist, all but one of them was founded during this period, and it is probable that many others exist which are not publicly known. We may mention here "The United Goodness Society," "The Apprehension of Goodness Society," "The Tao Yuan," "The Six Sages Union True Tao Society," and finally "The Study of Morality Society." The common characteristic of these various movements is that they attempt to bring together in a new synthesis certain elements that are found in the other religions of China together with certain innovations in some cases. They seem to be the result of the failure of any one of the established religions to meet the needs of the particular people who have been drawn to them. They have hoped that by the eclectic process they might make adequate provision for the meeting of those needs.

[33] *Chinese Recorder*, Vol. 59, p. 624.

RELIGION IN CHINA

"The Apprehension of Goodness Society" combines five religions, namely Confucianism, Buddhism, Taoism, Islam and Christianity as does also the "Tao Yuan." The "Six Sages Society" adds Judaism to the list. Since the "Tao Yuan" seems to be the most important of the group we permit ourselves to describe briefly its growth and general organization.

It had its origins in 1921, arising from a revelation vouchsafed to its founder by means of a planchette in 1920. It is interesting to note that the planchette figures in most of these new movements. The planchette takes many different forms, one of the commonest being that of suspending above a sand table something resembling a dagger, with the point barely touching the sand. The method of getting the revelation is for one, or in some cases two persons, to grasp the handle of the planchette and stand or sit quietly without making any conscious movement. One trying this for himself will soon observe that with the arms extended at length, grasping this dagger or stick, there is a certain amount of involuntary muscular movement which causes the dagger to make marks in the sand. These cryptic marks are then examined and are found sometimes to resemble word signs, which word signs, being interpreted, are held to be the revelation of God.

This scripture, revealed in 1920, served as the basis for the initiation of the organization. From the first it grew rapidly and within two years it had spread to a number of the principal cities and even beyond the borders of China. The aim of the movement is expressed in their literature as "the worship

MODERN TENDENCIES

of the Most Holy Primeval Father, the founders of the five religions, and the gods, saints, worthies and Buddhas throughout the world, together with the appreciation of the god-given, world-center scripture as the connecting link of the truths of the five religions." The scripture is kept secret, no non-member of the group being allowed to see it. When Mr. Twinem, who writes regarding the movement, asked if Lao-Tze had written the scripture, they replied, "The true scripture existed before the world, before God, before Lao-Tze" and invited him to become a member of the group and so receive a copy and learn for himself. The scripture is not yet complete, but was expected to be so within a period of twelve years. For some curious reason, when Mr. Twinem reported upon the movement, the scriptures were still being received by means of the planchette somewhere in Italy, through the medium of the French language."

The movement is not exclusive, permitting members of other religions to join it without renouncing their other faith, for all religions they think come from the great Tao, the Primeval Father. The two major emphases in Tao Yuan seem to be on meditation and philanthropy. They have a decalogue which stated briefly is as follows:

(1) Do not dishonor parents, (2) Do not lack virtue, (3) Do not lack goodness, (4) Do not lack righteousness, (5) Do not lack mercy, (6) Do not

---

²⁴ The writer is chiefly indebted for this brief sketch to Mr. Twinem's articles in *The Journal of Religion*, Vol. V, pp. 463 ff. and pp. 595 ff.

RELIGION IN CHINA

conceal goodness, (7) Do not be cruel, (8) Do not have secrets, (9) Do not have envy or spite, and (10) Do not blaspheme.

The movement is elaborately organized into six departments or courts, each of which has its executive superintendent, secretary and treasurer. Among the departments one of the most important is called the "Sitting Department," which has to do particularly with meditation. The technique is somewhat as follows: Sitting upon a stool the worshipper clasps his hands on his knees and meditates for a period of four minutes, four times a day. Reports of an elaborate sort are sent to headquarters regarding this phase of their worship. Much is made also of self examination, which is carried out by a well-elaborated system. There is provided for each worshipper a book in which at night all the offenses during the day are entered. It is interesting to note that the big offenses are failure to sit, impatience, smoking, drugs, drinking, gambling, carousing, while the minor offenses are slander, anger and careless words. A kind of penance is enforced upon those who commit offenses. Sitting is the most frequent penance. For ordinary lapses the period of sitting is increased four times, while in the case of major offenses it is increased twelvefold.

We have already noted that a common feature of the syncretic movements is the use of the penance which seems to come into them from Taoism, where it is familiarly used. The device of keeping books with reference to one's offenses is likewise a Taoistic contribution. Indeed, one is impressed with the num-

MODERN TENDENCIES

ber of elements that seem to have come from Taoism. This is interesting since, of all the religions of China, it is most difficult to discover what is happening to it today. Here and there reference may be found to the effect that the new age has thoroughly discredited it. Here in the syncretic faiths at least part of its teachings and techniques seem to be preserved. It is apparently in connection with these syncretic movements, therefore, that Taoism is playing its major part in the modern changes in China's religion.

Although the syncretic movements seem to have flourished and grown rapidly during the early years of their existence, they have in recent years practically disappeared. Whether they still exist but are carried on with such secrecy that their existence is not known, or whether because of the great pressure put upon them by the government they have been forced to discontinue, it is impossible to say. "This is the case with the Tung-shan-sha. The Wu-shang-she and the Tao-teh-hsioh-she. Even the once powerful Tao-yuan had to go into retirement or to sail wholly under the Red Swastika flag. In spite of all difficulties the Buddhist Association keeps on flourishing, especially in the great ports," [35] writes Dr. Reichelt.

The fact is that since the rise of communism and the struggle between the nationalists and the communist group has become so bitter, most secret societies have been suppressed by the government in

[35] Karl L. Reichelt, *Chinese Recorder,* Vol. 59, p. 175.

RELIGION IN CHINA

the interest of public safety. Since there was a good deal of secrecy about the rise of these newer movements they have been much affected by this government policy.

What the result of the thoroughgoing revolution of the political, social and intellectual life of China will ultimately have on religion, it is impossible to prophesy. With the breakdown of the family it would seem almost inevitable that the present almost universal custom of ancestor worship, called by some the real religion of China, should undergo a serious change. Indeed, in an attempt to discover what people at present are thinking about this a writer in the *Chinese Recorder* quotes the following statement:

"Present-day Chinese maintain an unfavorable attitude towards ancestor Worship. The introduction of Occidental material philosophy has, to a great extent, loosened the hold of tradition and customs upon the minds of people. As a result, reverence for ancestors is giving way to dollarists or dollarocracy. Ancestor Worship had its origins in the bequest of property from ancestors and the notion that ancestors would, as deities or spirits, afford protection to their offspring or favor them with the blessings of prosperity and plenty. But present-day Chinese begin to doubt the existence of the soul or spirit; they have become indifferent as to what should be done with the deceased, even if this means that they themselves should be no more. The young materialists believe that death ends everything; the deceased have entirely severed their relationships with their survivors; and it is an extravagance to worship the no more sensible beings who probably do not have any actual existence. Again, many people do

MODERN TENDENCIES

not inherit any property or real estate from their ancestors, and so it is absolutely unnecessary to offer them sacrifices which they cannot possibly enjoy or appreciate. Although it may be a mere ceremony to remember their part in rearing and raising children, the latter can repay their service with filial piety and obedience in their life time better than after their death.

"This great change of attitude is of great significance in the minds of the Chinese. While the extreme form of Ancestor Worship has sacrificed the personality of the younger generation—a most pernicious influence of the institution—the utter disregard of it has over-individualized the youth, who seek for small families, self-enlargement (though not necessarily aggrandizement), and pleasure in this life alone. That nepotism is shattered need not trouble us, but that absence of sympathy for members of the same blood also becomes pronounced is another matter altogether." [26]

This attitude, if it should become generalized, would spell the ultimate decline of the practice, but it is only fair to state that in the same article others are quoted who take a much more favorable attitude toward the institution. With the sort of general education that is being developed and the gradual raising of the standard of literacy among the people, of course many of their ancient superstitions will be sloughed off. The contributions of the non-theistic humanism of the past will make its appeal to many of the modern generation, to whom super-naturalism is no longer a tenable position and whose pride in their cultural heritage leads them to look into their past for guidance. But it seems likely also that

[26] "Present-Day Attitude Towards Ancestor Worship," *Chinese Recorder*, Vol. 59, p. 231.

RELIGION IN CHINA

Christianity and Islam, particularly Christianity, if it comes to an expression wrought out by the Chinese themselves consonant with the values of the older Chinese culture, will play an important rôle in the future development of religion in China.

CHAPTER IV

MODERN TENDENCIES IN JAPANESE RELIGIONS

THE story of the spectacular rise of Japan to a great modern world power is so familiar that it will not be necessary to spend much time in detailing the changes that have come about in Japan, which might normally be expected to produce corresponding changes in the various Japanese religions. Probably no nation in the world has undergone a more rapid transformation than that Island Empire, beginning less than eighty years ago with her opening to the commerce of the world by Commodore Perry. Since that time every influence that has operated to mold the life of the West has also been operative in Japan. To come from a position of complete obscurity to that of one of the five great powers of the world in less than a century reveals qualities within the Japanese people that may well challenge the interest and attention of men everywhere.

The Industrialization of Japan

From a nation primarily agricultural, Japan is very rapidly becoming an industrial people. Fifty years ago there were but two hundred factories in Japan employing but fifteen hundred workers. There

RELIGION IN JAPAN

has been a steady increase in the industrial population, particularly since the Russo-Japanese War, but it was during and after the great World War that the great percentage of increase took place. By 1921, the number of factories had risen to 49,380 and the workers to 1,700,000, more than half of the increase after 1914. By 1928 the factories had increased still further to 55,948. In 1929 factory employees numbered 2,066,642. Along with this industrializing process went naturally the shift of population from country to city. Between 1894 and 1925, the percentage of population in cities of 10,000 or more rose from 16 to 36.6. Commerce, transportation, and other types of non-agricultural workers increased in somewhat similar proportions. At the present time about fifty per cent of the population is still agricultural. The very rapid progress of industrialization and urbanization brought all the long list of social ills to be found in any industrial land: bad housing, long hours, unhygienic working conditions, and city slums, with the usual accompaniment of vice, disease and poverty. The post-war slump in industry brought in its wake unemployment, and social unrest, which in turn made for the rise of radicalism, socialism, and communism, which greatly distressed the essentially conservative, capitalistic administration of Japan.

In 1920 the communist movement took root in Japan, capturing large sections both of the labor-peasant group and the students of the higher schools, colleges and universities. Ruthlessly suppressed again and again, both in labor and student groups

MODERN TENDENCIES

by wholesale arrest and imprisonment, it has continued to recruit followers. By no means is the whole of the proletarian group communistic, but a sufficiently large percentage is either openly so or generously sympathetic to it, so that no little alarm is occasioned as to the future, particularly since the Manhood Suffrage Act of 1928 has increased the voting strength of labor from three million to fourteen million.[1] Student communist groups are to be found in all the higher schools and colleges, eager students of the works of Marx and Lenin. Naturally religion is not popular with this group. Indeed, it is chiefly among the student and labor groups that the definite Anti-religious Movement has recently made headway. The movement in organized form first appeared in 1930, founded by a Mr. U. Akita, who about that time returned from Russia with a crusading passion against religion. Over twenty books and pamphlets were published in that year, denouncing religion as an enemy to mankind in true Marxian fashion. In 1931 the movement was very active under the two organizations, "Han-skukyo, Toso-Domei" (The Anti Religion Fighting Alliance) and "Nippon-Han-Skukyo-Domei" (Anti-religion Union). They carried their campaign into the rural villages, preaching revolt among the youth, especially against the priests and temples, the "visible symbols of religion . . . an ally of the hated capi-

[1] A correspondent objects that while the right of suffrage was extended to well over ten million people, there are still qualifications which restrict the franchise so that while it reaches well down toward the bottom of the middle class it is not yet a labor vote in any complete way.

RELIGION IN JAPAN

talistic system." The success of the movement was in part registered in the refusal of the Swiheisha or pariah group to contribute to the Hongwanji temple funds in 1930 and 1931, and in numerous student strikes in Buddhist colleges and universities. However, Mr. Kawashiri, who contributes the above information,[2] believes that while the student circle in general is materialistic and indifferent to religion, it is, so far, little affected by the anti-religious movement. As will be indicated in more detail later, the government is anxiously considering what may be done to offset this, and some are inclined to look in the direction of religion as the most effective means to be employed. This fact, to those who have been under Marxian influence, will only bring confirmation of the dictum that "religion is the opium of the people."

"Apropos of the government's fear of communism," writes Dr. Charles W. Iglehart,[3] "a whole string of events have been happening within the last five years by way of attempting both to encourage religious activities and teachings, and to regulate and control all religious agencies. There has never been a time in recent years when the government—the Department of Education—has so desired the support of religion both within and without the schools. But it has always been on the assumption that religion was an upholder of the status quo, and that it would help make loyal citizens, who would resist the encroachments of communism, and 'dangerous thoughts.'

"Twice within that time the Diet has presented and

[2] Kawashiri, Seishu, "The Anti-Religious Movement and its Significance," *The Japan Christian Yearbook 1932*, pp. 53-63.
[3] Personal correspondence.

MODERN TENDENCIES

tried to pass a so-called Religious Bill, which would have recognized religion, Christianity included, with wider prestige than ever before, but which would also have carried with it control. Both times the Shintoists and Buddhists were ready to acquiesce in it,—the Shintoists eagerly and the Buddhists passively, when both times it was blocked by the power of Christian resistance. You can get an idea of the influence of Christian feeling from this fact. Curiously enough, the immediate weight of the opposition was a group of non-Christian Peers who supported the Christian point of view because they believed in the work of the Salvation Army and saw that by such a law, which did not recognize lay workers, it would be disfranchised—a strange team!"

All this was bound to have its effect on religion. Ancestor worship is an important element in Japanese religion. Writing of the future of Japanese Shintoism, Yone Noguchi declares:

"The fact that modern civilization is driving people away from the birthplace of their ancestors is certainly weakening the conception of ancestor worship, in that it deprives them of the opportunity for observing the religious rites toward departed spirits. Again, the atmosphere of the city, exciting and unpoetically scientific, does not tend to cherish the somewhat ghostly and shadowy sense of ancestor worship."

He further reflects that since the devotion of the Japanese people to the Imperial house is in part based on ancestor worship, the loss of a sense of obligation to worship their ancestors may have far-reaching political results as well, for he says:

"Even the imperial house would be powerless against our changing concepts of ancestor worship. The

RELIGION IN JAPAN

spiritual insularity which has once been broken cannot be so easily mended." [4]

Again, the relative failure of the current religions—Shinto, Buddhism, and Christianity—to meet adequately the needs of the people involved in the industrial struggle has led to a widespread abandonment of religion in any form by the workers.

The Cultural Invasion from the West

From a hermit nation with no outside connections, Japan has become neighbor to the world. Her commerce is found on all the seas, and the currents of life and thought that flow through the nations of the occident flow in almost equal volume through the land of the rising sun. Her contacts with the cultures of the West have been most intimate through innumerable students sent abroad to study, through the travel of the West to the East, and the travel of Japanese through the West. Eager in her desire to modernize herself, she has laid under tribute almost every important phase of western civilization. In nothing has she been more assiduous than in her promotion of education. From a nation overwhelmingly illiterate in the middle of the last century, she has today the highest percentage of literacy among the nations of the world. She has a higher percentage of her school-age group in school than any other country in the world. While the vast majority of her citizens receive only an elementary education, she has not neglected higher education, but has numerous highly

[4] Yone Noguchi, "The Future of Japanese Shintoism," *Nation*, Vol. 102:512-13.

MODERN TENDENCIES

efficient schools, ranging all the way from high schools, normal schools, technical schools, up to great universities offering wide opportunity for graduate and professional study and taking their places on a level with the great universities of Europe and America.

The teaching of the occidental languages in the schools has brought a world of literature within the understanding of Japanese students, and the more important works of a scientific political and philosophical sort have been translated into Japanese. These have brought their freight of ideas and ideals, which have been very influential in the making of the modern Japanese mind. Not that Japan has slavishly followed the West. She has, it is true, been an avid borrower, but a fair study of the use she has made of her borrowings reveals clearly that she has always adapted her borrowings to her own peculiar genius. Nevertheless all this impact of foreign cultures has wrought mightily in changing the fabric of Japanese life and thought, including her religion. The teaching of religion had been barred from the schools as a result of the educational reform of 1886 on the ground that a "religious universalism was incompatible with nationalistic ethics. Although this measure of exclusion had the merit of keeping the schools free from sectarian strife, it worked to make antagonism towards religion almost a creed of the educational circles. The majority of the teachers identified religious faith with superstition or regarded it as tolerable only for the sake of the com-

RELIGION IN JAPAN

mon people."[5] The leaders of the present generation are products of schools in which this attitude prevailed. It is not remarkable, therefore, that their attitudes toward religion today are what they are.

Not the least of the influences that have wrought upon the native religions of Japan has been the missionary work of the Christian church,[6] which has succeeded in establishing itself in such fashion that it is today one of the three religions of Japan, on an equal footing so far as governmental control is concerned with Shinto and Buddhism.

Under the circumstances it is not surprising that one finds a great deal of religious confusion in Japan. One Japanese writer characterizes the practices of the typical Japanese community as a "jazz of religions." A Buddhist, writing of his own religious experience, in which he had gone from a non-religious or skeptical religious position to that of a convert to one of the Buddhist schools, writes as follows:

"And yet the reader must not take me to be a perfect convert to Jodoism. There is still left in me some-

[5] Anesaki, *History of Japanese Religion* (London: Kegan Paul Trench, 1930), pp. 364-65.

[6] It ought to be said that in this chapter the author has as in the other chapters omitted practically all discussion of the movements within Christianity except as these are related rather definitely to the movements in the so-called native religions. The omission has led a friendly critic to declare that one "gets no adequate feeling for the creative part Christian thinking and feeling, even apart from the organic life of the churches, is playing in the modern situation." This is doubtless true and is much to be regretted, but it is simply one of a number of limitations imposed upon the writer by the nature of the survey in general and the exigencies of space—in an age of depression!

MODERN TENDENCIES

thing of the believer in salvation by works, something of a materialist and a skeptic, some influence of Christianity, Confucianism, and Shintoism, and," [he adds,] "unfortunately, this strange conglomeration will be found to be the spiritual stock of most Japanese of my years and training at the present time." [7]

Another writes:

"The complex life that we modern people live makes it impossible to say definitely and with assurance under what influences we have arrived at a certain kind of faith. In me I clearly see the influences of Christianity, Buddhism, Shinto, and Confucianism, and that is the religious and intellectual life of a modern Japanese." [8]

Still another writes:

"We believe in Shintoism and Buddhism and Christianity in about the way that we take to the conglomeration of the Eastern and Western modes of life. You can't say a girl is a Christian because she attends church any more than you can say she is Western because she is dressed in foreign style. At the same time she is no more Buddhist if she burns incense before a Buddhist grave. She is just the sum total of all these and no more. If you put Shinto, Buddhism, and Christianity together and call that religion, there is more religion in Japan than anywhere else in the world. But if you ask if the ordinary Japanese is religious in the original sense of any of these three religions, you can hardly say that he is. The very fact that there are so many forms of religion promiscuously assembled in the same community and the same household and observed by the same person, prevents any particular religious

[7] M. G. Mori, *Buddhism and Faith,* preface iv.
[8] "The Religion of Modern Japan," *Transpacific,* Vol. 13 (April 10, 1926), p. 5.

RELIGION IN JAPAN

spirit from taking root in the spiritual life of the race." [*]

In general, however, one may discover in Japan four distinct tendencies: first, a general tendency within Shinto to reassert itself as the peculiarly national faith of Japan, manifesting itself among other ways in the rapid rise and spread of new Shinto sects; second, a notable revival of Buddhism, revealing itself chiefly in an emphasis on the social values of religion; third, a notable humanistic trend closely allied to like trends in western nations. A fourth tendency not yet so prominent but beginning to show itself is that of coöperation between the chief religions of Japan in practical social effort.

Tendencies in Shintoism

In the face of the extreme modernizing influences that are everywhere touching Japanese life, there is a distinct tendency—one may, if he so desires, call it a defense reaction—to accentuate certain elements within the old religions, particularly Shinto. Bound up as it is in an unusual way with national feeling, it gathers to itself many of those who are moved by highly patriotic motives to preserve the national culture in the face of the innovations that come into Japan from without.

The western world is fairly familiar with the effort on the part of the Japanese government to make Shinto a national cult of loyalty and secure its general practice even among Buddhists and Chris-

[*] *Ibid.*, Vol. 16 (July 28, 1929), p. 7.

MODERN TENDENCIES

tians, by separating what is known as Ko-Shinto or State Shinto, called also Shrine Shinto, from Zoku-Shinto or Sectarian Shinto.[10] This was done, of course, before the beginning of the present century, but there has been no tendency to abandon it thus far; indeed, in recent years the government has taken repeated steps to intensify the cult. A correspondent long resident in Japan [11] and a close observer of religious trends cities two instances of this, namely:

"The Coronation, which was the occasion for the most thorough diffusion of State Shinto ideas and practices of recent years. We had hymns to the Emperor, prayers in all the schools of the Empire, facing Ise when the Emperor went into the sacred enclosure, all sorts of ceremonies at the state and local shrines, and tons of literature inspired and sent out by the government.

"The erection and integration in the life of Japan of the Meiji Shrine in Tokyo. This is the focus of the national cult on its recreational side, of national games,

[10] State Shinto is declared by the government to be not a religion but a system of state ceremonials in which all Japanese citizens, whether Shinto, Buddhist, or Christian, may properly engage without prejudice to their own faiths. It is carefully distinguished from Sectarian Shinto administratively, the latter standing on the same plane as Buddhism and Christianity and being administered by the bureau of Religions. The fact, however, that the state ceremonial invokes largely the same gods as Sectarian Shinto and uses much the same ceremonial, makes the government's claim seem a specious one to Buddhists and Christians, a device by which constitutional freedom of worship may be theoretically maintained while still carrying on the ancient religion of Japan. For an excellent discussion of this question see, D. C. Holtom, "Modern Shinto as a State Religion," *Japan Mission Year Book, 1930*, pp. 38-61. Also *Id.* 1931, pp. 51-66, "Recent Discussion Regarding State Shinto," by the same writer.

[11] Dr. Charles W. Iglehart.

RELIGION IN JAPAN

etc.; and shares with Ise the chief place in the linking up of State Shinto with the army and national policy. There is being built up over the country a network of local shrines to the Emperor Meiji."

But over and beyond what the government itself has done, moved doubtless by the desire to secure the utmost of loyalty to the central government, there has been a marked non-official movement to accentuate the values of emperor worship and the place of Japan as central in the life of the world. Two separate types of support for this idea have appeared, one in the formation of new sects of Shinto, which stress these ideas, and a second in a rationalization of Shinto by modern Shinto scholars. While both of the two principal illustrations of this first tendency had their beginning before the opening of the present century, their chief progress has been made within the last twenty-five years, particularly since the Russo-Japanese War, which seems to have brought a new consciousness of world destiny to the people of Japan.

Tenrikyo and Omotokyo, the most outstanding illustrations of the tendency, were both founded by women. Both have a special center chosen by God which the members of the movement think to be the center from which will radiate influences for the remaking of the world. It will suffice to describe briefly the latter of the two, namely, Omotokyo. This, in the words of Anesaki, an eminent Buddhist scholar, was started "by a crazy old woman who believed herself to be the messenger of the Gods sent by them to effect a fundamental rebuilding of the

MODERN TENDENCIES

whole world." [12] She was an ignorant rag-gatherer, left a widow with eight children to support. On New Year's day, in 1892, while praying in a Shinto shrine, she became possessed with the spirit of the Earth God and began to prophesy and ran through the streets shouting unintelligible warnings to the people whom she passed. Although an ignorant, untutored woman, she wrote revelations on the walls of houses and on scraps of paper. She prophesied that the city of Ayabe was built on a sacred spot and that unless it was abandoned it would be burned. Her prophecy was fulfilled, but police, believing that she herself had brought about its fulfillment, arrested her and she was in prison for a time, but was later released to the custody of her relatives, who promised to keep her safely locked up. She lived thus as a prisoner until her death in 1918. During all this period she was writing incessantly. Tradition, which has already grown up about her, declares that she wrote six thousand volumes. She prophesied, so her followers claim, the war with Russia, and the World War. The movement which grew up about her has been under the skillful guidance of a son-in-law, a retired military officer, who has proved theologian to the cause and has developed a most interesting theology. The government has on more than one occasion attempted to suppress the movement, but despite their efforts it has gone on steadily increasing. Kenneth Saunders says, writing of it and similar sects in 1922:

[12] Anesaki, "Social Unrest and Spiritual Agitation in Japan," *Harvard Theological Review*, Vol. XV, pp. 305 ff.

RELIGION IN JAPAN

"These movements have gathered around them an amazing number of adherents of all classes: patrioteers, maniacs, earnest seekers, and many weak-minded persons; especially from the ranks of retired officers of the army and navy does Omotokyo recruit its most ardent supporters. They work cures and seem to work especially with those who have much leisure and limited intelligence." [13]

Omotokyo is characterized by one writer as "an imperial socialism, combining the characteristics of communism, millenarianism, mysticism, and patriotism." A typical statement of their belief in the central place of the emperor is indicated in the following quotation:

"The imperial family of Japan is parent not only of her sixty million but of all mankind on earth. In the eyes of the imperial family all races are one and the same. It is above all racial consideration. All human disputes, therefore, may be settled in accordance with its immaculate justice. The League of Nations, which proposes to save mankind from the horrors of war, can only attain its real objective by placing the imperial family at its head, for to attain its objective the League must have a strong punitive force of super-national and super-racial character, and this can be found only in the imperial family of Japan." [14]

An organ of the Tenrikyo movement, the Michi-no-tomo, in September, 1914, declared as follows:

"Japan is the parent nation of the world. It is the source whence the salvation of all nations proceeds. He

[13] Kenneth Saunders, "Glimpses of the Religious Life of New Japan," *Journal of Religion,* Vol. 2, p. 70.
[14] Quoted by A. Pieters, "Emperor Worship in Japan," *International Review of Missions,* Vol. 9, p. 355.

MODERN TENDENCIES

who is hostile to this nation opposes the will of God. For this reason we, the believers in Tenrikyo, are resolved to serve the divine and imperial will." [15]

For the most part, the reactionary movements have drawn their support from the more or less ignorant masses. A very interesting tendency has appeared, however, which attempts to discover in Shinto and in emperor worship, which is its center, the only proper religion for modern Japan. Dr. Genchi Kato, professor of comparative religions in the Imperial University, is the chief figure here. Dr. Kato, so far from thinking of Shinto as a primitive nature religion adapted to a rather simple type of national culture, holds that in it there are to be found those elements of universality which seem to express most adequately the religious life of Japan.[16] He makes emperor worship the central feature of his system and attributes to the emperor all the qualities that serve to make a God in religion. He represents him, i.e. the emperor, as of a two-fold nature. "When the emperor turns to the people below him he is Ahra-hito-kumi or Aki-tan-Kami (God incarnate), but when he turns toward the divine ancestors he occupies the position of a man." "Probably," writes a thoughtful student of Japanese religion, "no ancient Shintoist ever dreamed of such a thing as two natures in the Emperor or ever said that the standard of right and wrong, good and evil is found only in the Emperor's will." The writer thinks to see in the two-

[15] Quoted by A. Pieters, *loc. cit.*
[16] See Genchi Kato, *A Study of Shinto, the Religion of the Japanese Nation* (Tokyo, Meiji Japan Society, 1926).

RELIGION IN JAPAN

fold nature of the Emperor a reflection of the influence of Christian theology. "In Dr. Kato's work," writes Pieters, "we have the first attempt by a scholar trained in the method of modern thought to re-state the principles of Shinto in modern terms and to relate them to other departments of human knowledge. In other words, we have here the beginning of a Shinto systematic theology, the awakening to intellectual self-consciousness of an age-long and primitive religion. A man who has learned to think philosophically must either throw overboard the faith of his childhood or he must learn to re-state it in terms that can satisfy his intellect. . . . By far the greater number of men in Japan who have received the higher culture, adopt the former alternative and have no religion at all. If they continue to observe outwardly any religious rites they try to prove to themselves that these have no religious significance. It is intensely interesting, therefore, to find in Dr. Kato a man who has taken the other course."

He is not alone, however, in his advocacy of the central place of the emperor in religion, for another eminent scholar, Dr. Uesugi, writing in the *Sun* of April, 1913, with reference to the imperial rescript on education, said:

"The educational rescript is the fundamental principle of the moral activity of the Japanese people. It is a rescript from the Emperor. For this reason and for this reason alone, it is implicitly obeyed by the millions of Japanese. By obedience to that which the Emperor commands, we develop and perfect our lives, and by keeping all laws in this way we reach the highest step in moral progress. To serve him, never doubting, never

MODERN TENDENCIES

fearing, preserving thus our hearts in the highest peace and joy, giving ourselves up to him body and soul, turning aside to nothing else in zealous obedience to the doctrine of Mikadoism, this is indeed the marrow of Japanese ethics and the taproot of our national character. For this reason the imperial rescript transcends all criticism. The standard of right and wrong, good and evil, is found only in the imperial will." [17]

Dr. Iglehart, in a letter, notes regarding the modernization of Shinto that:

"The newer trend is not so much represented by Kato, centering in the person of the Emperor, as by a younger group who have selected one of the original progenitor gods from the old mythology,—away back before the Sun-Goddess, and find a monotheistic basis in him for all that follows in Shinto theology, including, of course, all that Kato holds about the Emperor."

Along with this reëmphasis on Shinto, even in its more reactionary forms, there has gone also a tendency toward modernization, especially in their methods of propaganda and appeal, very similar to that which has occurred in Buddhism, as will be indicated later.

The Revival of Buddhism

The second tendency to be noted is the revival that is taking place within Buddhism. It would be a mistake to suppose that all Buddhists or even all the many Buddhist sects are involved in it. As a matter of fact, travelers and even Buddhist writers themselves are constantly calling attention to the low

[17] Quoted by A. Pieters, "Emperor Worship in Japan," *International Review of Missions*, Vol. 9, p. 355.

RELIGION IN JAPAN

estate to which Buddhism has fallen. But new currents of life and thought are flowing through large portions of the Japanese Buddhist world and all the evidence points to a continuous spread of the new tendencies. Among the various indications of the revival, space will permit discussion of but five:

1. The intellectual awakening.
2. The increasing adaptation of modern techniques of propaganda for the spread of Buddhism.
3. The new emphasis on social service.
4. The growing solidarity of the Buddhist world, and their consciousness of a world mission revealed in
5. The renewed missionary emphasis.

1. By the intellectual awakening is meant, first of all, their evident discovery of the changes that have taken place in the thought of the modern world through the advances made by science. Confronted by a new intellectual world they are making conscious effort not only to adjust their own thought to it, but to show that Buddhism, as no other faith, furnishes the very ground work for modern science. Here is no conflict between a static scriptural doctrine of creation by fiat; on the other hand the doctrine of evolution but reveals the logical way in which the world unfolds in accordance with Buddhist thought. Indeed, Pratt asserts:

"The Japanese are much interested in the science of the West; but they are also beginning to realize that the philosophy at the basis of all branches of the Mahayana is of a sort that is quite capable of making room for everything that science has yet discovered or is likely to discover. The more thoroughly educated

MODERN TENDENCIES

members of Jodo and Shin, for example, have already gotten back of the symbolism of their sects and are basing their lives and their religion intellectually not upon a naive mythology, but upon a profound philosophy. The same resource is open to the Nichiren and Shingon sects. And both Zen and Tendai consciously and explicitly rest upon a philosophy that has nothing to fear from science."[18]

This fact has been held as one of the points of superiority of Buddhism over Christianity and was, in an earlier day when the Christian teaching was much less modern but more closely tied up to a relatively hard and fast doctrine of the infallibility of the Bible, effectively used in opposing the advance of the western faith. With the modernization of the Christian outlook, this type of opposition has lost most of its strength. The historico-critical method has been freely applied to Buddhist scriptures, with the result that some of their most cherished traditions have been completely disproven. Of course there was opposition to it. The older scholars fought it bitterly, but, says Professor Addison, all the younger leaders "accept the evidences brought to light by the historical method. The conservatives are in the majority in such older sects as the Shingon and Tendai, but in the universities of the other sects the liberals are more numerous."[19]

The adjustment has not been so difficult among Buddhists, thinks Professor Addison, since:

[18] From J. B. Pratt, *The Pilgrimage of Buddhism*, p. 698. By permission of The Macmillan Company, publishers.
[19] J. T. Addison, "Religious Life in Japan," *Harvard Theological Review*, Vol. 18, p. 340.

RELIGION IN JAPAN

"Buddhists have never been taught to believe that a particular date or event was essential to the existence of their religion, still less that their scriptures were infallible. So the question of who wrote a book and when, interests scholars alone; it is not a matter, as with us, that can affect personal religion. If the Eternal Buddha of philosophy did not speak at this time through this man, then he spoke at another time through another man; and if at all times everywhere, the supreme Amida or Vairocana or Dharmakaya is revealing himself, what do dates and documents matter?" [20]

The Japanese Buddhist, never as dependent upon an historical Buddha as Christians upon the historical Jesus, are able to look with reasonable equanimity upon the workings of an historical method that reveals much of their faith as of comparatively late origin and unrelated historically to Gautama himself. A modern leader, Dr. Takakusu, editor of the *Chinese Tripitaka,* can say:

"No matter whether they [certain Buddhist ideals embodied in Amida or Mahavirocana] were discovered by Buddhist disciples many centuries ago or are discovered by ourselves today, it does not in the least affect any teaching of Buddha, as long as we know of the ideal of Buddha."

All of which sounds familiar to many a modern Christian whose faith in the ideals of Jesus would be undisturbed if the discovery were made that Jesus was not an historical figure at all.

As one manifestation of this phase of the revival, the completion of a new scholarly edition of the Buddhist scriptures in Chinese in fifty-five volumes

[20] Addison, *ibid.,* p. 341.

MODERN TENDENCIES

has been recently celebrated, and announcement is made of the early appearance of the scriptures in a monumental translation into Japanese. There is also noticeable a greatly increased literary activity among the Buddhist sects, most of which have presses of their own.

2. It must suffice merely to mention in passing some of the more obvious changes in their methods of work, most of which bear the clear marks of Christian influence. While some of the methods had been adopted before the beginning of the century, most of the development has taken place within the period of this study. Preaching, for example, has been made a regular part of the temple service in a number of Buddhist sects, particularly the Zen, Nichiren and Shin, and to a lesser degree in Jodo, Shingon, and even the more conservative Tendai. Preaching missions are conducted by some sects in the prisons, in the neglected districts, and sometimes in the streets. The Shinshu sect alone has over two thousand preaching stations aside from its temples. The Sunday School has likewise been taken over and adapted to Buddhist uses. The techniques that have proven useful in Christianity are employed with notable success. One hears even of Buddhist Sunday school picnics. Teacher training classes are carried on for the preparation of teachers. A proposed Sunday school workers' conference of the Christian churches was somewhat startled to get a request that Buddhist teachers be admitted to participation in the conference. Representatives have been sent to study religious education in some of the best schools of re-

RELIGION IN JAPAN

ligion in America, with the view of returning and promoting a modern system of religious education in Buddhism.

Some of the songs sung by Buddhist children are taken over almost bodily from Christianity. Two such adaptations follow:

"There's a land of sunshine
There's a land of flowers
Pure and always happy
Of birds and songs and bowers.

Chorus

"It's a happy land, it's a happy land
It's the 'Pure Land' of the blest
Where all is love and peace and joy
A home of sweetest rest!

"What's the use of weeping
What's the use to sigh
With Amida guiding
We'll reach there by and by.

"Trust to dear Amida
With his loving care
Shall find its garden path
And all these pleasures share."
E. T. DUNLAP.[11]

NAMU AMIDA

"Namu Amida, the shadows are descending
Veil from our eyes the bright radiance of day
Night with its perils o'er us is impending
Only Thy presence our fears can allay.

"Namu Amida, while helpless we slumber
Shed thou about us the light of Thy love

[11] *Young East*, Vol. 2, p. 57.

MODERN TENDENCIES

Dread and alarm have no power to encumber
Hearts that are trusting Thy watch-care above.

"Namu Amida, when death-shadows falling
Hide from our sight all we treasured before
Shine through the gloom, faith and courage recalling
Bring us in triumph to peace evermore."
                                A. R. ZORN.[23]

The extent of the influence of the Sunday school movement may be appreciated when it is known that as long ago as 1920, the latest complete statistics available, there were 6,928 Sunday schools, with 18,750 teachers and 788,146 pupils.[22] The numbers would be considerably greater at present.

The Salvation Army has been working in Japan since the last decade of the last century. There is now a Buddhist Salvation Army doing somewhat similar work. There are flourishing Young Men's Buddhist Associations and Young Women's Buddhist Associations, though instead of being united in a single national organization as in America, they are related to the various sects. The Shin sect alone reports more than 100,000 members. There are associations in most university centers. They carry on a program of evangelism and social work very much like the kindred Christian Associations. The men's association is very much stronger than the Y.W.B.A. There are, however, other societies which unite Buddhist women in active effort to spread their faith. For example, the Fujin Howakwai or Society for

[22] *Ibid.*, Vol. 2, p. 240.
[23] From J. B. Pratt, *op. cit.*, p. 583. By permission of The Macmillan Company, publishers.

RELIGION IN JAPAN

the Deepening of Devotion of the East Hongwanji sect has nearly 200,000 members.

The Christian festival seasons, Christmas and Easter, have become widely known among the Japanese. A Buddhist writer in *Young East* advocates their adaptation by Buddhists thus:

"The commemoration of Our Lord's holy vigil beneath the Bo-tree during the December holiday period will enable us all, especially the young people, to participate in the social activities and delights about us, without abandoning our position as followers of the Lord Buddha. Let us welcome, then, this Bodhi season and celebrate it in our homes. Let us set up our symbolic tree and adorn it with lights and ornaments, not forgetting to place at its foot a statue, or at least a picture of Him whom in this festival we honour. Then let us gather around it with our little ones and tell again the wondrous story of Him who, in His boundless love for suffering mankind, renounced all that men hold most precious in order to find the true way of eternal salvation. In order that the full spiritual value of this celebration may be realized by them, let us carefully point out to the children the inner significance of the trees, the lights, and the ornaments, as well as the Bodhi-gifts we present to them. So shall we lay an excellent foundation of religious truth in their young and impressionable minds for the teaching they will receive in the Sunday school during the ensuing year." [24]

In 1897 was begun the celebration of what they call the Lumbini Festival or Buddha's birthday. It falls on April eighth each year. A writer in *Young East* notes, among other features of the three-day celebration in 1926, an evangelistic campaign in

[24] *Young East*, December, 1926, p. 230.

MODERN TENDENCIES

various sections of the capital, series of lectures on Buddhism by noted scholars, a radio broadcast of a life of Buddha for children, chorus singing of hymns of praise to Buddha, the dropping of lotus petals made of paper over the city from aëroplanes, the publication and distribution of special books and pamphlets commemorating the event.[15] All the most modern up-to-date means available are being employed in the interest of their faith.

3. Buddhism, especially Mahayana, has never wholly lacked the social note in its teaching and practice, but the present century has witnessed a remarkable increase in organized social effort on the part of Buddhists in Japan, especially if we include education, as we may well do, among the social activities. In this regard Buddhists are like Shintoists. Anesaki, generalizing on the situation, writes:

"Wide is the gap between the extremes (irreligion on the one hand and the most reactionary movements on the other), but common features can be discovered in them all, namely, that social and particularly economic considerations are brought into close relation with the spiritual, and that the intuitive or instinctive nature of religion is emphasized in antagonism to the doctrinal and ecclesiastical systems."[16]

The most recent available statistics show that the Buddhists maintain 211 institutions for educating and fostering children, including orphanages; 147 for helping working people to obtain higher educa-

[15] *Ibid.* (April, 1926), pp. 370-371.
[16] Anesaki, "Social Unrest and Spiritual Agitation," *Harvard Theological Review*, Vol. 15, p. 305.

RELIGION IN JAPAN

tion; 139 institutions for giving advice and other assistance, such as labor exchanges; 47 hospitals and 20 schools for the blind and deaf.[27] Pratt noted that in 1919 they maintained 462 institutions for the care of ex-convicts alone. Professor Addison mentions still other forms of social work, describing in some detail a Buddhist settlement in Tokyo which, under the direction of a Buddhist priest who studied social settlement work in the United States, employs seven full-time, paid workers and thirty-eight part-time, volunteer workers. The activities of the settlement include a domestic science school for girls, an elementary schools for boys and men, a crêche, a kindergarten, a Sunday School, a free dispensary, a baby clinic with a section for prenatal care and instruction, a legal service department, an employment agency, and clubs for boys and girls, young men and women.[28] *Young East* reports an active functioning temperance society and organized opposition to the system of licensed public prostitution.[29]

In the field of education Buddhism has shown not a little activity. As in America, religion is banned from the public schools. Buddhists have, therefore, founded schools in which they hope, as do Christian schools, to provide a wholesome religious environment. Statistics for 1925 indicate that there were then about one hundred primary schools; over a hundred secondary; twenty-six middle schools for boys, thirteen for girls; forty special schools, ten

[27] *Japan Mission Yearbook 1931*, p. 69.
[28] Addison, *op. cit.*, p. 708.
[29] *Young East*, August, 1926, p. 103; February, 1927, p. 320.

MODERN TENDENCIES

colleges, and four universities, besides several theological schools.[20] In the universities there is instruction in Buddhism, its history, literature, doctrine and philosophy, in History of Religion, Psychology, Philosophy, ethics, literature, and history. The most conspicuous omission in the curriculum is that of the natural sciences.[21]

In addition to formal educational effort, Buddhism founds and maintains libraries and reading rooms; and publishes a large number of newspapers, magazines, pamphlets, and books. The *Japan Mission Year Book for 1931* [22] in an article on "Buddhism Today," based evidently on Buddhist sources, states that an average of about 190 new books on distinctively Buddhist subjects are published each year; that there are 219 monthly and 23 weekly or ten-day Buddhist periodicals issued by 31 Buddhist publishing houses.

Mention has already been made of the numerous Young Men's and Young Women's Buddhist Associations and the Salvation Army, which are channels through which much social service is performed.

One of the most remarkable recent movements in Japan has been that of Mr. Toyohiko Kagawa, a Christian minister, evangelist, social worker, writer, who has given a powerful social impetus to Christianity by his own self-sacrificing service through his Settlement in the slums of Osaka. He has become the founder of what he calls the Kingdom of

[20] Pratt, *op. cit.*, p. 588. By permission of The Macmillan Company, publishers.
[21] Addison, *op. cit.*, p. 347.
[22] P. 69.

RELIGION IN JAPAN

God movement [22] within Christianity. He has won an enviable place of leadership in the world of labor, on the one hand, and among those responsible for the social welfare work of the country, on the other. He is now adviser of the Social Welfare Department of the Municipality of Tokyo. As stated, Mr. Kagawa is a Christian and an ardent Christian propagandist, who dreams of a million converts to Christ, but his ministry of social helpfulness as the inevitable expression of religion, is furnishing a distinct stimulus to the Buddhists and Shintoists as well, if for no other reason (and it would be ungenerous to attribute low motives to these faiths) as a defense reaction.

4. The growing solidarity of the Buddhist world is evident from some recent attempts on the part of various Buddhist groups to get together for conference regarding their common problems. First of all there is a tendency for the various sects of Buddhism in Japan to draw together for certain specific purposes. Nichiren seems the least willing to coöperate with others. Among other unions there is the United Buddhist Organization, which is accredited with

[22] While Mr. Kagawa is the moving spirit, and by far the best known of those engaged in it, the Kingdom of God Movement is actually much bigger than any one man. It is a real people's movement among most of the denominations. If we were here telling the story of Christianity in Japan, considerable space would have to be given to it. It is a carefully planned-out campaign promoted through Protestant Christianity in Japan. In 1930 the emphasis was on evangelism, in 1931 emphasis was upon rural problems including educational, economic, social, leader-training, health and recreational features; in 1932 attention was focused on city and industrial problems. For details vide *Japan Christian Year Book*, volumes 1930, 1931, 1932.

MODERN TENDENCIES

sponsoring 367 of the 701 social institutions noted above. The publication of the *Chinese Tripitaka* was a union enterprise. One sees mentioned in Buddhist periodicals, such organizations as the "Liberal Buddhist Association," the "Federation of Buddhist Organizations for Children," and "The Buddhist Union to Reform the Buddhist World." The United Buddhist University is a union project shared by three sects. Another organization, The Eastern Buddhist Association, announces its purpose thus:

"1. The Association has as its object thorough study and world-wide propagation of Eastern Buddhism, which was developed by the Japanese race.

"2. The Association endeavors to make clear the historical facts of Eastern Buddhism which forms the essence of Japanese culture.

"3. The Association aims at criticism of matters relating to modern thought and solution of social and racial problems in the light of the spirit of Eastern Buddhism." [14]

The Interdenominational Association (Kakaishu Rengokai) among other activities publishes a magazine, *The Study of Religions,* edited by Professor Anesaki, one of the great Buddhist scholars of Japan. This association, according to Professor Addison, corresponds in some respects to the Federal Council of Churches in the United States. It unites all the major sects except Nichiren, and represents Buddhism, especially in matters relating to the imperial government and other public affairs.[15]

It was this association which, with a view to unit-

[14] *Young East* (July, 1925), p. 72.
[15] Addison, *op. cit.,* p. 338.

RELIGION IN JAPAN

ing the entire Mahayana Buddhist world, issued a call for a Far Eastern Buddhist conference with representatives from China, Korea and Formosa. The conference met in Tokyo, in November, 1925, with more than one thousand in attendance at the opening meeting. There were twenty-one official delegates from China, and three each from Korea and Formosa. Its purpose was to discuss means of relating more closely the various sects of Buddhism and the promotion of coöperation among them in the spread of their common faith. The chairman of the congress in his address remarked: "Special discussions on points of Buddhist doctrine by Japanese and Chinese workers are no doubt very important, but the fact that the religious leaders of the two nations have come together with the single purpose of discussing plans for spreading their religion throughout the world is more important than anything else." [**]

Other meetings of the Far Eastern Conference were projected, but as far as the writer has been able to discover none has yet been held. The next was to be called by the Chinese to meet in Peking. According to Pratt, however, Japanese Buddhists are not content with uniting only Mahayana. They would like, if possible, to bring both Mahayana and Hinayana together in a World Buddhist Conference, but thus far it is only a dream.

Apparently, from the remark of a Japanese Buddhist priest apropos of a statement that a delegate had been sent to Geneva to a religious conference,

[**] *Transpacific,* Vol. 12, p. 44 (November 7, 1925), p. 15.

MODERN TENDENCIES

Japanese Buddhism has not itself become as yet a unit. "It is about time," he declared, "for us to get together to discuss a general policy of Buddhist workers in their relation with people at home as well as abroad." [17]

5. Closely related to this phase of the revival is the renewed sense of world mission which has developed recently. Of course, Buddhism has been one of the great missionary religions of the world, but in recent centuries it has remained stationary. Once more it is feeling the urge to conquest and some of its leaders see in its teachings the only hope of the world. Here is a typical utterance:

"The spiritual fate of humanity hangs today in the balance and only Buddhism properly understood and practiced can save it from sinking into the abyss of nothingness, where even despair is forgotten and where all effort toward the divine is unknown. It is Buddhism that gives the logical and scientific basis for the brotherhood of humanity." [18]

It will be of interest to Western readers to know how the eastern Buddhist thinks of his task of preaching Buddhism to the West. Incidentally, light is thrown upon the modern aspects of that faith. We quote the rather lengthy statement of Mr. Dayal on the kind of men and women needed for such work, the preparation they should have, and the attitudes they should hold toward Christianity.

"The Buddhist missionaries in Europe must be men and women of wide culture. They must study the his-

[17] *Ibid.*, Vol. 16, p. 12 (August 4, 1929).
[18] *Transpacific*, vol. 17 (July 11, 1929), p. 16.

tory of philosophy and religion, Eastern and Western, before they begin to work. They must be experts and specialists in comparative religion. Such training will enable them to see that Buddhism is something higher than mere Hinayana or Mahayana. They will become original thinkers of the Buddhist 'movement,' and they will cease to be mere imitative priests and sectarians, who can only repeat the old formulæ of the Tripitaka and the later canonical works. We need new Nagarjunas and Bodhidharmas, not merely humble followers of Nargarjuna and Bodhidharma. Here is a great civilization in Europe, and the Buddhists must accomplish the task of preaching Buddhism to it. New methods of educating the missionaries must be adopted."[39]

"What should be the attitude of the Buddhist missionaries toward Christianity in Europe? Should they be hostile and exclusive, or should they appreciate and assimilate all that is good and noble in Christ? In my opinion, the Buddhist missionaries should also study the Bible and the history of Christianity very thoroughly. . . . A Buddhist missionary must first adopt and adapt all the good points of Christianity, and then proceed to criticize the errors of the Christian Church. If he only denounces and ridicules Christianity without studying it, he will make exactly the same mistake as the purblind and ignorant Christian missionaries in China, Japan, and India have committed for a hundred years. The Christian missionaries in India, China and Japan do not study and assimilate Hinduism, Confucianism and Buddhism: and they only denounce and criticize our great teachers and our sacred books. The result is that we do not listen to them at all, and we regard them as fools and fanatics. The Buddhists in Europe should not follow such a suicidal policy."[40]

"A missionary is a guide and a leader for his con-

[39] *Young East* (February, 1927), p. 300.
[40] *Ibid.*, p. 302.

MODERN TENDENCIES

gregation. He must decide many practical questions, and advise his disciples in their daily lives. It is a tremendous task. A Buddhist missionary who has not studied all the aspects of European civilization thoroughly, cannot help his disciples at all. Europe must solve labor problems, international problems, women's problems, ethical problems, religious problems, social problems, problems of all kinds in ever-increasing numbers. How will the Buddhist missionary deal with these educated and ambitious working men? How will he advise these clever, free, and idealistic women with short hair, short skirts, and bare arms? If he applies the simple, old rules of the venerable Tripitaka to these conditions, he will fail in his mission. The Buddhist missionary must himself become very modern and progressive in spirit and temperament. Then he will be able to guide and mould these active, inquisitive, daring, earnest and idealistic young men and women of Europe and America, in whose lily-white hands lies the future of the human race." [41]

The most active missionary sect, the Hongwanji, reports 84 centers, 130 priests, and 117,933 followers. Twenty-five of the centers, 36 priests, and 7,357 followers are in the United States. China, Hawaii, and the South Sea Islands are their other fields; Hawaii, the largest, with 64,750 followers. While it is true that most of this work is done among Japanese emigrants, it is by no means confined to them. Magazines and books and tracts are published in English, adapted especially to appeal to the educated Englishman and American. The quotation above from *Young East*, a Buddhist-English publication, makes it very clear that its missionary work is not to be limited to Japanese.

[41] *Ibid.*, p. 303.

RELIGION IN JAPAN

The New Humanism

The fourth tendency is that movement, among the intellectuals chiefly, which from the traditional point of view with reference to religion, would be considered non-religious. Those, however, who would call modern humanism a religion would certainly classify representatives of this group as religious. Confucian influence has been fairly strong in Japan. It has been in its Japanese expression even less concerned with supernaturalism than in China. Those who in the modern day find themselves dissatisfied with the intellectual offerings of current religion, whether it be Shinto, Buddhism or Christianity, find Confucian humanism congenial to their spirits. The peculiar institution known as State Shinto, which by government declaration is not a religion, may, it seems to the present writer, be accepted and practiced by this humanistic group without any feeling that they are sharing the beliefs of Shinto as a religion, and thus fulfill for them a real need that men ordinarily call religious. It is true that there is a large group of intellectuals who have thrown over completely their beliefs in any of the traditional faiths. A census of student belief in the University of Tokyo early in the 'twenties will serve as an illustration of this fact. Out of the total of 4,608, 2,989 listed themselves as agnostic, 1,511 as atheists, and only 118 as adhering to Christianity, Buddhism or Shinto. It is common enough in the articles dealing with Japanese religions to discover statements like the following:

MODERN TENDENCIES

"It may be said without fear of valid contradiction that the majority of educated young men in Japan are skeptics—I had almost written 'normally godless.' By the latter phrase I mean that save in exceptional circumstances they neither recognize nor worship a God or gods." [42]

Or this:

"But the majority of educated people still think . . . that a religion is necessary only to those who have not received higher education." [43]

Yet many among these are by no means satisfied that Japan be without religion. What they urge, rather, is a new religion of humanity which finds its chief ally in the progress of modern science and would seek to achieve its major goods through scientific control of the natural world and of society. It is the distinctively human values that receive their chief emphasis and even where their intellectual objections to the traditional religions have not wholly dethroned the gods, there is a strong insistence upon humanizing them, whether Shinto, Buddhist, or Christian. This bears so close a resemblance to the protest that is observable in our own intellectual world that detailed discussion of it is unnecessary.

Inter-Religion Coöperation

There are other minor tendencies discernible, but perhaps none more significant than the recent trend toward a larger coöperation between the religions, particularly in their practical social program. An evi-

[42] M. G. Mori, *Buddhism and Faith*, pp. 26, 30.
[43] *Ibid.*, p. 26.

RELIGION IN JAPAN

dence of this is found in an all-religions conference held in June, 1928, in which Shinto, Buddhism and Christianity united for a three-day discussion of their common problems. The conference divided itself into four sections to consider Thought Problems, World Peace, Religious Education and Social Problems.

The Thought section emphasized:

"the responsibility of religious leaders for opposing communistic and anarchist ideas which are a menace to national order. They recommended the establishment of a research bureau for harmonizing the thought of East and West, and also expressed a hope that the Japan Religious Association would "conduct a research in order to formulate a sane social creed." [44]

The World Peace section recommended that religious leaders support the League of Nations and its principles, approved the Treaty to outlaw war, advocated the removal of racial discrimination, and recommended that helpful material regarding international peace be incorporated in textbooks.

The Religious Education section drew up a memorial to the government to "modify their attitude toward religious education, religious instruction and ceremonies, so that the law would not discount religion." [45] They recommended establishing religious courses in normal schools, and establishing a religious research commission in the Department of Education.

The Social Problem division dealt with the "extermination of leprosy, juvenile courts, child welfare, abolition of prostitution, prohibition of liquor to

[44] *The Japan Mission Year Book, 1929*, p. 66.
[45] *Ibid.*, p. 67.

MODERN TENDENCIES

those under twenty-five, abolishing liquor in religious gatherings, and the employment of shrines, temples and churches for neighborhood welfare work." [46]

It is interesting to note that all three felt themselves on common ground in the attempt to maintain spiritual values in the face of an advancing secularism.

Another evidence of coöperation among the religions of Japan is to be seen in "The Japan National Committee for the Promotion of International Peace through Religion." In this are combined Buddhist, Shinto and Christian forces. In May, 1931, this committee promoted a conference in Tokyo with the view "to gain concerted actions of all religious sects on the principle of love for peace and to promote the peace movement through religious faith." Three hundred and forty-two religious leaders attended the conference, of whom 128 were Buddhists, 107 Shintoists and 75 Christians.[47]

That a degree of syncretism is present is evident in the writings of many modern Japanese. Some of them are quite consciously attempting to form an eclectic faith adequate for the modern day and age. "A new God fashioned from the substance of all existing gods is the thing which we now badly want," [48] writes Professor K. Sugimori of the Waseda University, and this may be taken as typical of the thought of many.

[46] *Ibid.*
[47] *Japan Christian Year Book, 1932*, pp. 35-36.
[48] *Principles of Moral Empire* (London: University of London Press, 1917), preface, p. v.

RELIGION IN JAPAN

Thus we have seen Japan like the rest of the world in the midst of change, economic, political, social and intellectual such as is not surpassed anywhere unless possibly in China. Religion is there as everywhere trying to come to terms with this change. It has done it in the form of reaction on the one hand, reassertion of the old national, indigenous faith, now centered in the person of the Mikado, as a religion of unquestioning loyalty and patriotism; on the other hand, one finds an attempt at modernization of that faith by a rationalizing process and by the use of modern techniques borrowed largely from the vigorous missionary faith, Christianity. Buddhism has undergone this same modernization in method. It has become evangelistic; it has become educational, stressing not only religious education but secular education as well, touched, however, by the religious spirit. It has become a significant social force in the life of the Japanese people in the midst of their rapidly shifting from an agricultural to an industrial type of civilization. It has awakened intellectually; it has reinterpreted and reëvaluated much of its heritage from the past. It has become aware of a certain unity in its diversity and swings in the direction of a greater degree of union within Japan itself, but at the same time becomes increasingly conscious of its relation to the world of Northern or Mahayana Buddhism. Some even dream of a united world Buddhism including Hinayana or Southern Buddhism. It has become once more positively missionary in its interest and is making an effort to extend the blessings of Buddhism as the one force adequate to meet

MODERN TENDENCIES

the demands of a world torn by hatred, greed, suspicion, and racial and national strife.

A new humanism, something of a religion of humanity, appeals to an increasing number of thoughtful Japanese who no longer find satisfaction in the religions as they exist, while some seek by the method of syncretism to build a faith that will be adequate for Japan's need, where no single religion nor all of them together have succeeded.

Religion and Nationalism

In very recent months, indeed, while this study was being written, the Manchurian situation and the Shanghai incident followed by international protests and the League of Nations' intervention, created a new set of conditions which could not but affect seriously Japan's religions. It is still too early to assess the true effects, but two or three statements may be made with some certainty. It was to be expected that heightening of nationalistic feeling would tend to intensify loyalty to a religion already closely associated with the peculiar national culture and national aspirations, such as Shinto, and the nation would be expected, as has always happened, to use that religion to intensify patriotic devotion. Apparently this has happened. A correspondent who was in Japan during the greater part of this period, notes that Shinto has been immensely strengthened by the national crisis. Every regiment, he declares, "lines up before the Meiji shrine before leaving for Manchuria. The local shrines have never been so busy since the Russian War." [49]

[49] Dr. Charles W. Iglehart.

RELIGION IN JAPAN

Buddhism and Christianity, both ostensibly religions of peace, might have been expected to protest against the military policy of the nations. At least Christianity, after the very harsh criticism it has met for its failure to oppose effectively the World War, might have been expected to react thus. What has happened? So far as we have been able to discover, no protest has come from organized Buddhism, indeed, in the words of a correspondent in Japan, "there comes as near being unanimous consent from the population as one could well imagine from seventy million people."

In the case of Christianity there has been official protest on more than one occasion from the National Christian Council, the one group that could speak for Christianity as a whole. To quote one of these in part must suffice. It was directed to the Japanese premier:

"As we look at the present state of confusion in international relations we are grieved at the tendency that has arisen to regard our country as . . . a violator of the covenant of the League of Nations. We are eager that such suspicions should be speedily removed and trust that our government will take adequate measures to bring this about. We sincerely hope that they will make clear both at home and abroad that the attitude of our people is one of regard for the league, the nine-power treaty and the Kellogg pact, and we pray that in their spirit a speedy settlement of the present dispute may be found." [50]

That it required real courage to voice such a protest, none who have followed carefully the recent

[50] Quoted by T. T. Brumbaugh in *The Christian Century*, Vol. 49 (May 18, 1932), p. 648.

MODERN TENDENCIES

trend of events in Japan can deny. What effect, if any, these protests have had upon the attitude of the government and of the war-inflamed population in general toward Christianity is not yet known.

Certain it is that observers will watch with interest the outcome of the whole matter in its effect upon the religious life of Japan and upon the fortunes of the three great religions which share amongst themselves the loyalty of the Japanese people.

CHAPTER V

TWENTIETH-CENTURY TENDENCIES IN ISLAM

AMONG all the religions of the world Islam would probably be considered by the average individual as the most rigid and unyielding, the least likely to undergo serious change. Yet Islam is, at the present time, in the midst of exactly the same sort of a struggle which religion is experiencing elsewhere, and, whether voluntarily or no, is suffering far-reaching modifications in her age-old beliefs, practices and organization. What are the major changes that the present century has produced?

Before proceeding to note these, it will be worth our while to indicate briefly the influences that have operated to bring about these changes. It is very clear that for the most part they have not been self-generated, for here, as in the farther East, the impact of the West must be charged with heavy responsibility for the revolutions that have come about in Islamic lands. Along with the impact of the West have come inevitably those factors that have made religious change inevitable. To be sure, there had been contact between Europe and the Near East long before the opening of the present century. Indeed, not a few changes had been wrought in the fabric of Mohammedan life before the opening of the

MODERN TENDENCIES

twentieth century. But the more intimate contacts and the more powerful influences have been the contribution of the present century and the contacts of the earlier centuries. Perhaps the two cultures were too near the same level to exert drastic influences one upon the other. We may list very briefly the various economic, political and cultural influences that have played the major rôle in this overturn of the civilization of the Near East.

Economic Changes in the World of Islam

First consider, for example, the economic impact. The building of railroads, and in more recent times the establishment of motor-bus lines, and still later air lines, has opened up to the currents of world thought the remoter centers of the Moslem world. Today one may traverse in a few hours by plane or in a few days by rail or motor car, desert distances that had effectually separated population centers from all contact with the world of progress for centuries. The telephone and telegraph lines and, latterly, radio stations bring to the most remote corners of the Islamic world the latest ideas that are abroad in even the most progressive sections of modern life. In short, the Moslem world has been effectually opened to contact with a world which only a few decades ago was scarcely dreamed of.

Along with improved communication and transportation has gone modern business with its different ideals and practices that stand in sharp contrast to the age-old, religiously sanctioned customs of Islam. For instance, consider the question of interest which

IN ISLAM

plays so basic a part in the modern business world, but which is expressly prohibited in the law of the Prophet. For the exploitation of the abundant resources of Moslem lands, large sums of capital become necessary, but capital can be secured, according to western standards, only on the payment of interest. What shall be the attitude of the Moslem, who may have capital to lend, or who may desire to borrow from foreign capitalists for business purposes? Shall he be untrue to his faith, which strictly forbids it, or shall he manage, by some sort of a rationalization, to justify the principle of interest payment, as have both Jews and Christians? Here appears a very practical problem which the Moslem world has had to meet. Or again—modern business and industry is very apt to occasion urban development which speeds up life and therefore raises a bar to the performance of established religious customs, for example, the daily prayers of the Moslem. The muezzin's call to prayer from the minaret of the mosque may be drowned by the honk of automobiles or the noisy clang of the street car gongs. "Can a city business man be asked to kneel in his good clothes five times a day in wet and muddy streets," asks a Moslem of the West, who settles the matter for himself by replying "Of course not," and advocating an abandonment of this time-honored custom. Moslem law, which until very recently, was the law of most of the Near and Middle East, was forged in a desert environment and adapted to a relatively simple nomadic or agricultural population. How shall it be applied to the vexing problems which the new world

MODERN TENDENCIES

of industrial expansion forces upon men? Some one has humorously said, "Mohammed may have left detailed instructions for camel drivers, but he had nothing to say about drivers of Ford cars." How shall these new questions and new problems be solved? Shall religion determine the answer? Is there not in these situations the seed of profound change?

Political Ferment in Moslem Lands

But again, consider briefly the political changes that have been experienced in the world of Islam within the present century. The whole growth of nationalism, perhaps the most notable phenomenon in the field of politics, is having a very profound effect upon Islam. One writer, who is well acquainted with Near Eastern trends, declares:

"Nationalism then with its practical policy of self-determination, is the outstanding primary idea fermenting in the mind of Moslem youth today. . . .

"In the mind of Moslem youth the idea of the nation has irreparably torn into fragments the enormous, heavy tapestry of Pan-Islamism. Nothing parallel to this has happened in the mind of any generation of youth since the Reformation shattered the unity of the Holy Roman Empire." [1]

Almost every Moslem state throughout the Near East has, within the past decade, become very strongly nationalistic. Turkey has led the movement. As early as 1909 the Young Turk movement

[1] Basil Mathews, in *The Moslem World Today* (by J. R. Mott), p. 63. Reprinted with permission from Doubleday, Doran and Company, Inc., publishers.

IN ISLAM

arose in Turkey, largely as a result of the impact of the West. Certain reforms of a political nature resulted from this movement, though by no means all that its partisans had hoped for. Turkey went into the World War as the "sick man of Europe" on the side of the Central Powers. She came out of it so sick that many thought that she could not live. But she failed to die. Rather, under the vigorous leadership of Mustapha Kemal, she abolished the Sultanate, created the great national assembly at Angora, won notable diplomatic victories at peace conferences, and, finally, at the Lausanne Conference practically dictated her own terms to the representatives of the Allied Powers and took her place once more as a vigorous, forward-looking nation, which Europe could by no means neglect or ignore. Under the direction of Mustapha Kemal, who could have been Sultan, but who remained as President-Dictator, the whole direction of Turkish history has been changed. He and his able advisers have definitely chosen to "go West," that is, to follow the European or Occidental, rather than the Oriental, pattern in her future development. This has had, and is yet to have, most far-reaching influence upon the whole of the Near and Middle East and upon the faith of the Prophet throughout the world. For Turkey had been the very center of the Moslem world, and its Sultan had been the Caliph, or successor to the Prophet, for all of the Moslems. Could democracy and Islam exist together? Was it possible for a republican state, which had, through her unfortunate war experience, lost the political hegemony over a great

MODERN TENDENCIES

part of the Moslem world, to retain her leadership of the Moslems in the field of religion? Arabia, Egypt, Palestine, Trans-Jordania, Iraq and Syria ceased to acknowledge her as their over-lord. Thus the apparent political solidarity of the greater part of the Islamic world had at a blow disappeared. Formerly the more timorous of the Christian world had cherished the fear that a Pan-Islamic movement, which would set the Moslem world over against the Christian, might develop. One of the popular bogies of the pre-World-War period had been the fear of *Jihad,* or a united Islamic war against the Christian world. But the World War laid once and for all that fearsome threat, for when, after Turkey had entered the world struggle on the side of the Central Powers, the Turkish Sultan and Caliph of all the Moslems solemnly issued the call to *Jihad,* it fell on deaf ears. Instead of responding to the call, Mohammedan India threw her enormous resources to the side of Great Britain. French North Africa, which is ninety per cent or more Moslem, literally poured her soldiers into France, and Moslem faced fellow-Moslem across No Man's Land. The dream of the world solidarity of Islam was shattered. It was a terrific blow. In such a shock there was the suggestion of far-reaching change.

With the growth of democracy in Islam the increasingly powerful revolutionary government at Angora abolished the Sultanate, but the Sultan was also Caliph. What should they do about that? Had they the right to abolish the Caliphate? They were not quite prepared, as yet, to take so important a

IN ISLAM

step as the abolition of the Caliphate, so in dismissing their political ruler, the government appointed one who should act as Caliph, performing all of the functions of a non-political character belonging to that office; that is, they separated the religious from the political functions, and for two years the Caliph carried on in Constantinople, while the effective government of Turkey centered in Angora. But the situation was an anomalous one, and in 1924, with but a few hours notice, the Caliph, the great head of the Moslem world, recognized but a little while before as the "shadow of God on earth, Caliph of all the Moslems" was ordered to gather his personal possessions together and leave the country as a permanent exile. Naturally, this drastic action caused the utmost consternation throughout the Moslem world. Who should be Caliph or substitute for the Prophet? As might have been expected, various claimants arose for the position, but there was no unanimous agreement on the part of the Moslem nations. A great Pan-Islamic congress was called and met in 1926 to discuss the whole matter of the Caliphate. They discussed four issues: (1) the definition of the Caliphate, (2) the qualifications necessary for a true Caliph, (3) the manner in which the Caliph should operate in future, and (4) the question as to whether it were possible to find any one who could fulfill the legal conditions of the Caliphate at the present time. The upshot of the conference was a definition of the Caliphate as "the office of spiritual and temporal chief of the Moslems," but no agreement could be reached with reference to the

MODERN TENDENCIES

other questions. The conference ended without having made any marked progress toward the continuation of the office. This congress had been called by Moslem doctors at Al Azhar University in Cairo. The Wahhabi chieftain, Ibn Saud of Arabia, evidently not content with that assembly, called a world Moslem congress of his own, which he hoped to continue as an annual conference. It met in the pilgrim season of 1926 in Mecca, but a number of the important Moslem countries had failed to send delegates, including Turkey, Persia, and Iraq. There is no record in the reports of the congress of any adequate discussion of the Caliphate. Indeed, a recent writer in the *Moslem World* says that the question was not raised, though many other matters affecting the Moslem world were discussed. A third international Islamic conference was held in Jerusalem in 1931, to discuss problems raised by the Zionist movement and again there was no discussion of the Caliphate.[2] The office of Caliph, if indeed it exists, has no incumbent. But the matter may not be considered settled, for from time to time, press dispatches note the rise of interested claimants for the honor. As recently as September 19 (1931), a newspaper dispatch declared that the former ruler of Egypt was offering himself as a candidate for the office which he desires to see established at Jerusalem, as the second holiest of the Moslem cities.

The same dispatch mentioned still another candidate, the former Caliph and Sultan of Turkey, who

[2] Alfred Nielsen, "The Islamic Conference at Jerusalem," *The Moslem World*, Vol. 22 (October, 1932), pp. 340-55.

IN ISLAM

was being backed by certain groups of Moslems to resume his function with his seat of office in India, under British protectorate. A still later dispatch of September 29, 1931, stated that the former Caliph and Sultan of Turkey had agreed to resume his pontifical duties with temporal powers at Jerusalem. One of the Moslem leaders, head of the Pan-Islamic movement in India, who was a delegate to the Round Table Conference in London, was said to be negotiating some sort of an agreement between the former Caliph and the British government. It is interesting that India, the most numerous Moslem group in the world and a wholly non-Arab population, seems to be the most deeply concerned over the question of the Caliph. So ardent were they in the support of the Caliph in Turkey, that there is said to have been a near revolution among the Moslem groups of India when Britain took an attitude hostile to the Caliphate in Turkey.

Naturally, the abolition of the Caliphate was a matter of deep concern among Moslems. Some one has said that it would be a somewhat parallel case if it should occur to Mussolini one day to announce that he had abolished the papacy. To be sure, the Pope and the Caliph did not exercise parallel functions, yet each was the head and center of a great religion, and to some the Caliphate was so important that it was openly questioned whether or not prayer could be made if the office were abolished. The impression that one gathers from a study of the whole situation is that the unity of the Islamic world has been effectually broken, and that with it has gone

MODERN TENDENCIES

the Pan-Islamic dream which for so many years was cherished among Moslems.

But Turkey has not been alone in undergoing political change. Nationalism has swept across the entire Near and Middle East, carrying with it a variety of reforms of a political and social character, which are apt to have far-reaching consequences in the field of religion as well. As early as 1907 there were beginnings of republican revolt in Persia. In 1920 the Shah was deposed and a popular soldier-conqueror became dictator and still later the founder of a new dynasty, but one limited by a constitution that admits of a degree of democratic participation in government totally unknown to older Persia. The new Shah has his face definitely turned westward. He is particularly watching Turkey and has adopted not a few of the reforms which Mustapha Kemal has introduced among the Turks, such as the abolition of the native male headdress. Popular education of both boys and girls has received new impetus. A remarkable development in public building, and road construction has been carried on which has greatly modified Persian life. Women have acquired a degree of liberty unknown until very recently and though not as yet officially unveiled, are taking an increasingly prominent part in the building of a new Persia. While there has been no modification in the legal attitude toward religion, for Islam is still the state religion, there has been a noteworthy growth of the spirit of tolerance, so that other faiths, while enjoying no legal freedom, are relatively unhampered in carrying on their work. Where in the

IN ISLAM

past, conversion to Christianity frequently enough meant death, it occasions only minor inconvenience today in the larger cities. That would not hold true of the more remote villages.

Important reforms affecting marriage and therefore the status of women have been recently decreed:

"A law became effective in Persia on September 24 [1931], which permits women to seek a divorce from their husbands and establishes the marriageable age at sixteen years for women and eighteen for men. Persia like India has been discredited by its child marriages. Apparently the custom of temporary marriage by agreement of adults has not been changed."[a]

Even Afghanistan, perhaps the least known and the most inaccessible of the Moslem nations, has felt the influence of the West. The sovereign Amanullah, himself modern, wished to modernize his people, but his attempt proved abortive. When he decreed a number of reforms like those of Turkey, the abolition of the veil for women, the substitution of European hat and dress for the time-honored and religiously sanctioned native costumes, he failed to take into account the depth of religious conservatism of his people. The result was a revolt of the reactionary group, which obliged the ruler to abdicate in favor of an orthodox administration. It is true, doubtless, as Mr. Ikbal Ali Shah observes, that the reaction was not wholly or perhaps even chiefly for religious, but economic reasons; but the net result has apparently been to strengthen orthodoxy.

Egypt since 1919 has vigorously sought her own

[a] *Current History* (November, 1931), Vol. 35, p. 309.

MODERN TENDENCIES

independence from the protectorship of England. Arabia, which was lost by Turkey at the close of the war, has become independent and fairly well consolidated under the control of Ibn Saud, a staunch Wahhabi Moslem who is thought by many to aspire to the Caliphate himself. Mesopotamia or, as now known, Iraq, Trans-Jordania, and Palestine, the two latter still under British mandate, are rapidly being modernized. Iraq has recently come to complete autonomy, her independence having being recognized by the mandatory power, Great Britain. Syria and the Lebanon, under French mandate, have been a center of intrigue and revolutionary activity, and even in India, where Islam is a minority group, the relationship of the Islamic population to the nationalist aspirations of India has been a matter of very great importance. With such kaleidoscopic political changes throughout the entire Moslem world, it is little wonder that religion has undergone the necessity of some very significant reform. We may properly add one other political influence which has not been without its effect, particularly upon Turkey and Persia; namely, the propaganda of Bolshevism which, during the period immediately following after the World War, was most zealously spread throughout the Islamic world. Persia particularly, by reason of her proximity to the Russian border and her fairly intimate relationship with Russia in the years immediately after the war, was subject to Bolshevik influences. Naturally, with their strong anti-religious prejudice, they would tend to affect the attitude of the Moslem leaders toward religion.

IN ISLAM

Other Cultural Influences Affecting Islam

Among what may be called the social or cultural influences that have wrought religious change, must of necessity be named the network of schools which have been carried on throughout the entire Near and Middle East by the Christian missionary societies of both Europe and America or by private philanthropy. Such institutions as Robert College at Constantinople, the Syrian College at Beirut, the Women's College, also at Constantinople, and others of the same sort have had a most powerful liberalizing influence. The other contributions and the work of the Near East Relief Organization made a very deep impression upon Islam. It would have been strange had not Christianity, thus brought into intimate contact with Islam, tended to modify in some degree at least the religious beliefs and practices of the followers of the Prophet. Partly as a result of the educational work of the missionary societies, popular education has been widely extended through Moslem lands. The general percentage of literacy has risen rapidly. With increasing numbers of people able to read, the dissemination of ideas, before limited to a comparatively few people, has been made possible even to the more remote parts of the countries. The development of the press has been little short of phenomenal. The number of periodicals, as well as books issued yearly throughout these lands has increased by leaps and bounds. Thus the Moslem world discovers what the rest of the world is thinking and doing. Is it not impossible

MODERN TENDENCIES

under such circumstances that religion should continue to exert over them the same unlimited authority as before? Moreover, social conditions have been profoundly affected by these influences and since religious and social life are in Islam, as elsewhere, so intimately inter-related, religion also changes.

With the introduction of schools and the new learning and the much heralded scientific method, it was inevitable that men should begin to question and to probe into the religion of the Prophet, just as they had in the Christian faith at an earlier period. It was natural that the same exacting tests that have been applied by the methods of historical criticism to the Christian Bible should be applied to the Koran in Islam. It could not be otherwise.

Perhaps one of the most potent of the influences for social change is to be noted in the introduction of the moving picture, which today carries in vivid, picturesque fashion the American and European standards of behavior and ideas of both men and women into the most remote corners of the Moslem world. Mr. Basil Matthews, who knows well the Moslem world, writes:

"Adolescent boys and girls, the latter with their mothers in the harem galleries, witness at the cinema pictures of Western romance, in which men and women meet on an equal plane and where women have the freedom of the wide world—a world in which the relations of the sexes are presented in terms of the choice of youth by youth on a plane of personal attachment and choice. Mary Pickford, Pola Negri and Gloria Swanson, when appearing on the film before tens of thou-

IN ISLAM

sands of women and girls in an environment of Moslem social conditions and among people of relatively low standards of literacy, are likely to be more potent instruments of social revolution than a hundred books on the theory of the family." [4]

Thus, in brief, we have noted the chief influences which seem to be making for change in Islam. What actual effects have these produced?

In Islam, as in most of the religions considered, there may be discerned four main types of reaction: namely, the indifferent, the radical, the liberal, and the fundamentalist, each manifesting itself, however, in peculiar fashion in different sections of the Islamic world. In addition may be noted a new and vigorous modern missionary emphasis, especially in Indian Islam. Which tendency is the most important? It is difficult to say. One writer asserts what is probably true of Islam, as it is of other religions as well, that the vast majority hold a conservative position. The editor of the *Near East and India* declares that:

"The mass of evidence so far available seems to point to the fact that the main tendency in Islam in matters of faith and outward observance is toward the growth of indifference, if not of irreligion." [5]

Indifference is indicated by the comparative calm with which the rather drastic reforms in Turkey and elsewhere have been received by the masses of the people. Much of what is frequently

[4] *Op. cit.*, p. 67. Reprinted with permission from Doubleday, Doran and Company, Inc., publishers.
[5] "Transformation of Islam," *Near East*, Vol. 35 (1929), p. 164.

MODERN TENDENCIES

charged to irreligion might more properly be described as a mere luke-warmness in the belief and practice of a given faith. Probably the attitude of "don't care" is the most serious one from the standpoint of most of the religions of the world. Not a few leaders would frankly say that they prefer active hostility to the deadly attitude of "it doesn't matter."

The Radical Reaction

The radical tendency seems to take two chief forms: (a) that of skepticism or agnosticism with reference to Islam as a religion and philosophy, but its retention as a desirable socio-political scheme, if only it proves capable of certain modification; (b) a complete abandonment of Islam, both as a religio-philosophical system and a socio-political scheme; or, where the attitude does not extend to complete abandonment, it expresses itself at least as regarding the Moslem faith in the light of a serious handicap to progress. Just as has happened elsewhere in the world, within Christianity as well as other religions, modern scientific progress, obviously at variance with many of the traditional religious explanations of the world, has led to a complete abandonment of religion by many. Within Christianity, Latin America provides the most familiar example of this attitude on a grand scale, but it is no less true in Islam, for they are reading much the same kind of books, both scientific and critical literature, as well as fiction, which presents the "pagan superficial aspects of the structure of the social order of western Europe." A writer discussing this kind

IN ISLAM

of reading, so widely done by Moslem youth, declares:

"The widespread influence of these varied types of literature leads to an outlook that is not Islamic and is not Christian . . . it may be described as a careless, unsystematic agnosticism cheerfully cynical in outlook on the world, with few enthusiasms save those accompanying the assertions of independence."[6]

Less serious-minded representatives of this group, either uninterested in reform or from sheer apathy and indifference, continue to accept the minimum social control of the system consistent with their own ideas of personal comfort and peace of mind. They are lacking either in energy or conviction sufficient to motivate them to engage in the costly struggle for change. Lord Cromer, writing in particular concerning European influences upon the Moslems of Egypt, declares:

"The truth is that in passing through the European educational mill the young Egyptian Moslem loses his Islamism, or at all events he loses the best part of it. He cuts himself adrift from the sheet anchor of his creed. He no longer believes that he is always in the presence of his Creator, to whom he will some day have to render an account of his actions. He may still, however, take advantage of the least worthy portions of his nominal religion, those portions, namely, which in so far as they tolerate a lax moral code adapt themselves to his tastes and to his convenience in the affairs of this world."[7]

[6] From *The Moslem World Today*, by J. R. Mott, p. 68. Reprinted with permission from Doubleday, Doran and Company, Inc., publishers.
[7] Lord Cromer, *Modern Egypt*, Vol. 2, pp. 229 ff.

MODERN TENDENCIES

Yet others, and their number is on the increase, no longer think of religion in any form as a real necessity in this modern age. Religion, they think, doubtless has value for the unlettered poor, the unreflective masses of people, but for the man of education and culture it is no longer vital; that is, religion does not seem to them a necessity in any personal sense. To be sure, it is a valuable social control and the accumulated social values of Islam are not to be lightly disregarded. Its value in the creation of a sense of social solidarity renders it a formidable bulwark against the aggression of Occidental civilization. On this account they would retain it, though not without certain reforms sufficient to eliminate its major weaknesses without destroying its distinctly Moslem character. It is quite the fashion now in magazine articles as well as book titles to write of "The Near East Goes West," "Turkey Faces West," etc. Yet in each of the countries where the invasion of the West threatens, there are many who would hold on to Islam, precisely because it is at odds with certain things for which the West stands and which they deem ill-fitted for their own people.

Others, and perhaps a more numerous group of serious-minded radicals, not only no longer subscribe to Islam as a philosophy or as a religion but attack it vigorously as a socio-political system, because they hold that in this realm it is a weighty handicap to progress. While this spirit is manifested to a degree in Egypt, Persia, and even Afghanistan, it is in Turkey that it has found its chief expression.

IN ISLAM

It is there that the leaders have most insistently demanded a complete abandonment of Islam and a total reorganization of social and political life on a rational basis entirely apart from religion. An editorial which appeared in a Turkish daily newspaper in Constantinople is typical of a very widely accepted point of view, particularly in Turkey. It makes all religion a bar to progress. The author writes:

"In the discussion of religion, the progress of humanity has been very slow and very trivial. The humanity of today has not progressed a hand's breadth beyond what was known in Hindustan ten thousand years ago regarding the beginning and the end. Today we are simply repeating the ideas thought ten thousand years ago on the top of the Himalaya Mountains by the Indian. Civilization, the product of the work and life of human beings, is an entirely different thing. In view of its course in history it can very clearly be seen that it is completely irreligious and perhaps an entirely human thing.

"Possibly those may be found who would call social events, which are necessitated by religion, the outcome of civilization. These also can only be considered so in a roundabout manner. Aside from this, no religion has ever taken any people by the hand and helped them up the ladder of civilization nor has helping them up ever been possible to religion, nor is it now possible. It is now necessary to know that religion and civilization are two entirely different things. All through the period in which Christianity was master of the situation, it has hindered the development of civilization, that is, the enlightenment of minds and spirits. Therefore, the term 'Christian civilization' is nonsense.

"At the same time, the term 'Moslem civilization' is also nonsense. All that Islam did in the way of civilization was to build upon and carry forward the Greek

MODERN TENDENCIES

civilization. In the same way, the present world civilization also is nothing but the continuation and improvement of the Greek and Roman civilizations. Even religions have been helped and improved by this current of civilization. However, they themselves have not been able to forward the cause of humanity in the least. By means of their inherent conservatism, they have done their best to hinder the progress of humanity and they have actually tried to push humanity backward; but a single step forward—never." [*]

Still another Turkish editor charges that the backwardness of Turkey and Persia is due directly to the religion of the Prophet. He writes of Mohammedanism as an Arab religion in which Turkey, a non-Arabian people, can as a nation have no part:

"The disintegration of Turkish people in the past has been due chiefly to three causes, the first of which is religious. A cloak cut out and modeled for Arabia (i.e. Islam) has been forcefully put around our necks, which has kept us tied to our bedsteads and so prevented the free development of our normal abilities. God says in the Koran: 'Verily we have sent down the Koran in the Arabic language, so that you may understand it.' From these words it is evident that the Koran has been addressed to the Arabs, and the Turks can have no share in it. In the early ages of superstition it was only natural that each people should have a god of its own creation, and consequently it was very natural that the revengeful Arab should have a mighty, revengeful god. . . . The Arabs have ruined us [the Turks] by forcing upon us a god of their own creation. This god does not lack some good and noble qualities, but he has such attributes as have paralyzed our national and normal

[*] Quoted by T. H. P. Sailer, *The Moslem Faces the Future* (New York: Missionary Education Movement, 1926), pp. 172-174.

IN ISLAM

growth. Our minds have remained puzzled in the midst of contradictions. The cause of the Persian disintegration is also the same thing."[9]

This editor thinks of religion as an other-worldly affair, wholly unconcerned with the ever-present social problems that arise in the modern world. Elsewhere he writes:

"Especially in the East, religion today is a science of the hereafter, and as regards its present influence on us, religion ruins this present world. . . . Let the high moral principles of religion exist in its source books as much as you please . . . still cleanliness will continue to be found, not in Moslem but in non-Moslem wards of the city, attention to science will be observed among non-Moslems more than among Moslems, care for the acquiring of wealth and comfort and for the removal of poverty will be noticed more among non-Moslems than among Moslems. A people's religion is made up of convictions which are active and dominant in their practices and deeds. It is obvious to what depths and to what conceptions the Moslem beliefs, which rule in our spirits and consciences, have lowered us. . . . There is no religion among us which is worthy of serious attention and support. We face the high duty of making our people religious in this worthy sense by means of well-ordered moral training. . . . In America religion is put forward and exalted from the point of view of its usefulness with regard to building up and restoring the world and making men happy. . . . The Moslems of Persia and India, of Khiva, of Bukhara, and even of Turkestan still continue to say: 'Religion and the world are mutually contradictory; wherever there is religion, no importance is given to the present life.'

"We are not unaware of the fact that other factors

[9] *Ibid.*, pp. 170-171.

MODERN TENDENCIES

also were present in the fall and ruin of the Moslem East, but no one of these factors with its baneful thought possesses degenerative and destructive power to the degree of the religious. Until the conception of religion acquires a character and a power elevating instead of degenerating, constructive instead of destructive, and until it changes its flavor, to mention its name—in the East—will continue to be fatal. Therefore, Turkish leaders are called upon to create for the Turk a new lordship of conscience, free from silly tales." [10]

But if religion is inadequate to the task of molding moral and social life, where must men look for a force adequate to that task? To science and a rational philosophy! Mr. Lootfy Levonian, writing on "Moslem Criticism of Religion," quotes a Turkish contributor to *Ikdam*, a Constantinople daily paper, as expressing the solution popular today among the Turkish literati:

"What is the motive power of morality? Among primitive and conservative peoples and individuals it is knowledge. The human race has practiced these two methods in the past for thousands of years.
"In ancient times religion and service, morality and philosophy were combined together. Later the priests and the clergy through religious organizations have brought corruption and spoiled this early purity. . . . It is science and philosophy which will establish true and pure morality. It is knowledge which will bring individuals into the fulness of perfect manhood. Philosophic morality does not need any reward. Religious morality is easy. Religion quickly reaches its goal because it appeals to the ignorant, whereas philosophy appeals only to the learned. This increases the responsibility of the non-religious communities. Every person

[10] *Ibid.*, pp. 171-172.

IN ISLAM

ought to be enlightened. This is the meaning of democracy. . . . This is true for Turkey today. The Turkish nation has accepted the principle of non-religious democracy, therefore it is knowledge which will ultimately establish order in the Turkish community."[11]

How influential a group this represents in Turkey is evident from the radical changes which the Turkish government has recently put into effect. Not to mention the entire list, note the following:

First, as already noted, came in 1924 the abolition of the Caliphate, a most drastic step and one which had tremendous consequences throughout the Islamic world, greater perhaps in India than anywhere else. Of possibly even greater local significance was the abolition of the office of the Commissariat of Sheriat, or the "Religious and Pious Foundation Department," and the distribution of this function between the ministry of education and a presidency of religious affairs attached to the Prime Minister's office. This removed from the Cabinet the active head of the Islamic Church in Turkey who had previously exercised jurisdiction over the Sheriat or ecclesiastical courts where all questions of marriage, divorce and inheritance were handled. Thus a powerful influence for the maintenance of Islam was removed from a position of power. It will be noted that the state and religion were still related. It was not until 1928 that the clause which declared Islam to be the state religion was abolished.

Moslem theological seminaries with their large

[11] L. Levonian, "Moslem Criticism of Religion," *International Review of Missions*, Vol. 19, pp. 89-90.

MODERN TENDENCIES

endowments and vast properties were confiscated for state purposes; the reactionary dervish orders and like religious organizations were abolished, their monasteries being converted into secular educational institutions; the Moslem sacred day, Friday, was abandoned for the Christian Sunday as the day of rest; and the Moslem calendar gave way to the Gregorian.

Considered by many to be the end of religion in Turkey, by others it was hailed as a boon to religion. The complaint of at least one writer is not at the separation of church and state, but the fact that though now separated, the state still, through its Presidency of Religious Affairs, attempts to control religion. Thus she writes:

"The Islamic Community is chained to the policy of the government. The situation is a serious impediment to the spiritual growth of Islam in Turkey and there is always a danger in it of the use of religion for social ends.

"Now that the state has freed itself entirely from religious control, it should in turn leave Islam alone. Not only should it declare, 'Every Major Turkish citizen is free to adopt the religion he [or she] wishes to adopt,' but it should also allow the Moslem community to teach its religion to its youth. Now that the schools give no religious instruction, and the religious institutions are abolished, the Islamic community, if it is going to last as a religious community, must create its own means of religious teaching, its own moral and spiritual sanctions. Further, in the ritual and in the fundamentals of worship, there are likely to be changes among the Moslems in Turkey. Those changes should be allowed to take place without governmental interference. The occasional proposals by the university professors of new

IN ISLAM

forms of worship in Islam—such as substituting organ music for vocal music, entering the mosques without taking off the shoes, placing benches so that the faithful may pray seated, and doing away with a number of complicated body movements in prayer—have met with profound displeasure. All these changes might take place by the wishes of the people, but governmental interference in this most sacred part of men's rights would constitute a dangerous precedent. It would fetter the religious life of the Turks and bring politics into religion. The fundamental meaning of the long and very interesting phases of secularization is that Turkish psychology separates this world from the next. To take religion out of the political state, but at the same time to keep the state in religious affairs, is one of the contradictory aspects of the last phase which must be corrected." [12]

The Liberal Tendency

The third general tendency is what may be termed the liberal tendency, which takes a mediating position between the radical and the conservative and seeks, by means of reinterpretation, modification, and reform to conserve in this modern age the essential values of Islam. Within this general group various shades of opinion, of course, are to be found.

Here belong an increasing number of Moslems who recognize and welcome all progress, whether scientific, economic or political and who find nothing in this attitude incompatible with the faith of the Prophet. Religion is not static, they hold, but subject to evolution. Change of certain forms and beliefs is inevitable, but this in no wise affects the

[12] Halidé Edib, *Turkey Faces West* (New Haven: Yale University Press, 1930), pp. 230-231.

MODERN TENDENCIES

fundamental values in Islam. There are many reverent, constructive modernists among the followers of the Prophet, who are directing their efforts toward a reinterpretation of Islam which will render it capable of appeal to the modern generation, upon whom a world of swift change is forcing many new ideas.

"Science and knowledge have always been encouraged in Islam" [writes a modern Moslem]. "Throughout Islamic history you will not find people being persecuted for the sake of their having made discoveries in science and art. Islam has ever been the champion of rationalism and scientific research. Islam claims to be a rational faith and undertakes to satisfy reason and conscience both." [13]

Mr. Syed Amir 'Ali sums up the thought of a very large number of Moslems when he declares:

"The Islam of Muhammad contains nothing which in itself bars the progress of the intellectual development of humanity. The wonderful adaptability of the Islamic precepts to all ages and nations; their entire concordance with the light of reason; the absence of all mysterious doctrines to cast a shade of sentimental ignorance round the primal truths implanted in the human breast—all prove that Islam represents the latest development of the religious faculties of our being." [14]

A writer in the *Islamic Review* declares that if Mohammedanism is to appeal to the minds of educated and thinking Muslims, and to the West, it must be reformed. He declares that they err who

[13] *Moslem Sunrise*, January, 1924.
[14] M. T. Titus, *Indian Islam* (London: Oxford University Press, 1930), pp. 216-217.

IN ISLAM

say that Islam cannot be reformed. He points out that innovations have been introduced ever since the Prophet. He cites particularly the four orthodox schools of Islamic law, each differing to a degree from the other. If the *agreements* of the past have come to be accepted as authoritative, why may not Muslims of today in a World Muslim Congress decide on matters pertinent to the present day?—for he quotes Mohammed as saying, "Whatever Muslims find good, that is good with God." The only condition the author would place upon such reforms would be that they be true to the Spirit of Islam.[15]

This liberal tendency expresses itself in three rather characteristic ways: first, as a "back to the Koran" or "back to the Prophet" movement; second, reform of non-essentials which do not affect "the spirit of Islam"; third, actual modern criticism of the Koran.

While, as Dr. Murray Titus says, "The belief of all the modernists is 'that the Islam of Mohammed and the Islam of the Qur'an is without blemish and without spot and that its genuine and chief principles are in perfect harmony with nature and reason,'" there are many whose liberalism would by no means extend to any historical criticism of the Koran itself to discover the real Mohammed. What they mean is that there has grown up about the Koran and about Mohammed a vast deal of tradition and practice, which has tended to obscure the figure of the Prophet as he is seen in the Koran

[15] Muhammad Shahidu 'l-Lah, *Islamic Review*, Vol. 17, pp. 211-218.

MODERN TENDENCIES

itself. An Afghan, writing of the modernization of Islam, thinks of it merely as a return to the genuine Islam uncorrupted by priestcraft. He says:

"In the New Dark Age of my faith, from which we have just emerged into the sunny vistas of real religion, a curious politico-religious system had grown; and it is indeed by reason of our forebears having been seen so long under that influence that the average European wonders whether we have not definitely divorced Islam by our modernization. The truth is that the organization of the Doctors of Moslem Law, backed by autocratic Eastern monarchs was the very antithesis of the words of the Koran. In Turkey, for instance, no man was permitted to consult the Holy Book of Islam and seek interpretation for himself; despite the fact that the only reason for which the faithful places his book above every other Revealed Law is that any man can have his cue directly from it. The Prophet himself emphasized this fact repeatedly and thereby meant to destroy the human tendency of priestcraft. This particular teaching was so deep that it was not until many political cross-currents amongst the Moslem States had much weakened the spiritual essence that the clergy at last won the battle which they had fought for at least a thousand years."[16]

When ecclesiastics frowned upon women parading the streets in Stamboul, the young men were able to silence the objections by quoting the Koran to prove that the Koran enjoined only modesty and not the cruel practice of closing women in the houses.[17]

Another Moslem writer affords an interesting illustration of the adaptation of Islam to the mod-

[16] Ikbal Ali Shah, "The Modernization of Islam," *Contemporary Review*, Vol. 135, pp. 263-264.
[17] *Ibid.*, p. 265.

ern world. He moves in the direction of liberalization in Moslem practice by a resort to a clever reinterpretation of the Koran. The question involved is that of taking interest which is condemned in Islam, as it was formerly in the religion of the Hebrews. He writes:

"Interest has been prohibited in three places in the Qur'-an (2:276; 3:125; 30:38) and everywhere it has been mentioned in contrast with *sadaqah* (charity) or *zakat* (poor-rate). In prohibiting interest the premises were that it is always an oppression to take interest, and that Muslims shall always be governed by their own laws and that no non-Muslim shall be able to exact interest from Muslims. Now none of these conditions exist in India. It is certainly no oppression to take interest from the British Government. And then, though a pious Mussulman cannot take interest, he is bound to give interest in India. The result has been that the Muslims are being impoverished and the other people are being enriched at their expense. In prohibiting interest the Qur'-an says: 'Do not oppress, and do not be oppressed' (2:279). But though we cannot oppress we are being oppressed. That the Quranic prohibition against interest is not to be taken universally has been admitted by some legislators who hold that it is legal in non-Muslim countries." [18]

Still another illustration in proof of the modernity of the Koran is to be found in the fact that it foretells the most modern scientific discoveries. In a lengthy series of articles on the supernaturalism of the Koran in the *Islamic Review*, the author, Mr. Syed Maqbool Ahmed, attempts to show how mar-

[18] Muhammad Shahidu 'l-Lah, "Modernization in the Light of the Development of Islam," *Islamic Review*, Vol. 17, p. 214.

MODERN TENDENCIES

velously the Koran has foreshadowed most of the advances in the modern world of science. We quote here as an example of his method of exegesis his statement regarding modern methods of transportation:

"In one of its chapters the Qur'-an describes certain gifts of Nature given to the Arabs. Only the other day when reading I was struck by the remarkably striking nature of this verse. It reads: 'And He made the horses, mules, and asses for you to ride on them and as an ornament, and God shall create other things which you do not know' (xvi. 9). Just mark the last sentence. The Arabs of the time of Muhammad, and in fact the whole world down to the time when machines were employed as a means of transport, did not know of any objects other than horses, mules, and donkeys that would serve them as carriers from one place to another. Probably they had heard or known of elephants, camels, and some other animals as beasts of burden, or the ship that glided on the sea, which the Qur'-an also includes in the category as one of the great gifts of God to mankind. But what are those things which will be created afterwards and of which the Arabs did not know? Surely not a new animal. After reading the latter portion of the verse quoted above, who could say that the Qur-'an had not foreseen the age of locomotive engines and motor-cars? When the railway was approaching the gate of Medina and motor-cars were making trips between Jedda and Mecca, the fanatics wailed that the sanctity of the holy places was being defiled by these inventions of devils. It seemed that they had forgotten the promise embodied in the words of the above-quoted verse through His blessed Prophet some thirteen centuries ago. This is one of the many reasons that we call the Qur-'an a living book in all ages." [19]

[19] The *Islamic Review*, Vol. 17, 1929, p. 247.

IN ISLAM

"Back to the Prophet" means, generally speaking, back to the idealized figure of the Prophet. The method of idealization will be illustrated in the discussion of the reactionary trend, where the defense of the Prophet against many charges is to be sketched.[20] Dr. Murray Titus has this to say of the idealizing tendency:

"A new emphasis is being placed today on the character of the Prophet of Islam, and a process of idealization is going on which represents him as the perfect model for mankind (insan-ul-kamil). This is not only at variance with the historical 'lives,' such as that of Ibn Hisham, but even to the express statements of Muhammad himself, as set forth in the Qur'an, where he asks forgiveness for his own sins. The whole purpose of this new effort would seem to be to offset the character of the 'sinless Christ of Christianity,' as well as to arouse a new enthusiasm for Islam by recognizing that religion thrives best when it can lay claim to a person in whom centre all the highest spiritual and moral values, and around whom loyal followers can rally. In the new apologetic it is no longer the Qur'an and the Shari'at (the Law) to which men are called, but to Muhammad himself."[21]

Whether Mr. Titus is correct in his judgment that this trend arises out of opposition to Christianity or in the desire to find a figure that will appeal to the modern world, the tendency seems definitely to be present, and it is tendencies that we are here concerned with.

After all, many declare, the important consideration is the real spirit of Islam, and not any particu-

[20] See p. 159 ff.
[21] M. T. Titus, *Indian Islam*, pp. 209-210.

MODERN TENDENCIES

lar detail of belief or practice. "The time has arrived, according to Sir Ahmed Hussain, for a break, not with Islam itself, but with its traditional exponents, 'who have degraded the religion by paying undue attention to formulas and forms to the exclusion and neglect of its living spirit and reality.' " [22] Or again, in the words of a great Indian modernist, S. Khuda Buksh:

"There is nothing strange in the view that laws must accommodate themselves to circumstance. Such is the true spirit of Islam! Universalism is its keynote, unity of God its sole slogan; brotherhood of man its cardinal tenet; a will to conquer its refreshing inspiration. The rest is the creation of theology and not the essentials of Islam. And such is the Islam of the modern Muslims, the true Islam of the Prophet." [23]

Lord Headley, an English Moslem, expresses the feeling that is very common among the Moslems of the West when he suggests that certain innovations in the cult would add greatly to the attractiveness of Islam to Westerners. He thinks that the use of music, not necessarily in the mosque proper but in the rooms adjoining where lectures and meetings are held, would be a distinct help, and he would gladly see certain of the great Christian hymns supplied with Moslem words. He would place less emphasis on the formal requirements of prayer five times a day at appointed hours, since in a great city men engaged in active business life do not find the oppor-

[22] Quoted by M. T. Titus, *Indian Islam*, p. 207.
[23] S. Khuda Buksh, "Awakening of Islam," *New World*, Vol. 20, pp. 13-14.

IN ISLAM

tunity for prostration and the conventional devotional forms. Nor is it absolutely necessary, though desirable, he thinks, that ablutions be made before meals, the essential thing being the food and, of course, the gratitude of the consumer, which should be properly expressed. His whole contention is that these are relatively inconsequential matters which, entirely in the spirit of Islam, may be dispensed with where the demands of the modern world make it difficult or impossible to carry them out. It is in line with Lord Headley's feeling that these are not of the essence of Islam and that they may be dispensed with without seriously crippling it, that many in Turkey are advocating reforms "such as substituting organ music for vocal music, entering the mosque without taking off the shoes, placing benches so that the faithful may pray while seated, doing away with a number of complicated bodily movements in prayer."

The really liberal attitude is expressed, however, in the modern approach to the Koran and Moslem tradition. It would have been strange if in a world that had called to the bar of historic-scientific investigation, the Christian and Jewish scriptures, the Koran, the sacred book of the Moslems, had escaped this ordeal. While thus far the number of those who have approached the book critically is not perhaps very large, the tendency is, nevertheless, there and is becoming increasingly prominent. Dr. Margoliuth, in discussing the ideas of modern Islam, calls attention to the fact that even if the material in the Koran

MODERN TENDENCIES

relating to Mohammed were not seriously affected by modern criticism, they could not escape the effects of the application of the critical method to the Bible, from which the Koran has taken so much material. "For example," says Dr. Margoliuth, "if it is held that neither Abraham nor Ishmael can be regarded as historic characters, serious consequences arise for those passages in the Koran wherein the two are connected with the building of the Kaabah and other deeds and sayings ascribed to them." "When recently," he continues, "a professor of Arabic literature in the University of Cairo expressed doubts as to the historicity of Abraham and Ishmael, the book in which the passages occurred aroused a storm. . . . The professor adopted the course of declaring himself an orthodox Moslem and withdrawing his works from circulation, a new edition being substituted, from which the obnoxious passage had been removed." [24] Of course, it is true that the conservative Moslems, many of them, take the attitude that the results of the higher criticism of the Christian scriptures serves only to prove the untrustworthiness of those scriptures, whereas the real truth is to be found only in the Koran.

Dr. Titus cites among Indian modernists Professor Khuda Buksh, who "freely admits the debt of Islam to Christianity, Judaism, and pre-Islamic Arabia, and holds that Islam was thus developed by Mohammed into an eclectic system"; and Syed Amir Ali, who "makes bold to state that the Koran is the

[24] D. S. Margoliuth, "Ideas of Modern Islam," *Moslem World*, Vol. 20, p. 239.

IN ISLAM

product of the mind of Mohammed and reflects the processes of development of his religious consciousness." He refers to still another without naming him who, speaking of the Koran, calls it "a collection of sermons, commands, and instructions delivered and issued from time to time as occasion required . . . and you have to interpret the Koran quite naturally as neither book or historic document." [15] In Egypt, Taha Hussein, of the Egyptian University at Cairo, in a book on pre-Islamic poetry "tried to demonstrate a new thesis about the origins of Arabic poetry, showing that a few of the greatest masterpieces have nothing to do with Mohammed and had been interpolated in later times; they are of pre-Islamic origins though they form part of the Koran." We have already noted the consternation which this publication caused among the savants of the orthodox University of Al Azhar.

That modernism is making some strides in Egypt is evidenced by the fact that when a writer, Sheik Abdul Razek, published recently a book on *Islam and the Principles of Government,* in which he propounded the theory that the Moslem code is intended solely as a guide to personal conduct and not for purposes of the state, denying thus the fundamental significance of the Caliphate in Islamic thought, he was tried by the supreme council of Al Azhar for heresy, but so great was the pressure brought by the younger group in Egypt that he had to be acquitted. [16]

[15] M. T. Titus, *op. cit.,* pp. 215-216.
[16] Felix Valyi, "Ferment in the Arabic World," *The Nation,* Vol. 131, p. 78.

MODERN TENDENCIES

He has since been proclaimed by the Arabic press as the champion of free thought.[27]

The Reactionary Group

The fourth trend to be noted is a strong orthodox fundamentalist defense or reassertion of the characteristic beliefs of an Islam, which will brook no compromise with modern thought. The most ardent Christian fundamentalism seems comparatively mild in contrast with the extreme obscurantism of this group. They stand for a full defense of historic Islam. When the modern critics assail the plenary inspiration of the Koran, they hasten to defend it by the most interesting and devious methods and attempt to bring every part of it into the completest agreement. For these followers of the Prophet the Koran is a book sent from Heaven in a much more literal sense than Christians have ever claimed for their scriptures, and the most elaborate efforts are made to prove the divine quality of the book. A careful student of present-day Islam declares:

"As regards the defense of Islam, the old orthodoxy has written a whole library of books on the miraculous eloquence of the Koran and its sublime beauties. Rahmatu'llah says that its divine nature is proved by the fact that one never grows tired of reading it. Ibn Taymiyya says that, since the smallest verse of the Koran is a miracle of eloquence and elegance, the whole book contains thousands of miracles. Al Jili says that

[27] Mr. Arthur Jeffery, of The American University of Cairo, a careful student of the trends in Islam, writing in *The International Review of Missions*, Vol. 21, pp. 497-515, October, 1932, under the suggestive title, "Three Cairo Modernists," recounts the experiences of these men in great detail.

IN ISLAM

all that is contained in all religious books is contained in the Koran, that all the Koran is contained in the *Bismillah* (the conventional phrase which heads each sura but one), that all the Bismillah is contained in the B, and all that is in the B is contained in the point that is beneath it in the Arabic script."[28]

A writer in the *Islamic Review*, which is sometimes to be found advocating reforms, writes regarding the Koran:

"Almost all religions except Islam have suffered in their purity from human influences and human tampering. Fortunately for the Muslims, they receive their inspiration from a Book which is admittedly the same to-day as it was when delivered to us by the Founder of our Faith. We have accepted it as the Last Word of God, and we believe that every word of it comes directly from Him. It is not the work of Muhammed, nor has the purport of its message been translated into any words of his. Everything in it—its teachings as well as the language in which those teachings were couched—is from God. This is an orthodox belief, and though Islam has in the course of time given rise to various schools of thought, there has been no difference of opinion in the Islamic world as to the origin and significance of the Qur'-an."[29]

Concerning proposed reforms in the prayer and ritual of the faith, he further declares:

"they cannot admit of any change or allow of any reformation. Everything of this nature has been ordained for us by the Qur'-an; and if all the injunctions

[28] From John R. Mott, *Moslem World Today*, p. 316, from the article by Mr. Jeffrey on the "New Apologetic in Islam." Reprinted with permission from Doubleday, Doran and Company, Inc., publishers.
[29] *Islamic Review*, Vol. 17, p. 138.

MODERN TENDENCIES

in the Qur'-an are from God, as we do most firmly believe, we cannot take exception to any of the so-called formalities in our prayers. A Muslim is bound to observe them in the letter as well as in the spirit—letter and spirit in such a case being identical." [20]

There is strong orthodox opposition to translations of the Koran into the vernacular, particularly by Arab Moslems, though the non-Arab group more generally favor putting it in the modern languages of the faithful. Mr. Marmaduke Pickthall, who has recently made a translation into English, desiring the approval of the learned *ulemas* of the great Moslem University Al Azhar, went to Egypt to secure it.

It is interesting to note that while approving of his translation into English, the *ulemas* of Al Azhar held that it should be printed with Arabic text on the opposite page. Mr. Pickthall justified his refusal to do this on the score of expense, and the fact that English readers would be repelled on opening the book to find it half full of Arabic. He climaxed his justification, however, with the quoting a verse of the Koran: "So, whosoever hath attacked you, attack him with the like of that wherewith he hath attacked you." Now the other English translations held to be for purposes of attack on Islam had not included the Arabic text. Hence, this version designed to attack them should be like them in this respect. His argument carried conviction, for said one of his advisers, the former rector of Al Azhar, "If you feel so strongly convinced that you are right,

[20] *Islamic Review*, Vol. 17, p. 139.

IN ISLAM

go in God's name in the way that is clear to you and pay no heed to what any of us say."

It is interesting that even Mr. Pickthall does not call his translation the Koran, but the *Meaning of the Glorious Quran*. That fact removes much of the occasion for objections. Said the present rector of Al Azhar on first hearing of it, "If he calls it that, there can be no objection." Afterward, however, he did refuse to sanction it.[21]

That the unbending rigidity even of the great bulwark of orthodoxy, Al Azhar, is in the process of breaking seems to be evidenced to Mr. Pickthall by the Egyptian attitude toward his translation which, though pronounced as unfit to be authorized in Egypt, was at the same time recognized as the best of all translations. Commenting on their refusal to sanction it, Mr. Pickthall writes:

"There is something hopeful in the actual condemnation, the terms of which are wonderfully mild, one might almost say favorable, to the translation as compared with former pronouncements of the same authority. It marks the close of a long chapter in the history of relations between the Arabs and non-Arabs . . . since the position that all translation of the Qur'-an is sinful has been quite abandoned. A translation of the Qur'-an by a Muslim has been examined and a literary reason has been given for its condemnation. That is a great step forward."[22]

But when a noted professor of Arabic literature, writing on pre-Islamic poetry, attempted to use the

[21] M. Pickthall, "Arabs and Non-Arabs," *Islamic Culture*, Vol. 5, p. 431.
[22] *Ibid*, p. 433.

MODERN TENDENCIES

critical method in dealing with certain poems found in the Koran and arrived at conclusions at variance with orthodox views, regarding the perfect sanctity of the Koran, the *ulemas* of Al Azhar raised a storm of protest. Copies of the book were bought up and burned, and a demand was made that the offending professor be dismissed from the Egyptian University at Cairo, where he taught.

When Mohammed's character is assailed, the orthodox hasten to defend it, finding not only justification for all that he did, but discovering as well some high and worthy purpose in everything, even those phases of his life which the modern world most condemns—namely, his relationship to and treatment of women. What these relationships were the Koran states clearly. The Koran is an infallible book. One may not, therefore, dismiss it or explain it according to some historico-critical method in such way as to minimize the more objectionable features. These must, therefore, be justified. Their methods of justification are, indeed, interesting. We quote again from Mr. Jeffrey's excellent discussion of the new apologetic in Islam. He writes:

"Obliged by their theory to accept these as facts they have evolved the theory of the all-round man. Every prophet, they say, came with a special message to his own age. The age of Jesus was given to debauchery and needed an example of asceticism; so Jesus was an ascetic. But Mohammed was the seal of the prophets, the culmination of the prophetic line; so it was necessary that he should give men an all-round example. He was married to give men an example of married relations; he went to war to give men an ex-

IN ISLAM

ample of courage in the fight; and so on. In answer to the question why Mohammed needed so many wives, they say that marriage is the most important of human relationships, and men need more detailed example there than in other things; so, as men marry different types of women, it was necessary for the Prophet to give in his own life an example of how life should be lived with each kind of woman. Thus, with Khadija, he gave an example of how to live with a wife older than oneself; with 'Aisha, how to live with one younger than oneself; and so on, with all his wives according to their several types." [33]

The attitude of the Prophet toward women, manifested in such characteristic institutions as polygamy and divorce, is defended freely. Polygamy, they declare, is the Moslem solution of the social evil. Instead of thinking, therefore, of the polygamous marriages of the Prophet as evidence of sensuality and indulgence, Muhammad Ali, translator of the Koran, finds in his plural marriages a noble social service. He says:

"Up to a good old age of fifty-three, when one outgrows the passions of youth, the Prophet led his life in the company of but one wife, thereby setting an example that monogamy must be the rule of life under normal conditions. And as a matter of fact, this is exactly the purport of the Qur'-anic teachings. But as a universal religion, Islam must needs provide for all sorts of abnormalities. Polygamy is one such provision, permissible only when certain abnormal conditions call for it. When such conditions do arise, polygamy becomes a necessity, and if it is not allowed then, the

[33] From John R. Mott, *The Moslem World Today*, p. 306. Reprinted with permission from Doubleday, Doran and Company, Inc., publishers.

MODERN TENDENCIES

result is immoral sexual intercourse. The society becomes corrupt. Unmarried mothers and natural children become a part of it. Polygamy is, under such circumstances, the only effective preventive. Call it a necessary evil, or what you will, it is the only safeguard against moral turpitude. The Prophet was to be a perfect exemplar for mankind. Hence it was necessary that, notwithstanding his spending the whole of his youth—nay, even the major portion of his old age—with a single wife, he should have taken more wives than one, when war had increased the female element."[24]

In further proof of the disinterestedness with which the Prophet took these wives, Muhammad Ali notes:

"The perpetual state of war created disparity between the male and female elements of the society. Husbands having fallen on the field of battle, their widows had to be provided for. But bread and butter is not the only provision needed in such cases, as is supposed by certain short-sighted statesmen. Their sex-requirements must be looked after, otherwise moral corruption would inevitably result, and ultimately lead to the ruin of a whole nation. But a reformer, with whom morals are all in all, could not content himself with making provisions merely for their eating and drinking. The Prophet was jealous of their chastity, far more than of their physical needs. It became, therefore, necessary to sanction polygamy under the circumstances. This is the reason that the Prophet had to take a number of wives in the Medinite period of his life. We must note that all of his wives were either widows or divorced women. Where self-indulgence is the motive, the choice seldom falls on widows. Passion must needs have virginity for its gratification. And there was no dearth of virgins. It would have been an enviable privilege for any Muslim

[24] Muhammad Ali, "Muhammad the Prophet," *Islamic Review*, Vol. 19, pp. 404-405.

IN ISLAM

to be the father-in-law of the Prophet. But the object was a far nobler one—the protection of the widows of his friends. Thus as many as five of his wives were such as had lost their husbands on the battlefield or otherwise. . . . So in polygamy alone lay the moral safety of the Muslim society situated as it then was." [25]

The seclusion of women, as it has been so generally practiced within the Islamic world, is looked upon as a protective device wrought out for the purpose of saving women from the evils of the world. A present-day Moslem theologian of the great Mohammedan University of Al Azhar of Cairo, Egypt, recently wrote:

"I am certain that God made the veil compulsory for the women of believers, when I realize what the consequences of unveiling are, and what curses it brings on all people. This is clearly shown to every observer.

"Women go unveiled in France, Germany and Italy. They go out alone and participate with the men in their social life in England and other European countries and in America. Observe the conditions in these countries. Where is morality? Where is dignity and modesty? How numerous are the painful love stories and how great the calamity of prostitution, adultery and vice? And what is prostitution, that disease fatal to both male and female, but the outcome of unveiling, which many deceivers claim to be a better custom than that sanctioned by our prophets?

"To unveil is to stray from the religion of God Almighty. It is a great setback to the nation. It is nothing but foolishness and weakness. It is a great catastrophe, contrary to the book of God and the regulations of his prophet. Moreover, many today proclaim that woman should leave her harem and participate with men in their

[25] Muhammad Ali, "The Prophet's Wives," *Islamic Review*, Vol. 17, pp. 410-411.

MODERN TENDENCIES

activities. They encourage women to mingle with many people in clubs and meetings. For all this there is no excuse except that of blind imitation of the West. The worst of it is that those who are proclaiming this new practice are among the prominent men of our nation.

"Who is the woman you are trying to civilize and whom you encourage to participate in every phase of life? Women in Egypt are the weakest-minded of all on earth and the slowest to understand. They are still innocent of life and know nothing of either religion or education. To demand that they be unveiled is a crime and an unpardonable sin in the eyes of God.

"So have mercy on our country. Do not cause her to fall into destruction and do not lead her into evil." [20]

One further justification for Mohammed's plural marriage is noted by Muhammad Ali. He writes:

"Thus it has been clearly set forth that the Prophet's household was not the place for ministering to carnal cravings. The object was far more sublime—the preservation of what they heard and learned through their frequent association with the Prophet for the benefit of mankind in general and their own sex in particular . . . there are a hundred-and-one morals of a man that do not find manifestation but in relation to the fair sex. Again, there are certain points of Islamic law which appertain to the female sex exclusively and cannot find promulgation but through members of the same sex. In order that the world might not be deprived of those sayings and doings that could only find expression in the household, and in order that these things might be handed down to posterity, it was assigned to the Prophet's wives to watch all they heard or saw, and communicate the same to others. Thus the Prophet's marriages were intended as a means towards the realization of a religious object of great importance. There

[20] *Voices from the Near East* (New York: Missionary Education Movement, 1927), p. 51.

IN ISLAM

is many a point in the Islamic code which the Prophet could not explain to women direct. He could do it through his wives."[27]

Reactionism is to be found all over the Moslem world, but, as may well be imagined, the most pronounced resistance to modern civilization is to be found in the less accessible regions. When, for example, King Amanullah of Afghanistan attempted to follow the lead of the Turkish reformers in the abolition of certain characteristic Moslem institutions, he found himself very quickly opposed by armed resistance which obliged him to abdicate the throne and brought into power a strong reactionary Moslem administration. While it is probably true that not all of the opposition was on religious grounds, since the matter of changing costume has its serious economic aspects as well, probably it was the major factor in the revolt against King Amanullah. In Persia there has been a considerable resistance to modernization, particularly in the matter of dress reform, but that opposition has not been able to stem the tide of reform.

Probably the most ardent Moslem fundamentalists are to be found in Arabia, the ancient home of the Prophet, where the Wahhabis have quite recently come into the position of political dominance. Wahhabism is not the product of the present century, for it was particularly active about a century ago in Arabia. There has, however, been a recrudescence of the Wahhabi spirit in reaction to the threat of mod-

[27] Muhammad Ali, "The Prophet's Wives," quoted in the *Islamic Review*, Vol. 17, p. 409.

MODERN TENDENCIES

ernism. In 1924-25 the Wahhabi Sultan, Ibn Saud, managed to get control of western Arabia, including the sacred cities of Mecca and Medina. While thoroughly conservative in their whole program, the Wahhabis are particularly opposed to certain practices that have grown up in Islam, such as the worship of saints. It was feared at first that they would forbid the annual pilgrimages of Moslems to the sacred cities, but this fear has not been justified. They have, however, enforced certain somewhat puritanical rules against the use of tobacco; and they have destroyed most of the tombs, which were the centers for the prayers to the saints, which intercession, the Wahhabis hold, is polytheistic and hence contrary to the Islamic idea of the unity of God. Eldon Rutter, who recently visited the holy cities, tells of the extensive desecration of shrines, such as the birthplace of Mohammed, which is now only a camel's resting place. Writing of one of the great cemeteries, Mr. Rutter says:

"It was like the broken remains of a town which had been demolished by an earthquake . . . demolished and gone were the great white dogs that marked the graves of the members of Mohammed's family, of the great Khalifah Othman. . . ."[38]

However, even in Cairo, which is probably the intellectual center of the Moslem world, and in the great Moslem University Al Azhar, extreme conservatism still holds sway, as indicated above, in their attitude toward critics of the Koran. But in

[38] Eldon Rutter, *The Holy Cities of Arabia* (New York: G. P. Putnam Sons, 1928), Vol. 2, p. 256.

IN ISLAM

some respects even this old Moslem university is beginning to change. Arthur Jeffery notes that within the last few years Al Azhar has changed from an aggregation of students ranging from infants to graybeards to one in which most of the elementary classes are gone, and where European trained teachers have been introduced into some classes to teach modern subjects. The whole curriculum is being reformed, so that while the old-style training will not be entirely lost the majority of students will get a training aimed to fit them for the modern economic world. The present director of Religious Education, under whose department Al Azhar is administered, is a wide-awake young Muslim, the product of European training.

Modern Missionary Movement in Islam

Not the least interesting of the trends in the Moslem world is the re-awakening of the missionary spirit of Islam. Of course it has from the first been missionary. No other world religion has surpassed it in this respect. But even missionary religions pass through periods of relative inactivity. It appears, e.g., that the unprecedented missionary drive of Protestant Christianity of the present century is beginning to slow down. Islam has not been in recent centuries so zealous in her outthrust. But the present century has seen the stirrings of a new life, especially in India, and a new type of Moslem missionary effort has developed in recent years.

It has always been said that every Moslem who goes abroad is a missionary. In a sense that has been

MODERN TENDENCIES

true. But awakened Islam is not disposed to rely wholly on such lay missionary effort. It has begun to organize itself for an active propaganda by trained representatives, deliberately chosen and sent even to foreign fields, to spread the gospel of Mohammed. The group most active in this effort is the comparatively recent Ahmadiya movement, which came into being in the latter half of the nineteenth century, founded by the figure now held by his followers as Madhi or the Messiah who was to come. This movement maintains missions in a number of countries including England and the United States, and is actively propagating Islam as understood and interpreted by their founder. They publish an extensive periodical literature in various languages. The better known magazines are the *Islamic Review* and the *Review of Religions*. The American publication issued by the Ahmadiya representative in Chicago is published only occasionally as funds permit. The modern era of depression has temporarily affected their financial resources, as in the case of Christian missions, so that their activity has been necessarily somewhat lessened.

Islam, as represented by these modern missionaries is, as might be expected, an Islam calculated to appeal to the interests and moral feelings of the peoples to whom the missionaries go. The emphasis in their teaching falls upon those things in Islam best calculated to appeal to the moral sensibilities of western people. A vigorous defense of the character of the Prophet along lines not dissimilar to those suggested in an earlier paragraph [20] presents an idealized pic-

[20] See above, pp. 216-218.

IN ISLAM

ture of the Prophet which, to the modern Christian, looks very much like a copy of the figure of Jesus. As one Christian missionary writer says, it

"is just taking over the picture of Jesus and applying it to Mohammed. His complete trust in God, his refraining from showing the slightest impatience, his calm and severe manner, his noble and dignified manners, his unshaken activity and zeal in the performance of duties entrusted to him, his perseverance, his fearlessness of his enemies, his forgiveness of injuries, charity, courage."[40]

According to the teaching of this group, the essential meaning of Islam is Peace, and Islam offers to a war-torn world the only guarantee of world peace. Islam is a world brotherhood, they say. It binds men and women of all races and all countries into a common unity. All men are brothers, whether rich or poor, whether black, or brown, or white, for Islam raises no color barriers between men. Islam is the world's greatest enemy of alcohol. Likewise it offers to do more for women than any other faith. The Prophet was the protector of woman. He gave her political rights and economic rights unequaled by any other religion in the world, and the Koran is quoted as holding the essential equality of men and women. "Man and woman have been created out of the same essence," "Women are the garment of men as men are the garment of women." So far from acknowledging any indebtedness on the part of the Islamic world to Christianity and to western civilization, the apologists of this group, as well as other Moslems, are apt to see in any good that is to be found in

[40] Quoted in *The Moslem World Today*, John R. Mott, Editor, p. 320. Reprinted with permission from Doubleday, Doran and Company, Inc., publishers.

MODERN TENDENCIES

European civilization, some element borrowed from Islam. Thus to Islam, they say, is due the abolition of slavery. To Islam the West is indebted for religious toleration and improvement of the status of women. In the political realm democracy as a substitute for autocracy has its source in Islamic teaching; and when "pussy-foot" Johnson, the world temperance organizer, visited Egypt and recounted the progress made in temperance reform in the United States, they said, "Ah, now you are becoming good Moslems." Islam holds the clue to the solution of the vexed problems of the present economic order. A recent article by Sufi M. R. Bengalee in the *Moslem Sunrise* analyzes the evils of capitalism and finds in three Moslem principles the solution of the problem. He ends his discussion:

"In short, Islam removes the evils of capitalism by its laws of inheritance, by the institution of Zakat, and by prohibiting the giving and taking of interest. Islam protects the poor from the clutches of the Shylocks and creates a middle class which is the backbone of society." [41]

Another writer sums up this whole position in the following statement:

"Islam has been the greatest social and democratic force in the world, and the future lies at the feet of Islam and nowhere else. The one distinctive feature of Islam is that it is a living religion . . . the door of prophecy it keeps open at all times, and its devotees can have a direct communion with God like the Prophet of old." [42]

[41] *Moslem Sunrise*, Vol. 4, p. 16, April, 1931.
[42] *Ibid.*, January, 1924.

IN ISLAM

Missionaries have been sent, within recent years, from India to China, and a pronounced awakening of the Chinese Islam seems to be taking place. News comes of vigorous propaganda, efforts being carried on in various parts of China. Lectures, periodicals, and the organization of clubs and Young Men's Moslem Associations on lines similar to the Young Men's Christian Association are the methods employed. Recently a translation of the Koran has been projected. An International Moslem Association has been formed for the Farther East for the propagation of Islam since "none of the actually prevailing religions in the world is sufficiently fit for the promotion of human welfare at the present age." [48] Reports are found of a revival of Islam in the Dutch East Indies. Moslem deputations have been sent to South Africa and lectures on Islam given in many places. Writing of this recent expansion of Islam, Mr. W. Wilson Cash declares:

"While Islam has a different connotation in different countries and although the faith is weakened in some areas by modern thought, yet a study of the activities of Moslems to-day shows Islam as strongly missionary, with its organization world-wide. Behind all lies the old ideal of a universal faith representative of an empire without frontiers and theocratic in government, yet, with all this historical idealism, Islam has shown in recent years a remarkable power of adaptability and a progressive spirit in the furtherance of its cause. Modern methods, such as propaganda through literature and lectures, have replaced the sword; a modern presentation of the religion has been substituted for Islam as it

[48] Quoted by W. W. Cash, *The Expansion of Islam* (London: Edinburgh House Press, 1928), p. 234.

MODERN TENDENCIES

is still preached in the orthodox centres. And so, in spite of Turkey's anti-caliphate action, modernism, western thought, agnosticism and other influence, Islam still holds up its head proudly and challenges the world." [44]

However, Moslem missionary activity is not only being carried on in foreign countries. In India there is a very active society for the propagation of Islam, with headquarters in Ambala, Punjab. According to Mr. Titus:

"The Central Jam'iyat-i-Tabligh-ul-Islam (Society for the Propagation of Islam), with headquarters in Ambala City, Punjab, is a strong, growing organization of India-wide character, with not only provincial but district organizations as well. Its twofold task is said to be (1) to prevent apostasy by seeking to counteract the efforts of the Arya Samaj Shuddhi Movement, and the work of Christian Missions; and (2) to send missionaries to teach backward Muslims. To accomplish these objects a campaign is being carried on to raise twenty-five lakhs of rupees (Rs. 2,500,000 or about £190,000)." [45]

To mention only one more, there is an important society with headquarters at Poona, which sets forth its aims as follows:

"(1) To place the teachings of Islam in their true light before Moslems in particular and non-Moslems generally;

"(2) To care for orphans and neglected children irrespective of caste and creed by means of orphanages, boys' and girls' homes, and industrial schools;

"(3) To uplift the untouchables;

"(4) To carry on general relief work." [46]

[44] W. W. Cash, *op. cit.*, pp. 236-237.
[45] M. T. Titus, *Indian Islam* (London: Oxford University Press, 1930), p. 201.
[46] W. W. Cash, *op. cit.*, p. 221.

IN ISLAM

By means of these vigorous missionary efforts, the Moslems hope to accomplish three major objectives: namely, (1) that of strengthening the faith of believers, (2) the defense against attack and encouragement from other religions, and (3) the conversion of non-Moslems. They are very aptly using the methods proven most effective by Christian missionaries in their work throughout the world.

But in all of this missionary propaganda, both at home and abroad, Moslem leaders are confronted with the necessity of one very considerable modification. With the dream of Pan-Islam practically dissipated, the suppression of church and state already an accomplished fact in some sections and threatened in still others, the Islam that is preached must be no longer a theocratic Islam, but a religion which finds its *raison d'être* precisely that of Protestant Christianity in other lands, and it will have to justify itself in the light of such demands as that fact imposes upon it. Therein lies the real test of Islam's ability to endure as a potent, living religion in this modern world of change.

Thus we have seen that the world of Islam is in a state of intense ferment—political, social, economic and intellectual. Fundamentalist Islam, in some centers, opposes energetically any demand for modernization. Radicalism flies to the opposite extreme of indifference, if not entire irreligion. Liberalism, attempting to hold on to the essential values of Islam, while admitting the possibility of change in non-essential features, is attempting thereby to render its faith operative as a potent influence upon the modern

MODERN TENDENCIES

age. It is too soon yet to prophesy whether or not Islam will be able to meet the challenge of this onrushing wave of modernity, but there are many signs that the followers of the Prophet are still a vital, living force and that out of this conflict with the forces of change there is apt to emerge a vigorous, dynamic religion, purged of much of the accidental and non-essential, which will be able to carry on effectively among the peoples of the world. One thing becomes increasingly clear as one sees the closer *rapprochement* between the reform groups in Islam and in Christianity; that is, that the two are allies in a common cause, fighting the common battle of the spiritual view of life versus the secular materialistic view. Such a conviction calls not for conflict between the groups but for increasing mutual understanding and coöperation.

CHAPTER VI

RELIGION IN RUSSIA

TRADITIONALLY the Russians are among the most religious peoples in the world. Their literature, their art, their architecture, their social life, their political organization, all until recently were thought to reflect a deeply religious nature. Yet the present age is witnessing a most determined effort to root religion completely out of the life of the Russian people.

Again and again religions, particularly Christianity, have undergone persecution and attempts to destroy them, but at no time in the history of the world has there ever been so consistent, deliberate and resolute an attack, not only on Christianity or Mohammedanism or Judaism, but upon religion itself. The Soviet government has relentlessly set out to destroy the last vestige of religion in the vast territory which it controls.

In most of the other religions which we have thus far studied, an evolution has been going forward slowly, destined to change materially the forms of belief and practice of each of the great faiths. But here in Russia one sees not simply evolution. Here is revolution of the most spectacular type. Here is not an attempt to change but an attempt to eliminate completely all religion.

MODERN TENDENCIES

It would not be quite fair, of course, to say that there has been no religious evolution, for religion is not yet dead in Russia, nor is it now quite what it was before the beginning of the revolution, but the main facts to be observed with reference to religion in Russia lately lie not in those attempts that are being made to mold religion so that it can be kept alive, but the destructive attitudes which the Soviet leaders have taken toward it.

The Church in Old Russia

Christianity had come to Russia late in the first millennium after Christ. In 1448 it had won its independence from Constantinople. Near the end of the sixteenth century it had won the patriarchal rank. In the eighteenth century it had seen the elimination of this office for political reasons and the establishment of the Holy Synod, with the control lodged solely in the hands of the ruling Czar, by reason of his right to appoint the members of the Synod and the chief ecclesiastical officer, known as the High Procurator. This latter functionary has been described as "the eye of the Czar," whose business it was to keep sharp oversight of the ecclesiastical hierarchy and see to it that it conducted the affairs of the church in accord with the emperor's will. He was able to veto any act passed by the Synod and indeed nothing of importance could be done without first gaining his consent. Singularly enough, this office was held by a layman and it was not unusual for the Synod to be presided over by an armed military figure. In this way the Czar was the effective

RELIGION IN RUSSIA

head of the church in Russia and might use it for his own ends.

Previous to 1917 there had been little change within the church for more than a century. It is true that there was some unrest and a demand that a council or Sobor should be called for the purpose of considering reform. Just after the revolution of 1905, the Czar, fearing lest his power be destroyed, quieted the church by promising to summon a council, but down to the day of his abdication he had never yet found it convenient to issue a call. Almost immediately after the abdication of the Czar and the setting up of the provisional government, a council was called together and met in the summer of 1917 to consider certain needed reforms. In none of the suggested changes, however, was there anything that looked toward any serious modification in the relations between church and state. The report of the council makes it very clear that they considered the Kerensky régime but temporary and that they looked forward to an early restoration of the monarchy in some form or other. In fact, they were still debating the advisability of restoring the patriarchate when the October revolution broke out and threw Russia into the hands of the Bolshevik party, led by Lenin and Trotzky.

The Church and the Revolution

Although the provisional government which came into power after the abdication of the Czar, took no extreme position with reference to the church, it soon became evident that things were not to go on

MODERN TENDENCIES

wholly as before. The Orthodox church had always enjoyed a place of privilege as the only recognized legal religion of the empire. Technically, all other sects and divisions of the church were under the ban. Within four months after the overthrow of the Czar, the provisional government had passed a law granting full religious liberty. Thus, for the first time, so far as freedom to carry out their peculiar religious forms were concerned, other religions stood on the same level as the Holy Orthodox Church.

The only other change of consequence, and this was largely a change of name rather than of function, was the dismissal of the *ober-procuror* through whom the personal control of the church by the Czar had been carried out, and the transfer of his functions to what was called the Ministry of Confessions. With this control, the provisional government was apparently content to allow such reorganization within the church as might become necessary under the new régime, to be worked out by a council or Sobor of the church.

It will be recalled that the Czar had promised the convocation of such a Sobor as early as 1906, but the assembly had never been convened. Now therefore, a pre-sobor committee was appointed to work out a proposed program for such a gathering, to be held later in the year. The action of this committee running closely parallel to another, non-official meeting of laymen in process in Moscow, indicates clearly that the church had as yet little conception of what the future held for it, for in the proposals here suggested there is no abatement in any sense of the

RELIGION IN RUSSIA

claims to the place of privilege and power which the church had always enjoyed. Rather, the advantage lay in their being freer from the control of government under the suggested relationship, while no less privileged in matters of support and influence with the government.

The Sobor met in August, 1917, and its temper was distinctly that of hostility to any interference of the government with its prerogatives. Partly because of the need of a strong centralization of the church's power to deal with or to meet possible encroachment upon it, there was an insistent demand for the restoration of the patriarchate. This matter was debated heatedly over a considerable period and indeed was still under consideration when the Kerensky government fell and the Bolsheviki assumed control of things. Doubtless the vote to restore the patriarchate was hastened by this occurrence, for only five days later the decision was made to name a patriarch, and Tikhon, the Metropolitan of Moscow, was named the official head of the church. His enthronement took place on November 21st.

The Church and the Soviet Government

It soon became evident that the temper of the Soviet government was distinctly less favorable to the church than that of the overthrown provisional group. Within less than a month there was passed a drastic law decreeing the nationalization of all land including the lands of the church and other like organizations. This was followed shortly by another law which took the schools out of the hands of the

MODERN TENDENCIES

church, lodging all of them under the control of the state. Thus at a stroke, not only was the education and training of the children taken away from the church; but even its theological seminaries and training schools were held subject to the law. This was a serious blow.

But other blows were to fall. Next came the law which took the registration of births and the solemnization of marriage out of the control of the church and made both of them mere civil matters. Heretofore the government had maintained no registration of births or marriages, the church being left in entire control of these functions. By a single order they passed forever beyond its control and the registries of births, which the church had kept for so many years, were ordered transferred to civil offices as rapidly as these latter could be formed. To be sure, there was no prohibition of the ecclesiastical forms of matrimony, but the only regularly binding form was that of the civil registry. This was a sharp attack upon one of the cardinal doctrines of the church, which made matrimony not a mere contract, but a sacrament.

Thus far the income of the church had not been seriously disturbed. Now followed a decree of the Soviet cutting off the financial support of its worship features, although they did continue for a limited period the payment of certain subsidies for the general direction of the church. It was, however, in the act of January 23, 1918, barely four months after the establishment of the Soviet control, that the most drastic of all the ecclesiastical legislation up to that

RELIGION IN RUSSIA

point was decreed. Heretofore, though much curtailed at a number of points, the church was still related intimately to the state.

The first article of the new act stated simply that the church is separated from the state. Naturally many changes followed this simple statement. Performance of all religious ceremonies in connection with state functions was to be eliminated. All use of religious phraseology in state documents was to disappear. Complete freedom of conscience permitting one to exercise any religion or none was guaranteed. All religious vows and oaths were abrogated. Civil registry of births and marriages was reaffirmed. The complete separation of the schools from the church was reiterated and all religious instruction was definitely eliminated from the schools, public or private. All preferential treatment that had been accorded the clergy was done away with. The right of the church to own property was denied and the complete withdrawal of state support to the church was ordered.

A mere recital of these various strictures upon the church can give little indication of the terrific loss which they entailed upon the establishment. Gone at a stroke was all special privilege and the proud Orthodox Church, which had known no rival and which had enjoyed a power and distinction seldom equaled in the history of the church, was shorn of its dignity, and its power and influence completely set at naught. Its vast wealth of extensive properties, those for cult purposes and those which gave income, were at a moment's notice taken away. Supported

MODERN TENDENCIES

generously by the imperial government for centuries, it had developed no plan of voluntary self-support among its people. With less than a month's notice it was obliged to find some means of substituting voluntary contributions for state subsidy.

Formerly able to control schools and to make use even of government schools for the indoctrination of its constituency, it now suddenly found itself without any means of carrying on any sort of formal religious education, indeed even the training of its own priesthood, outside the homes of its members.

It is not to be wondered at, therefore, that the church vigorously opposed these innovations with all of the power at its command, and it ought to be said that the odds were not wholly on the side of the government, for, if all the factors in the situation be taken into account, after all the Soviet government was a very small minority rule. The vast masses of Russia were still members of the Orthodox Church. There were multiplied thousands of priests, monks and teachers scattered throughout the entire length and breadth of the land. It must forever go down as an act of sheer audacity on the part of the Soviet government to attempt so rigorous a control of an institution which seemed to be the expression of the very soul of Russia and which contained such elements of power within itself.

The protests were various. Ringing addresses of opposition from the Sobor went out to the churches. Orders to resist the surrender of properties and of registries were dispatched. Not a little violence occurred in the clash between the officers of the gov-

RELIGION IN RUSSIA

ernment and the defenders of the church prerogatives, yet slowly, steadily, the Lenin government carried forward its policies.

It is idle to speculate as to what might have happened had the church accepted the new policies and sought without serious opposition to mold itself to the new political conditions. Whether it might not have won some concessions from the government and thus have been able to carry on in some degree its organization is an open question. The fact of its vigorous opposition to the proposed reform, its evident sympathy for the return of monarchy, although it ought to be said that there was a distinct party in the church which did not favor such a return— these things undoubtedly put iron into the spirits of the leaders of new Russia and induced them to enact measures of increasing severity as time went on.

Of course the Soviet government did not prohibit the carrying on of the church's worship. Although the properties of the church were nationalized, nevertheless it decreed that the use of these should be allowed free of charge to the local church organizations, stipulating that there must be at least twenty members to constitute a church. The only condition laid upon the congregations was that they maintain the buildings, keep them in repair, insure them, and pay such taxes as might be levied upon them. Comparatively few churches were closed. Indeed, down to the present time, counting all those that have been closed during the later period of greater severity, the great majority of orthodox churches in Russia have not been transferred to other purposes.

MODERN TENDENCIES

Some churches, of course, were taken over for other social purposes, such as clubs or museums or lecture halls, but according to the statement of the Soviet government, only in cases where the local sentiment favored such a transformation. Some of the more notable cathedrals, especially in Moscow and Leningrad, were taken over by the government, repaired, reconditioned and made to serve as museums or centers of some government activity, but at all events they still remained in the service of the people.

From time to time additional decrees were issued, interpreting more specifically the general law of January the twenty-third, but now and then adding some new item to the long list of restrictions.

The constitution of the Soviet republic passed in July, 1918, made explicit a great many things that had been merely assumed in the more general legislation of January, particular detail with reference to education and religious instruction being added. In 1922, in the interpretation of the law regarding religious education, it was declared that though persons under eighteen years of age might not be given formal religious instruction in schools, they might after eighteen be instructed in theological courses for the priesthood. Thus the way was definitely opened for the resumption of a limited amount of training of priests, but the financial distress occasioned by the removal of the church's support has made the establishment of theological seminaries an exceedingly difficult matter. In 1927 Professor Spinka could write that in all Russia there were but two seminaries

RELIGION IN RUSSIA

for the training of priests, and these very small and ill-equipped, carrying on under conditions of extreme privation.[1]

In 1924, a little more liberty in the matter of religious education of children was permitted, in that groups of not more than three, even when not of the same family, might be instructed by a teacher other than a parent, but not in a school or church building. Additional legislation increased the disabilities under which the clergy were placed. Doubtless on the supposition that they were opposed to the Soviet program, they were not allowed to vote or to hold office or to teach in schools or to become members of coöperative societies. These disabilities have become still further increased in recent years as will appear later.

As a result of the determined opposition to the Soviet program, on the part of the clergy, numerous leaders including priests, bishops and metropolitans were exiled or imprisoned, but it was the great famine of 1921 which gave the occasion for the most serious breach between the church and the government and brought down upon the church the most serious persecutions of the earlier years of the republic. In 1921 there was a great drought in the valley of the Volga. This in itself would not have been sufficient, perhaps, to produce a widespread famine,

[1] Matthew Spinka, *The Church and the Russian Revolution* (New York: The Macmillan Co., 1927), p. 157. The writer is indebted to Dr. Spinka's book and Julius Hecker's *Religion Under the Soviet* (New York: Vanguard Press, 1927) for much of the material employed in this survey of the relation the Soviets to the Orthodox Church.

MODERN TENDENCIES

had there been in existence the normal reserve of grain left over from the previous year. But there was no such reserve. In 1919 the Soviet government had confiscated the food surplus of the peasants for the use of the workers in the cities. Angered at this invasion of their rights, the peasants planted in 1920 only enough to meet their own needs. As a result, the disastrous drought of 1921 found them without any surplus with which to meet the emergency.

The suffering of the people was very great. Something over five million people starved to death. The entire world was moved to sympathy by the distress of these people and from every quarter there poured into Russia large relief sums in the attempt to save the starving people.

Within Russia the Soviet government was, or claimed to be, doing all that it could to handle the situation. The church was, it must be said, active in the collection of funds and the disposal of relief, but the suggestion early appeared that if the wealth of the church, represented by the accumulation of jewels and precious metal in the adornments of the church, were sold, a sufficient fund could be provided to secure relief for the people. Accordingly, the press of Russia called upon the church to sacrifice its ornaments to that end and presently the Soviet government itself made the request.

The patriarch, fearing the pressure of public opinion, did decree that all unconsecrated possessions of value in the local churches be sold and the proceeds of the sale be applied to relief, but this represented only a small, almost negligible sum,

RELIGION IN RUSSIA

for the great wealth of ornament had been consecrated. Finally the Soviet government deliberately ordered the church, for the benefit of the starving population, to dispossess itself of all those jewels and objects of value which were not of direct use in the cult. This the patriarch in a communication to the state refused to do, for, he maintained, permission to do so would be uncanonical and would render those granting permission subject to excommunication according to the law of the church. Perhaps no more serious blunder was committed by the leadership of the church than this. Here were starving millions of Russia's own people clamoring for food, and over against this cry was placed only an ancient canon of the church. That is, over against deep humanitarian need was placed ecclesiastical law, and the sympathies of the entire world were upon the side of the government, which seemed to be standing for the supplying of human need. Nor did the Soviet government fail to make use of this charge against the church, though it has since been pointed out by many writers that at the same time the Soviet was condemning the church for the refusal to sacrifice its jewels for the support of the starving people, an equally great source of wealth which was not hallowed by religious faith was in the hands of the Soviet government, in the form of the crown jewels, which were only the relics of an order which no one could accuse the Soviet of desiring to immortalize. It is doubtless true that the Soviet was here playing politics, but perhaps it was embittered in its attitude by the meeting

MODERN TENDENCIES

just a little before this of a Russian ecclesiastical group in Europe, which called for the overthrow of the new government and the return of the monarchy in the person of one of the Romanoffs.

The church resisted bitterly the attempt to confiscate these various jewels and as a result during the conflict in many communities not a few deaths and numerous arrests of church leaders for trial and imprisonment took place, with many banishments to Siberia and not a few executions of high church leaders. Henceforth it could hardly be expected that the Soviet government would make concession to the Orthodox Church.

There can be little doubt that the church lost heavily by the stand of the church leaders, in placing the canon law of the church above the really desperate need of starving people. They lost in the sight of the world outside Russia and they lost with great numbers of their own faithful followers, in addition to incurring the even deeper enmity of the Soviet government.

Partly as a result of this and other refusals to conform to Soviet policy, the patriarch was arrested and imprisoned. This gave the opportunity to a group of leaders within the church who had steadfastly opposed the patriarch's policy to assert themselves. A group of them came together and asked the patriarch to retire, which he did, appointing as his successor the Metropolitan of Yaroslav. The liberal leaders issued a statement in which they very sharply criticized the attitude of the patriarch on famine relief and his general resistance to the state, and further issued a call for a council or Sobor designed to

RELIGION IN RUSSIA

end the civil war existing between the church and state. This marks a very definite change in the attitude of the church toward the government.

The Sobor met in 1923 and was under the control of the progressive element. They condemned definitely the past counter-revolutionary efforts of the church, pointing out the fact that the Soviet power was the only one which had attempted by state methods to realize the ideals of the Kingdom of God, and they called upon the church to give coöperation to the government in the working out of the Soviet plans. They deposed the former patriarch Tikhon.

After the council, however, Tikhon repented publicly of his counter-revolutionary activities, was released from prison and became the center of a party which stood in opposition to the liberal groups within the church. These liberals who had started out under the name of the Living Church found themselves soon divided into two groups, one the Holy Synod group and the other the Living Church group. Over against these, both of them liberal movements, stood the patriarchal party. As a result of the council certain minor reforms were carried out within the church, but there were no striking changes and no outstanding leadership appeared to give it direction. The change of attitude toward the government, however, had the effect of allaying somewhat the rigor of the Soviet attack upon the church.

We have spoken thus far chiefly of the Orthodox Church. It ought not to be forgotten, however, that there were not a few sectarian groups within Russia, some of them off-shoots of the Orthodox Church,

MODERN TENDENCIES

but others of evangelical groups such as the Baptists and Methodists and others, which were carrying on some sort of missionary work in Russia. On the whole these groups had not fared so badly at the hands of the Soviet, since it was chiefly the Orthodox Church which symbolized the whole czarist power, while the sectarians, like the revolutionaries themselves, had been persecuted before the revolution. There was, therefore, a certain sense of fellow feeling which caused the Soviets to deal leniently with them. Many of these movements sympathized with at least some of the aims of the revolution and they readily acquiesced without any counter-revolutionary attempts against the religious restrictions which were placed upon them. Indeed, they seemed to be almost a part of the revolution, and began to attract considerable numbers of those who found themselves out of sympathy with the attitude of the Orthodox Church. The Baptists, in particular, experienced a phenomenal growth and were extending in every direction. The evangelicals, unlike the Orthodox Church, went beyond the mere performance of their rites. They were actively propagandist and did a great deal of social service work which seemed to be quite in line with the aim of the Soviet government. They opened club rooms, libraries, recreation centers and clinics, and strongly attracted the Russian people to them. Then too, they were religions of an active, aggressive, more or less revolutionary character from the standpoint of the Orthodox Church, so they flourished for a period of several years.

RELIGION IN RUSSIA

The Anti-Religious Campaign

Meanwhile, the Soviet authorities were becoming more and more active in dealing with religion, but not simply in the suppression of the religious cult. They were wise enough to know that mere suppression in matters of religion was not likely to succeed, so they early began the campaign of active propaganda of an anti-religious character, designed to destroy the belief of the Russian people in religion. The Communist party itself was frankly atheistic, assuming, though apparently not insisting upon, the formal declaration of non-belief in God as a condition of entrance into the party, but their anti-religious attitude was not so strongly marked as that of the Komsomol or young communist group who formed themselves into a Militant Godless Society and openly and aggressively made it their aim to ridicule and destroy all faith in God. This organization, which numbered in 1927 but one hundred thousand,[2] had in 1932 approximately three and one-half million members. Even the pioneer group or the Children's Communist movement was given a decisively anti-religious turn and the children made active propagandists against belief in God. The total membership of the above-mentioned organizations is reported in a recent article in *Asia* as about 15,500,000. To this number of active atheists must be added the greater number of the 16,000,000 members of the trade unions, and probably the vast majority of the Red army in which systematic anti-religious propaganda

[2] Eddy, *Challenge of Russia*, p. 183.

MODERN TENDENCIES

is regularly carried on. In 1928 there was one workers' anti-religious or Godless University, consisting of a definite series of lectures, usually twenty of three hours each, organized in Moscow by the workers. By 1931 there were eighty-three such universities.[3] All sorts of methods were used to uproot the religious faith of the people. Not the least effective of these methods was the exposure of the frauds that had been practiced in connection with the relics which the church had venerated. In a certain monastery in Kiev a very remarkable phenomenon had occurred: namely, the preservation or the non-corruption of the bodies of saints buried there. By exhibiting a criminal who, being buried under the same circumstances, was just as immune to the ravages of time, the Soviet authorities proved that it was no special providence which preserved the saints' remains. Museums were developed in various centers of Russia in which all sorts of exhibits of this character and others revealing the superstitions and the credulity of the people were shown. In Leningrad the noted St. Isaac's Cathedral houses the museum. In Novgorod it is found in St. Sophia Cathedral, in Kiev in the Cathedral of Vladimir, while the greatest of all in Moscow occupies part of the great Stratsvoi Monastery.

Typical exhibits in these museums are the evolutionary origin of life, history of religious beliefs from the primitive cults to Christianity, the church as a

[3] Lucia P. Lodge, "The Soviet Cult of Godlessness," *Asia*, Vol. 32:326-328, May, 1932. This article is an exceedingly interesting, detailed, and well-illustrated account of the anti-religious propaganda in Russia.

RELIGION IN RUSSIA

tool of capitalism, including correspondence to show how the church furnished to the state information received in the confessional, expensiveness of maintaining the priestly hierarchy, and evidence of fraud, for example in the supposed miraculous preservations of the saints. Museum trains were used to bring the same type of exhibits to those in smaller places. Posters were used effectively caricaturing in every possible way the older sanctities of religion. Perhaps the most common point of attack was upon the church as the oppressor of the people. Only through the destruction of the church and of all religion could the true aims of the Soviet revolution be achieved.

The Russian peasant had preserved and continued to practice ancient religious rituals in connection with the sowing and reaping of his crops. The land must be blessed by the priest or by some procession or religious ceremony. Prayers must be said by the accredited ministers to produce proper fertility. The Soviet authorities went out into the countryside and took up fields adjacent to those where religious ceremonials had been invoked to secure good crops. They employed tractors, plowed deeply and tended scientifically the growing grain to prove that not prayer or religion but machinery and intelligent scientific farming were the secrets of a good yield. This had no little effect upon the simple-minded peasants, for it thus appeared to them that not God but machinery and science were the most important factors in their lives.

Yet withal the people continued in large numbers

MODERN TENDENCIES

to practice many of their ancient rites. Although marriage was now a civil ceremony only, communists themselves sometimes secretly sought the blessing of the church upon their union.

The Soviet leaders, recognizing the large place which the rites of the church, its pageantry, its festivals, and its processions played in the lives of the people, early saw that if religion was to be eliminated some provision must be made for the satisfaction of the needs of the people which the church had for centuries met. Christenings, Easter, the saints' days had come to play so important a rôle in the life of Russia, particularly in the peasant group, that the authorities were in danger of failing in their attempts at the elimination of religion unless substitutes could be provided for these things.

In the early days of the revolution the younger communists had taken occasion at festival times to do everything to mock, deride, and caricature the religious practices. Wiser councils now prevail. There is now an attempt to provide festivals, pageants, processions, music, pictures, everything that the older régime provided, but to invest them with significance for the new communistic type of thought. If processions there must be, let them be such as to generate enthusiasm and passion for the social ideal of the state. If pageantry and dramatics appeal to the senses of the people, let them convey in an attractive way the ideals of the Soviet government. If the christening of infants in the church accompanied by appropriate and elaborate rituals minister to some deep interest of the people, let there

RELIGION IN RUSSIA

be communistic christenings which will likewise provide occasion for feasting and color and light. If confirmation by the church at puberty, signalized by feasting and gladness, is desirable, then let there be communistic confirmations which will induct the youth of Russia into the anti-religious societies with something of the same pomp and circumstance that surrounded the ceremony of the church. If the church made a great occasion of marriage, why may not communism offer to those who care for that phase of marriage an appropriate, dignified, meaningful ceremony as well as religion? And if at death the church lays away its followers with appropriate funeral ceremonial, looking toward a happy after-life, why should not communism provide for its dead equally satisfying funeral rituals in which, though believing in no on-going life of the individual whatsoever, they may eloquently dwell upon the contributions of the deceased to that order which is to come and to revolutionize life in the here-and-now through the triumph of the Soviet state.

It must be admitted that according to reports the success of these substitutions has not been great. It is exceedingly difficult, particularly among the highly conservative peasant group, to make a substitution for such ancient practices as those to which they have been accustomed, but it points in the direction of success as no mere effort at suppression could possibly do. It will be remembered also that the movement is still in its infancy and that many of the present crude methods may be refined and made very much more effective with the passing of the years—par-

MODERN TENDENCIES

ticularly with the passing of that generation which has known and practiced the older rites. The younger generation which has known the church only in its poverty, its distress, and its general impotence will without doubt feel differently about the matter.

If for a short time, the rigor of the Soviet attitude was somewhat eased, the year 1929 saw a strong change of attitude and there developed what must be recalled as the most disastrous religious persecution since the beginning of the republic. Up until 1929 the constitution of the Soviet republic allowed not only complete freedom of worship, but declared that "freedom of religious and anti-religious propaganda" is considered the right of all citizens. Now the article was changed to recognize the right of freedom of religious worship to all, but to restrict the right of propaganda to the anti-religious group.

This was a most serious blow, both to the orthodox group and to the sectarian societies. Up to that time, while working under very heavy handicaps, particularly as regards the training of the young, and being subjected constantly to the suspicion of counter-revolutionary activity, religious groups, including even the Orthodox Church, had, nevertheless, been privileged to extend themselves. To the sectarian and evangelistic groups had been accorded the opportunity for a very effective bit of propaganda which as already indicated had won them a very greatly increased following.

At a single stroke this privilege was withdrawn and they, as well as the orthodox group, were limited to the mere maintenance of the established services

RELIGION IN RUSSIA

for worship. They might perform no act of social service, maintain no meetings such as prayer meetings outside the regular established services for worship. Their right to circulate literature was sharply restricted. To the evangelistic and sectarian group this meant an even greater hardship than to the orthodox, since their chief appeal had lain not in the æsthetic realm, as has so often been said of the Orthodox Church, but precisely in the realm of social helpfulness and self-expression such as is common in evangelical circles. Shorn of these elements, there was comparatively little left to attract the people. The anti-religious drive coincided with the vigorous prosecution of the attempt to collectivize agriculture. Great pressure was put upon the peasants to enter the collectives, yet none could be a member of a collective without foreswearing his faith. Anti-religious feeling was intensified by the fact that the *kulaks* or rich farmers—rich only by the Russian standard, for they would be indescribably poor by the American standard—were frequently identified with the church. An object of social obloquy, like the village priest, he naturally tended to associate himself with the priest and the little remnant faithful to the church. This fact but added fuel to the flame of indignation against the church. It was the friend of privilege— a bulwark of the bourgeois opposition to the communistic ideal. The *kulaks* were counter-revolutionaries. So also was the church. As such they must both be dealt with rigorously by the state. It was not religious persecution at all, declared the government, but the putting down of counter-revolutionary oppo-

MODERN TENDENCIES

sition. The very life of the state demanded its suppression. It was the refusal of a large group of Mennonites, and therefore sectarian religionists, to forego their faith and enter the collectives and their consequent attempts to leave Russia that brought the matter sharply to the attention of the world.

Large numbers of churches were closed; the priests suffered fearfully. Unbearable taxes were levied on them; their children were denied all higher educational privileges and sometimes were even excluded from the village schools. In 1930 they were denied the use of the mails, telegraph and telephone, which restrictions entailed untold hardship upon them. Eddy reported in 1931 that, according to government statistics, fifty per cent of the ministers of religion had passed fifty years of age, while those under thirty were but five per cent of the total.[4] There was sharp resistance to this new aggression on the part of the state and so many were the atrocities committed by the Soviet government upon the religious group through execution, confiscation of property, exile, imprisonment and economic privation that the whole of the religious world was shocked beyond measure.

The pope made a vigorous protest against it. In many of the great parliaments of the world efforts were made to bring about some sort of intervention by government on the behalf of the persecuted religionists. As may well be imagined, this did not help the situation in Russia, for one of the charges, particularly against the sectarian group, was that

[4] G. Sherwood Eddy, *The Challenge of Russia* (New York: Farrar and Rinehart, 1931), p. 174.

they represented connections with the bourgeois world which had as its aim the destruction of the Soviet state. The protest of these capitalistic states could come to the Russian people only as confirmation of their charges. Happily, most of the nations recognized this possibility and withheld their protest.

To the arousing of world-wide opinion, however, the Soviet government could not be wholly indifferent, and after a prolonged period of bitter persecution, Stalin, the dictator, decreed that the vigorous aggressive Soviet policy of persecution must be relaxed. By that he did not mean that the campaign against religion must cease nor that the Soviet government had in any sense changed its traditional attitude toward religion.

If, declared *Izvestia*, organ of the Soviet government, they grant a measure of tolerance to religion,

"it is by no means by reason of its being in any way inclined to peace with any sort of popery, certainly not because of any weakening in our hatred towards religion and our attempt to destroy it. On the contrary, by our religious tolerance we simply conveniently limit the field of struggle and decline to use a worthless weapon. Our country is still full of a great number of believers. To challenge them to a final decisive battle, to proclaim them persecuted because of 'prohibition of faith,' would mean that we become supporters of the priests, because by such means we would immediately cast a significant part of these masses into the arms of the priests." [5]

If open persecution has ceased for a time, there is no letting up of the campaign against religion through

[5] *Izvestia*, June 8, 1929, quoted by Eddy, *op. cit.*, p. 175.

the young communist groups, which number today near six million youth and children, nor by the state itself through its schools. Gradually the believing teachers have been eliminated until not more than thirty or forty per cent remain. The former Commissar of Education, Lunacharsky, is quoted by *Izvestia* as saying, "The believing teacher in the Soviet school is an awkward contradiction, and departments of popular education are bound to use every opportunity to replace such teachers with new ones of anti-religious sentiments." [*] Atheistic universities have been established for the training of anti-religious youth leaders. Numerous papers, pamphlets, posters and books stream from the presses dedicated to but one end, the discrediting of religion.

It has become increasingly clear to the Soviet authorities that the success of their whole venture depends ultimately upon getting rid of religion. Why should this be so? What induces this extreme hostility to religion?

Communism vs. Religion

In the first place, the basic philosophy of communism is utterly opposed to religion. It is frankly and openly a sheer materialistic philosophy with no place in it for that which has been central in much of religion. From the days of Karl Marx this opposition has been unyielding. It was Marx who first declared religion to be the opiate of the people, a

[*] Quoted by W. H. Chamberlin, *Soviet Russia* (Boston: Little Brown and Co., 1930), p. 316.

RELIGION IN RUSSIA

sentiment which has been widely and enthusiastically propagated from the earliest days of the actual Russian revolution. Lenin himself was, if anything, more outspoken in his anti-religious opinion than Marx. Many years before the outbreak of the revolution he wrote:

"Religion is one of the forms of spiritual oppression, lying everywhere on the masses of the people, who are oppressed by eternal work for others, need and isolation. The helplessness of the exploited classes in their struggle with the exploiters just as inevitably generates faith in a better life beyond the grave, as the helplessness of the savage in his struggle with nature produces faith in gods, devils, miracles, etc. To him who works and is poor all his life, religion teaches passivity and patience in earthly life, consoling him with the hope of a heavenly reward. To those who live on the labor of others, religion teaches benevolence in earthly life, offering them a very cheap justification for all their exploiting existence and selling tickets to heavenly happiness at a reduced price. Religion is opium for the people." [7]

And in his subsequent writings he has rung the changes on this central thesis many times over. Again he writes:

"Every man who occupies himself with the construction of a God, or merely even agrees to it, prostitutes himself in the worst way, for he occupies himself not with activity, but with self-contemplation, and self-reflection, and tries thereby to deify his most unclean, most stupid, and most servile features or pettinesses." [8]

[7] Quoted by W. H. Chamberlin, *op. cit.*, p. 306.
[8] Quoted by René Fülop-Müller, *Mind and Face of Bolshevism* (New York: A. A. Knopf, 1928), pp. 73-74.

MODERN TENDENCIES

His attack is based upon religion as a bulwark of the privileged classes, a technique by which the exploited classes are held in easier subjection to the yoke through the promise of a compensation in another life for that which is denied them here. Communism knows nothing about another life. Whatever goods are to be enjoyed must be enjoyed here and now. Anything that under-cuts faith in the present life must therefore be completely destroyed. Communism knows no force outside of the state and the social order which can help to the realization of the dreams and hopes of humanity on this present plane. Therefore any teaching that inculcates dependence upon another, aside from the Soviet state and the present social order, must be suppressed, for it takes away that self-reliance and sureness which are required of those who would build in this present world a perfect state. Thus, like the ancient God of the Hebrews upon whom Israel depended for the realization of her dreams of a promised land and a prosperous state and who would "have no other gods before Him," the socialist state in Russia can brook no rival. At first the Orthodox Church in Russia, which had traditionally stood for privilege, was the object of its attack while the sectarians were given rather ample liberty. But the logic of its position ultimately drove the government not only to oppose the Orthodox faith but all religion, and they will not and cannot on their present philosophy permit the existence of the Christian or any other religion in any vigorous aggressive form.

Given this unrelenting opposition to religion, it sounds a bit strange to hear again and again from

RELIGION IN RUSSIA

all sorts of sources that communism is itself a religion. Yet it may be that in this interpretation of communism is to be found the best explanation of its intolerant attitude toward other faiths, since it is notoriously true that young, vigorous, aggressive, propagandist religions are highly intolerant of any rival faith.

Is Communism a Religion?

Is communism a religion? On the basis of any of the traditional definitions of religion, it would unquestionably have to be said that it is not, although it has many characteristics in common with traditional religion. But on the basis of some of the newer and more comprehensive definitions, there can be little question that it is in effect a religion. On the basis of what one writer has called a minimum definition of religion, namely, "devotion to a cause which goes beyond the warrant of pure rationality," or, if religion be defined as "the conservation of values" or "the coöperative quest for a completely satisfying life," communism may well be rated as a religion. Aside from the one limiting circumstance that it does not believe in a god, it presents very striking parallels to the more extreme forms of fundamentalist faiths whether Mohammedan or Christian. Reinhold Niebuhr thinks that on close analysis it approaches the maximum definition of religion, namely, "That the success of the cause and of the values associated with it is guaranteed by the character of the universe itself."[*] While "Communism

[*] Reinhold Niebuhr, "The Religion of Communism," *Atlantic Monthly*, Vol. 147, p. 416.

is ostensibly a highly scientific and irreligious social philosophy," writes Niebuhr, "in reality it is a new religion. Its virtues and vices are the virtues and vices of religion. The philosophy of Communism, which it characterizes as historical materialism, is already developing metaphysical pretensions among its devotees, which go beyond the realm of pure science and partake of the attributes of religious world views. . . . Ostensibly Communism makes no metaphysical pretensions but in reality it is confidence in the ultimate triumph of the proletarian cause that is supported not only by an analysis of history, but by a mystic and ultrarational faith that something in the character of reality itself is the guarantee of this triumph. For the Communist no less than for the devotee of other religions, the stars in their courses are on the side of the cause to which they are pledged." [10]

While not proving absolutely that communism is a religion, the following parallels indicate at least a very strong resemblance to religion. Evidently it occupies much the same place in the life of Russians that religion does among other peoples. One who has watched carefully the unfolding of religions that were at their inception non-theistic can well believe that the belief in God may appear in due time and thus enable even the more conservative to rate it as a religion.

First of all it, like religion, has a definite creed. It may be a materialistic creed, but a creed it is none

[10] Reinhold Niebuhr, "The Religion of Communism," *Atlantic Monthly*, Vol. 147, p. 462.

RELIGION IN RUSSIA

the less, and only those who adhere faithfully to the creed are worthy of membership in that inner group which controls Russia, the Communist party. It may be the firm and unyielding belief in the non-existence of God, but no Moslem has ever been more insistent on the oneness of Allah than are the communists that there is no God at all. Communism has its orthodoxy and it purges itself of heresy more frequently and more vigorously than any historic religious organization of the world. Every year there is a relentless weeding out of those who waver either in their faith or in their practice of the creed of communism. It is reported that last year more than one hundred thousand members of the party were expelled, and a very rigid test is made of those desiring to enter before they are permitted to join the party. The creed is the creed of Marx as interpreted and stated by Lenin, and to that thus far none have dared add. Indeed the movement like most religions may be said to have a sacred literature, for much the same regard for the writings of Marx and Lenin exists among communists as for the Bible among Jews and Christians. Some have made a parallelism between Marx and Lenin, on the one hand, and the Old and New Testaments, on the other. One would not do well to press the parallel too closely, but it is not without significance that communists seek support for their ideas in the works of these two great writers, very much as the Jew or Christian of the more orthodox persuasion cites chapter and verse of the Bible in justification for a certain idea which he holds. Here at least is potential, if not actual, scripture.

MODERN TENDENCIES

Like most great religions, communism has a great personal founder, who, if not worshipped, is at least venerated very highly and may, if the history of religions again repeats itself, come actually to be deified by the masses of unlettered people. There is but a thin line of separation between veneration and worship as may easily be seen in the case of Confucius in China, and of the Virgin Mary in Christianity. Of course not all religious founders are deified. Moses among the Hebrews was not. Mohammed in general has been held to be but a prophet, but what of Buddha, who started out with a belief as nontheistic if not as atheistic as Lenin's.

It is not at all likely, of course, that the enlightened communists will ever *worship* Lenin, however highly they may venerate him, but it is undeniably true that even to these people Lenin incarnates in a real way the ideal of communism. In him the theory focuses. It becomes personalized, and its very personalization gives it a certain dynamic or drive—perhaps only in the measure that it is thus more easily apprehended, but nevertheless a drive. The comparatively early death of Lenin before many of the problems involved in the practical building of the Soviet state emerged and before any serious failure could be assessed against him is a circumstance that distinctly favors a semi-apotheosis. Sun Yat Sen in China presents a not dissimilar case.

It is a well-known fact that Lenin's body has been preserved and is on exhibit in a great glass casket which is seen daily by multitudes of people. Preserved for several years in a temporary wooden

RELIGION IN RUSSIA

sarcophagus, it is now housed in a magnificent mausoleum in the great Red Square in Moscow. It may be, of course, that many or even most of the visitors are moved by mere curiosity or by an historic interest. It may be merely one of the sights of Moscow, as Napoleon's tomb is in Paris, but when it is said that groups of young people march to the tomb, there sing their stirring songs, pass by the figure of their leader and go away, as observers have noted, with a sort of exaltation similar to that furnished by worship, it is easy to prophesy that with the passing of time, unless communism suffers heavy reverses, this may develop more and more until, at least in the minds of the masses, a practical deification is accomplished. At least there is the possibility of his coming to hold a place like that of Mohammed in Islam. A recent writer, parodying the famous creed of Islam, says that the communist creed is "I believe in no God—and Lenin is his prophet."

The further circumstance that instead of the icon corner, which was formerly found in most homes and in many public places, the authorities have deliberately attempted and with much success, especially in public places, to substitute a Lenin corner, adds strength to the possibility of his becoming something of a religious figure. It is true that pictures of Lincoln and Washington are frequently found in homes and public places here in America, but in the Lenin corner there is the substitution of Lenin for a distinctly religious figure. Given the inclination of the Russian people to worship, it does not require an undue amount of credulity to believe that with the lapse of time he may become an actual figure to be worshipped. Already we are told the myth-making tendency is at work weaving stories about his life. And Lenin not yet ten years dead!

It has been facetiously and sacrilegiously said in Russia that there is a true communist trinity just as there was in orthodoxy: Marx, Lenin, and the Five Year Plan!

Like all great religions it offers salvation—not individual salvation, it is true, for communism has little regard for the individual as such. He is only of value in relation to the larger social group. But society is to be saved, and in a saved society the individual may find his own salvation. This doctrine of salvation is very clear. Society is lost. It needs a savior. To such a society communism, through the Soviet state, offers salvation—redemption. Society is in the power of the evil one, capitalism. If there is a devil, according to communism, capitalism plays that rôle. Victory over the evil one, destruction of the evil one, is the only hope for the redemption of society. Revolution affords the only method for its overthrow. Temporary class strife is an inevitable step in the achievement of the ultimate hope of communism, a universal brotherhood of men.

Mr. Fülop-Müller links this salvation doctrine with that of the older Russian sectarians. He writes:

"Bolshevism is, therefore, in many respects to be regarded as the political embodiment of the old Russian hope of the advent of the millennium, of the 'man-god.' All the laboriously thought-out doctrines of scientific

RELIGION IN RUSSIA

materialism, of dialectic and pseudo-Marxian ideology are, in the last resort, merely an attempt to conceal the religious and sectarian foundation of the Bolshevik doctrine of salvation, and to clothe it in modern garments. The whole apparatus of scholarship, as it has developed about Bolshevism, is merely subsidiary and accessory and cannot hide the fact that Lenin's teaching is fundamentally the old Russian gospel and that its adherents are sectarians." [11]

Gone, of course, is the idea of a personal immortality in a perfect heaven. That the communist scorns as an ideal selfish in the extreme. His goal is this-worldly. It must be made a present reality. His Kingdom of God is the perfect communist state wherein every constituent unit enjoys every advantage, and none shall be denied his just share of *all* the goods of life, whether material or spiritual. It is expressed, of course, in economic and political terms and guaranteed by no supernatural power, though it is to be achieved largely by Science spelled with a capital S, which comes perhaps nearest to representing *God* to the Russian. But, after all, it stands for very much the same ideal that the Hebrew prophet dreamed of and even Jesus and his followers preached. After all, it means the fulfillment of the deep-felt need of a humanity that has known great hardship and tribulation. To them it is effectively *salvation*. And that is what all religions have in one way or another offered.

Furthermore, there is nothing narrow and local about this salvation. It is for the whole world. Russian communism has no limited national salvation

[11] René Fülop-Müller, *op. cit.*, p. 88.

MODERN TENDENCIES

in its thought. It is in a true sense a salvation for the whole world. Hence in every quarter of the globe today there are emissaries of communism preaching the gospel of deliverance from a capitalist-cursed world. Indeed in a real sense there can be no local salvation. Ultimately "every knee must bow and every tongue confess" that communism is the redeemer of society. In all this, of course, there is logic, and they may well feel, surrounded as they are by hostile nations or at least nations based on a political and economic foundation diametrically opposed to their own, that the only hope of ultimate enjoyment of their creed lies in converting their neighbors. In a true sense communism is international. Russia is the leader, being the majority communist group of the world, but the Third International, which represents world communism, is equally interested in the promotion of communism in Turkey, India, the United States or South Africa. The international organization is largely officered, of course, by the very Russian leaders who control the government in Russia.

It, like other young religions, is highly missionary. It sends out its missionaries to all the world. Borodin for example went into China. Years after his recall, the leaders in China must still reckon with the results of his teaching. Other representatives are in India, South America, Mexico, and the United States—surely not so many as a recent congressional commission would have us believe, but undeniably they are here. No religion has ever been more aggressive or self-sacrificing in its preaching of the gospel. Surely here is a close parallelism to religion.

RELIGION IN RUSSIA

Like religion, communism has its own peculiar rituals and its own songs and music. We have already pointed out the development of substitutes of a communistic character for such ceremonies (before religious) as confirmation, marriage and burial. The leaders of communism are wise enough to know that no mere intellectual acceptance of their theory is sufficient to compel men's allegiance to their program. To the intellectual conviction must be added an emotional urge, and in the ringing songs, the inspiring martial music and in their elaborate rituals on certain ceremonial occasions this emotional urge is provided. Children in the lowest schools of Russia are taught to sing the songs expressive of the hopes and ideals of communism. Processions and public festivals formerly associated with religious ends, stir the ardor and fire the imaginations of the child, youth and the adult population of Russian cities and villages. In the songs they sing, just as in the songs of the church, may be found the aspirations and longings of the people for a new world, and in their confident, victorious affirmation of the truth of their ideal and the hope of its triumph there is to be found definite reinforcement of the will to do what their seers have dreamed of. Surely here again we have a striking parallel to religion, particularly to the evangelical type.

Finally, communism commands the extreme loyalty of its adherents and their near-fanatical devotion to its program to a degree seldom found apart from religion. Communism has its galaxy of martyrs who paid for the cause with their very lives by facing the firing squad or in the dungeon or in exile in the

MODERN TENDENCIES

frozen north. They are trained from childhood to be willing to sacrifice, to suffer, and if need be to die quite without a hope of personal immortality, but in the belief that in thus giving their lives they are lending life to the cause. In the Communist party itself there is a strain of asceticism and self-denial even among the most conspicuous leaders of the party. In a world that sets high store upon possessions and wealth, these members of the exclusive organization of communism pledge themselves to accept nothing beyond a moderate living wage, regardless of the type of work they are called upon to do. The dictator of all the Russians is paid at the rate of less than one hundred and twenty-five dollars per month. Among its younger members and even among the preparatory groups of children and youth who may look forward to membership in the party, there is generated a sense of loyalty and a desire to serve the common cause which sends them out as organizers or teachers or propagandists for the cause with all the ardor and enthusiasm which a young recruit to Christian service or foreign missionary service has in Christianity. It is this capacity to call out the best that is in men, to lead them to the consecration of life itself for the ideal which they hold, that links it up very closely in the mind of the present writer with a religion.[12]

[12] Many writers have held Communism to be a religion. Two interesting recent articles may be cited. H. R. Mussey, "Russia's New Religion," *The Nation*, Vol. 134 (May 4, 1932), pp. 572 ff., and S. K. Ratcliffe, "Russian Communism as a Religion," *The Yale Review*, new series, Vol. 21 (Winter, 1932), pp. 233-248.

RELIGION IN RUSSIA

Many even after reading this rather impressive list of parallels between communism and religion will still refuse to classify it as a religion itself. Perhaps they are right. If one who knows the history of religion and has watched the unfolding of like movements is unable to see in communism at least a potential religion, he will surely not fail to see that it occupies for those who accept it almost exactly the same place that religion does occupy in the lives of people generally. It will lack some of the elements that some of the faiths supply. It will offer some things that belong to none of the great religions, but at the heart of it, just as at the heart of religion everywhere, there is the eager questing for the satisfaction of the deeper human needs; and this quest many are coming to call religion, whether it expresses itself in traditional forms or not.

The Future of Religion in Russia

It appears from our survey that unless some overthrow of communism (at present difficult to foresee) should occur, religion of the orthodox type is doomed in Russia. If it survives it will survive as something quite different from what it has been in the past. Nor is it likely that the evangelical or sectarian religions will rise to meet Russia's need. The almost suddenness with which the much celebrated religiousness of the Russian peasant has given way before the onslaught of communistic anti-religious propaganda seems to be evidence either that the religiousness simply did not exist or that the needs of the people were being but poorly met. If com-

MODERN TENDENCIES

munism succeeds in meeting those needs, even though on the relatively low plane of physical satisfaction, it is likely that it can win the peasant to its faith. From an æsthetic standpoint doubtless a good deal will be lost, for the Russian church did have a certain contribution to make in that sphere, but as an actual living force in determining the life and character of the people communism may well prove to be a more effective agent. The overthrow of orthodoxy need not necessarily deeply affect the morality of Russia, for as it has been repeatedly pointed out by such writers as Maurice Hindus and Fülop-Müller, morality was not intimately bound up with religion in the old Russia. One need recall only the disgraceful episodes in the life of Rasputin and the apparent favor in which he stood in imperial as well as ecclesiastical circles to appreciate the apparent divorce between the orthodox religion and morals. On the other hand the communistic group, while defining morality in somewhat different terms from those of western religions, nevertheless finds in its doctrine and in its ideal an exceedingly effective incentive to morality as defined by itself. It is not so particular as to drinking, sex habits, gambling, and like vices as are certain religious groups, provided these practices do not militate against the accomplishment of their program. Comparatively large individual freedom within this limiting principle is given. The moral man in Russia is the man who lives most socially and contributes most to the realization of the communistic ideal. To the extent that the older sins against which evangelicalism has preached are anti-

RELIGION IN RUSSIA

social in their effects, communism attempts to eradicate them. In the Pioneer group, which is the childhood preparatory group leading ultimately to the Communistic party, the children are taught in the name of communism, most of the virtues that are inculcated through the Boy Scouts and similar movements in the West. A young Pioneer does not smoke, he does not drink, he does not swear. While doubtless there has been laxity, particularly in the realm of sex relations among the youth group, on the whole a degree of restraint, rather remarkable under all the circumstances, has been observed by the youth groups, particularly by members of the Komsomol, or the preparatory Communistic group. Most of the laxity in this regard is to be found not among those who are subject to the discipline of the party or its preparatory organization, but among those from whom the old inhibitions have largely fallen and who have not yet come under the restraining influence of the Communistic teaching itself.

The outcome of it all it is impossible to prophesy, but one who knows how consistently the people of the world have everywhere wrought out for themselves some sort of a religion, will not doubt that religion in some form or other, possibly very different from anything that the past has known, will persist and serve as one of the great formative factors in the on-going life of Russia.

CHAPTER VII

TENDENCIES IN JUDAISM

What Is Judaism?

IN writing of Judaism care must be exercised to understand just what is meant by the term. The present writer's interest in it is frankly as a religion, and his main emphasis must be upon religion. But to confine Judaism thus, only to religion, though he would find support for his usage, would leave out of account a very large number, indeed a considerable proportion, of those who call themselves Jews. One might conceivably attempt to use the term Jew [1] as a racial or cultural term, reserving the term Judaism for religious use alone, i.e. one might be a Jew, yet pretend no interest in Judaism as a religion. But even this would find opposition, for not a few Jewish writers distinctly regard Judaism as more than a religion, rather a civilization or culture of which religion constitutes an important phase but only one of many phases. It would seem to the present writer that some such distinction might well be made that would express the essential unity of the total Jewish group as a racial or cultural entity and yet allow for

[1] The term *Jewishness* has been used by Achad Haam to express this, but it has not come into general use.

IN JUDAISM

wide difference in religious belief, or indeed the rejection of religion entirely. Just as an American or a Frenchman may choose any one of many forms of religion and yet remain an American, so should there be some term to distinguish the synagogue from the non-synagogue group, without denying them a relationship to the total group which they are eager to acknowledge. But one must reckon with the situation as it exists and be on his guard in his use of terms.

There is a very large section of Jewry that has forsaken the traditional faith, whether in its orthodox, conservative or reformed phases, who nevertheless feel an essential kinship with these groups. André Maurois says, in effect, "I do not share the ideology of the Jewish masses, but I feel a vague mystic oneness with sixteen million people the world over, denominated Jews." It has frequently been pointed out that much, if not indeed most, of the really creative Jewish work in the realm of music, art, literature and science is being done by those who have abandoned all connection with the formal religious beliefs and practices of Judaism. To be as nearly accurate as possible, therefore, we shall, in discussing Judaism in the following pages, have to indicate by a qualifying phrase just the phase to which we refer, e.g. Judaism as a religion, or Judaism as a culture.

For those readers who may not be well acquainted with the major divisions within Judaism, a brief discussion of the traditional position of the three groups will be necessary in order to understand the

MODERN TENDENCIES

tendencies that are to be observed in each. We mention first the Reform group.

Reform Judaism

By the beginning of the twentieth century Judaism had already undergone its major reforms and had become relatively stabilized in two major groups: the Orthodox, representing "fundamentalist" Judaism, and Reform Judaism which stood for a rather radical departure from rigid orthodoxy. While not yet an organized movement the beginnings of the conservative group had already been made as will later appear.

The reform movement had developed first in Germany early in the nineteenth century, in part as a result of modifications in political and social life introduced by the French Revolution. This brought a relaxation of the restrictions upon the Jews which enabled them to leave the ghetto and to take their place in the larger world around them. This brought them into intimate contact with the currents of thought that were abroad in that period, broke down many of the older traditional ideas that they held and forced upon them the conviction that if they were to enjoy this new-won tolerance, they must abandon some of the older practices of their people and become more like the society of which they were now a part.

The beginning thus made had developed by the middle of the century to such a degree that there was a very wide gap between the extremes of thought within Judaism. Rabbinical conferences were held

IN JUDAISM

in Germany in 1844-46 which attempted to find a common basis of agreement, but Reform was not yet a vigorously organized movement. Individual congregations had adopted certain reforms in America as early as 1825, but it was not until the latter half of the nineteenth century that the American movement effected a definite, permanent organization. Possibly because the greater freedom which the Jew enjoyed in America called more insistently for some readjustment in his faith, Reform Judaism in America has been more consciously aggressive in its program than has been the case elsewhere.

Founded about 1869, by 1885 the Reform group had practically fixed its theological standards in the resolutions of the memorable Pittsburgh Conference. To summarize, their position was there declared, in effect, to be as follows:

That Judaism presents the highest conception of the God idea as taught in the Holy scriptures and developed and spiritualized by Jewish teachers in accordance with the moral and philosophical progress of the respective ages.

That the Bible is the record of the consecration of the Jewish people to its mission as the priest of the one God, and that it is of value as the most potent instrument of religious and moral instruction.

That modern discovery and scientific research are not antagonistic to the doctrines of Judaism, the Bible reflecting the primitive ideas of its own age and at times clothing its conceptions of divine Providence and Justice dealing with men in miraculous narratives.

MODERN TENDENCIES

That the Mosaic legislation furnished a system of training for the Jewish people for its mission during its national life in Palestine, but that only its moral laws are to be accepted now as binding, while only such ceremonies as tend to elevate and sanctify life are to be maintained.

That laws regulating diet, priestly purity and dress are not effective in modern times in impressing Jews with a spirit of priestly holiness.

That in the modern era of universal culture of heart and intellect is to be recognized the approaching of the Messianic hope for a kingdom of truth, justice and peace. That the Jews themselves are not a nation, but a religious community expecting neither a return to Palestine, nor a sacrificial worship under the sons of Aaron, nor the restoration of any of the laws concerning the Jewish state.

That there is necessity for preserving a historical identity with their own past, but that at the same time Christianity and Islam are to be recognized as daughter-religions aiding in spreading monotheistic and moral truth. That the spirit of broad humanity is an ally in the fulfillment of their mission and that the hand of fellowship is to be extended to all who operate with them in the establishment of the reign of truth and righteousness.

That the soul is immortal, grounding their belief in the divine nature of the human spirit, which finds bliss in righteousness and misery in wickedness. That ideas of Gehenna and Eden as abodes for everlasting punishment and reward—ideas not founded in Judaism—are to be rejected.

IN JUDAISM

That it is their duty, in accord with the spirit of Mosaic legislation concerning relations between the rich and the poor, to participate in the modern task of solving, on the basis of justice and righteousness, problems presented by the contrasts and evils of the present organization of society.

"This," declares Philipson, "still stands as the utterance most expressive of the teachings of Reform Judaism." [2]

Orthodoxy

It was in a sense the rise of the Reform movement which created orthodoxy, just as in Christianity it was modernism that created fundamentalism. That is, orthodoxy had been there through the centuries in the sense of the faithful practice of the observances prescribed in the code known as the Shulhan Aruk, and unfaltering belief in the dogmas underlying that code. But it was not a self-conscious group. In a real sense Judaism was but one until the rise of Reform. Orthodoxy is a term of contrast, a conscious reaction against the tendency to change, a passionate reaffirmation, in the face of opposition, of their unwavering faith in the religion of their fathers. By this it is not meant to infer that there had been no previous divisions in Judaism or that it had been completely static. What is meant is that the Orthodox simply became the champions of the Judaism which in the historic process had come down to them as authoritative, believed by themselves

[2] From David Philipson, *The Reform Movement in Judaism* (Revised Edition, 1930), p. 357. By permission of The Macmillan Company, publishers.

MODERN TENDENCIES

to be in the form in which it had been revealed by the God of Israel. The basis of their practice was the Shulhan Aruk, which, in turn, is based upon the Talmud and the Old Testament. Thus divine revelation was its basis, and with divine revelation man may not tamper. Fundamentalist Christians, who believe in the literal inspiration of the Bible to the very last word, will readily understand the feeling of the Orthodox. They were the defenders of a faith which had been attacked. Their answer to the attack was an even more strict attempt to fulfil the traditional requirements of the law and a positive aversion to any suggestion of change, even when the carrying on of ancient rites and customs entailed real sacrifice. Fear of the lengths to which the admission of any reform might lead induced them to set their faces steadfastly against even the most reasonable and necessary modifications to fit them for life in a modern urban environment, such as was the enforced lot of the greater number of Jews.

Conservatism

Between two extremes there is almost always a middle position. In the case of the Jewish group this was true. There were those whose leanings were orthodox in most ways but who were unable to go the whole way with the extreme literalists. There were in the Reform group those who were not a little troubled by the cavalier fashion with which traditional Judaism was handled by the more emancipated Reformed leaders. They believed there were profound values in traditional Judaism which would

IN JUDAISM

be irrevocably lost if such wholesale overnight changes were wrought in its fabric. While Solomon Schechter is generally accredited as the founder of conservative Judaism in America, it was Zacharias Frankel, a German rabbi of Breslau, who, in his insistence upon Historic Judaism, which he held was not a static but gradually evolving faith, is by many credited with being the father of the movement. The assumption by Dr. Schechter of the presidency of the newly reorganized Jewish Theological Seminary in 1902 is thought of generally as the beginning of American Conservatism, although the formal founding of the United Synagogue of America did not occur until 1913.

Conservative Judaism is not easy to define. Solomon Goldman in a recent book says of it:

"One experiences great uneasiness in writing about Conservative Judaism: one can never be quite certain that he is speaking for anybody but himself. Conservative Judaism has nowhere been defined, its program has never been clearly stated. One searches in vain the annual reports of the United Synagogue of America for even a trace of an attempt to deal with fundamentals or to state in unmistakable terminology the philosophy and program of the organization. This seems either to have been overlooked because of the pressure of more 'practical' affairs; or because of excessive politeness to have been studiously avoided." [*]

He further notes that the very term *Conservative* is misleading, for in its ordinary connotation it stands over against the progressive attitude, while as a

[*] Solomon Goldman, *A Rabbi Takes Stock* (New York: Harper and Brothers, 1931), pp. 3-4.

matter of fact Conservative Judaism believes thoroughly in the "worth of progressive modern ideas." The term Conservative was adopted, he asserts, because of the belief of the so-called conservatives "in conserving the permanent spiritual and cultural values in Judaism.[4] The Conservative Jew is rather "the conserving Jew." The author, a Conservative rabbi, declares, "the writer cannot describe a movement already in full swing, but one in the travail of birth. Neither can he present a body of fundamental beliefs shared by a large group. The most he can offer is a point of view held by a few men who can find no satisfaction either with Orthodoxy or Reform."[5]

Professor Meyer Waxman of the Hebrew Theological College, Chicago, defines Conservatism as a generic term covering everything from Orthodoxy to Reform. Rabbi Samuel M. Gup says of it:

"It has no clearcut unequivocal platform. What its theology is, whether it stands immovable upon the dogmas of Orthodoxy or tries to refine the Jewish elements of theology in the light of modern thought, presents a peck of troubles. As to its oft-proclaimed compact with Rabbinical Judaism, it runs from the extreme of Orthodoxy, on the one hand, to abrogation of the law whenever law conflicts with modernity, on the other. Its leaders uphold views which run to greater distances apart than do the views which Reform rabbis champion."[6]

This writer notes two distinct marks of Conservatism, first its insistence upon legalism. "Without

[4] *Ibid.*, p. 5.   [5] *Ibid.*, p. 5.
[6] Samuel M. Gup, *Currents in Jewish Religious Thought and Life in America in the Twentieth Century* (1931), p. 25.

IN JUDAISM

legalism there can be no Judaism . . . living Judaism consists in the preservation and continuance of rabbinical Judaism." In this it agrees with Orthodoxy. But, second, it claims "the right of the development of rabbinical traditions" which Orthodoxy denies. The Conservative admits, further, the legitimacy of the use of the critical method in the study of the Talmud. Schechter, the father of the present Conservative movement in America invoked as a guiding principle in the practice of the group the retention of whatever "Catholic Israel" had accepted and practiced regardless of its origin. But obviously a general principle such as this would fail to secure general uniformity, since the difficulty of proving the catholicity of any practice would always arise.

The complaint of Conservatism against Orthodoxy is that it is air-tight, that it refuses in theory to admit new ideas, though in real practice it compromises at many points. On the other hand Reform, according to Dr. Goldman, "has so deformed Judaism that it is largely to be blamed for the obstinacy with which Orthodoxy has resisted all suggestions of change. . . . It is indeed the negation of Judaism." [7]

Due to the failure of these two groups the synagogue has ceased to be a dynamic force in Jewish life. "The most vital endeavors of Jewry today are initiated and promoted by the 'unsynagogued.' The leaders in the upbuilding of Palestine and in Jewish education, the rejuvenators of the Hebrew language, the champions of modern Jewish knowledge, the promoters of Jewish art, all these with but few excep-

[7] Solomon Goldman, *op. cit.*, pp. 6-7.

tions are known not to be synagogue Jews." [9] The conclusion is that "Judaism must be redefined in terms of the whole of life. Nothing that enhances the physical, ethical, spiritual or æsthetic welfare of the individual dare be overlooked in its perspective." [9]

Apparently an important tenet in the Conservative creed is that the Jews are a people, a nation, dispersed to be sure but nevertheless a distinct people. Dr. Goldman characterizes as absurd the question so constantly in the mind of American Jewry, "Do Jews constitute a religious group or are they a nation?" and equally absurd the question "Can the Jews separate their religion from nationalism?" Religion is a part of their national heritage. Their mores, their folkways, their laws have been the inevitable outgrowth of the historical process through which they have passed. The Law was developed as the Jew's most effective method of maintaining his distinctiveness in an environment almost always hostile to him. "The nationhood of Israel," declares Rabbi Goldman, "is an ineluctable fact. The contention of the Jewish religionist is so much absurdity, for no people with a common ancestry, common longings, common experience and common memories can ever form merely an idealistic or voluntary union. . . . The Jews are a nation, no mere missionary society." [10]

Accepting the fact of the nationhood of the Jew there follow naturally certain responsibilities. It calls for a national language, not simply for the syna-

[9] Solomon Goldman, *op. cit.*, p. 9.
[9] *Ibid.*, p. 10.   [10] *Ibid.*, p. 16.

IN JUDAISM

gogue but as a literary medium and as a spoken language. This implies naturally a real Jewish education which no mere Sunday school can adequately provide. Jewish law and customs must be thoroughly examined. "We dare not take the attitude of either the Reform or Orthodox Jew regarding Jewish tradition. The former has been the proverbial bull in the china shop, the latter the proverbial ostrich. Jewish laws, customs and ceremonies must be searchingly studied. Many of them we will find obsolete. These we must lose no time in discarding. Many traditions we will have to retain because of their group-building value." [11] Obviously, of course, nationalism implies a national home, and Conservative Judaism becomes the ardent champion of Zionism. An Orthodox Jew may be a Zionist. Many of them are, though they might prefer to call themselves Messianists. An increasing number of Reform Jews are supporting Zionism of a sort. A Conservative may not be other than a Zionist if he is true to the full implications of his position.

Curiously enough, Conservatism includes some of the most radical Jewish thinkers from the standpoint of theology. A Conservative need not be liberal in theology—many of them are indeed very close to Orthodoxy—but he may be. There is room for a wide variety of theological opinion. Modern humanism finds a number of its followers among this group who seem in the faithfulness of their performance of Jewish ceremony to be most Orthodox. As one Reform rabbi expressed it, "The most radical Jews,

[11] *Ibid.*, p. 19.

MODERN TENDENCIES

from the theological point of view, who think of religion and its laws and ceremonies as merely a part of the folkways of the people, believe so heartily that in the persistence of these folkways lies the only hope of maintaining the distinctiveness of the Jewish people, that they go to an extreme in the punctilious observance of the requisite forms." Truly the term "Conservative" does seem to be confusing applied to such a group.

General Trends in Judaism

One of the marked tendencies in Judaism is not necessarily the changing of the three groups, already fairly well stabilized, but in the movement of the Jews from one group to another. This movement takes place chiefly among the younger group and as the economic status of individual Jews changes. Thus, for example, the newer immigrant Jewish groups congregate in the congested areas of the cities, the ghetto. Language and poverty hold many of them securely to the type of synagogues which minister there. The first generation may never leave the ghetto, but the public school and the contact of the younger group with outside groups, in workshops, in business, or in recreation tend to modify the traditional attitudes and weaken the ties of religion and racial custom. Economic success enables them to choose a more desirable residence neighborhood. Here Orthodox synagogues are seldom found, but the other groups are. Social prestige attaches in most communities to membership in the more liberal synagogues. Dissatisfaction with the rigidity

IN JUDAISM

of Orthodoxy and the difficulty in the modern American urban environment of observing strictly the ceremonial and dietary laws imposed by strict Orthodox Judaism, cause great numbers to abandon all relationship with the synagogue of whatever sort, while still maintaining with pride their racial character. Conservative and Reform Judaism attract some of them, but it is the lament of all the groups that such relatively large numbers are drifting away from Judaism as a religion. It is the deep concern of Orthodoxy to maintain its hold upon its younger members. It is the deep concern of the more liberal groups not only to hold their own young people—this is the same real difficulty which liberal religions of all sorts face—but how to reach and draw into the synagogue relationship that group which is becoming increasingly indifferent to religion in any form.

Repeated interviews with Jewish young people disclose a very common tendency toward the breakdown of traditional practices. It is a customary question when two young people of Orthodox training are about to be married and leave the paternal roof, "Are you going to have a 'kosher' home?" Most non-Jews are not acquainted with the fact that a 'kosher home' requires two sets of cooking utensils and two sets of tableware in order that certain foods may not be cooked or served in the same vessels. The economic factor enters here as a consideration. Shall this extra expense be incurred? It is difficult enough in this age of high-living costs for young folk to establish a home without any "extras."

MODERN TENDENCIES

Again, it is added expense to eat only "kosher" meat, that is, meat killed according to certain ceremonial requirements. This requires a special functionary in the packing house; the process is slower and therefore more expensive. Such added expense comes to the Jew in so much per pound extra on the retail price of meat. Strong conviction is required under the pressure of economic necessity to hold one to this extra drain upon his resources. Of course if one *believes it*—but there's the rub! So much of the liberalizing tendency pervades education, the theater, the press, the whole environment in which the young Jew develops, that it is increasingly difficult to maintain such beliefs—and so the drift. If one can still remain in the synagogue and be freed from certain of the observances, as Liberal Judaism advocates without reserve, and which Conservative Judaism holds more in the nature of desirable but not absolutely binding customs, the drift would seem inevitably to be away from Orthodoxy. The trouble is, of course, that many will not stop at half a loaf of freedom but go the whole way, leaving religion entirely in the discard. Unfortunately the drift does not stop with the mere separation from Judaism as a religion but tends toward a complete denationalization or loss of identity with the Jewish group. But our concern just now is with Judaism as a religion.

The economic factor operates in other ways as well to the same end. As influential a factor as any is the difficulty of maintaining the Jewish sabbath strictly in an environment organized on a Sunday holiday basis. If industry or commerce, in which the Jew

IN JUDAISM

must for the most part find his living, observes any seventh day of rest, it is Sunday and not Saturday. He is in competition—very keen competition indeed—with a system organized on a basis other than his own. The Jew would not be like the great majority of mankind if he were not appealed to by a rationalization of his faith, which would permit of the preservation of its essential values and at the same time allow of his adjustment to the economic system of which he forms a part, without the feeling that he is somehow proving disloyal to his faith.

A further factor in the drift of young Jewry from its faith lies in the desire to escape certain social disabilities. Living in an environment frankly prejudiced against the Jew, he who practices strictly the ways of his people is apt to think that he invites discrimination against himself. By erasing as many as possible of those habits and practices which set him off as a Jew, he thinks that he calls less attention to himself and that he may be more readily accepted by the larger social group. Curiously enough, the opposition of outside forces may operate in either of two ways. It may serve to force him back into his own group, and as a defense reaction he may be led to affirm his faith more strongly than ever. This fact is popularly exemplified in the well-known proverb, "The blood of martyrs is the seed of the church." Where the opposition is violent this is likely to be the result. But where it is comparatively mild, where it expresses itself in less outward, tangible fashion, where it is expressed mainly in mere attitudes of

MODERN TENDENCIES

dislike, depreciation, ridicule, or one of superiority, it lacks sufficient force to provoke vigorous reaction, and frequently results in an attempt to minimize the differences which lie at the root of the opposition. That is the situation today in America, generally speaking, in schools and colleges, in business, in industry, wherever the Jew and Christian are brought together. It is not to be wondered at, therefore, that there is a steady drift from the orthodox to the more liberal or to the non-profession of their religion in any form.

Zionism

The long history of Judaism has witnessed the frequent emergence of Zionistic hopes. The nineteenth century produced a considerable number of movements looking toward some sort of restoration of the Jews, to a home of their own where they would be free to develop in their own way without the handicap of a hostile environment. Their desire for such a home became intensified toward the latter part of the century, with the growing emphasis on nationalism that was abroad throughout Europe and the recrudescence of anti-Semitism which had been less marked since the French Revolution. The Jews had hoped that with the grant of political freedom they would also acquire social equality, but this was not to be. The rising nationalism rather turned sentiment against them, and the latter part of the nineteenth century witnessed a cruel revival of racial hatred against them. Suffering was not new to the Jews and the great mass of the people submitted

IN JUDAISM

passively to the conditions that were forced upon them. But Theodor Herzl, smarting under the injustices heaped upon his people, in 1895 wrote a pamphlet from the publication of which, in several languages in 1896, may be said to date the beginning of Modern Zionism. Antedating thus by four years the beginnings of the twentieth century it does not fall strictly within the limits of this study in its origin, but few Jewish ideas or movements have been more prominent among the Jewish groups, especially since the war. One of the very interesting trends observable is the shifting of Jewish thought of the various schools with reference to this idea.

The argument of Herzl was a simple one. Since the Jewish people were not to be allowed to assimilate themselves to the larger group through intermarriage, it was necessary, if the Jew were to survive that he have some place of his own where he could live his own life. He suggested either Argentine or Palestine as suitable for the purpose. As a method of carrying out such a scheme he suggested a "Jewish Company" capitalized at fifty million pounds, to develop plans made by a Society of Jews who should take into account the political and social factors involved in such a movement. It is a noteworthy fact that Herzl was not moved chiefly, or possibly at all, by religious considerations. No theological support was invoked at the beginning. Absolute separation of religion and state was an integral part of his plan. But he did later come to recognize the practical value of the religious sanction to a large section of Jewry.

MODERN TENDENCIES

It was in 1897 that the First Jewish Congress met in Basle. Contrary to reasonable expectation the reception of the idea was by no means enthusiastic. In certain sections of Europe where anti-Semitism flourished, Herzl was hailed as a deliverer; also a small group of intellectuals were attracted to him. But there was much opposition to it. Extreme Orthodoxy opposed it partly on the ground that under the leadership of men who were themselves not followers of the Jewish faith, the movement would not advance the real cause of Judaism. Others stood out against it because it seemed to them that it was a human attempt to do what they had always believed God would one day do. To them it was something of an impertinence. If men would but trust God He would fulfil His promises. A Messiah would arise and Israel would be led back. They could not see the hand of Providence in the plan of Herzl.

Liberal Jews opposed it, as logically they must do, on the basis of such declarations as those made at Pittsburgh. Two main objections were raised by them, namely that in the first place Judaism stood not for a people or a nation but for a religion. The old national Judaism had ceased at the dispersion. The Jews had become citizens of the world. To withdraw from the world and to become only an obscure nation would be to cut themselves off from any effective influence upon the world; and second, that this influence of Judaism upon the world constituted the real mission of the Jew. K. Kohler, for example, took the position that Judaism was "designed to interlink all nations and sects, classes and races of

IN JUDAISM

men; its duty is to be a cosmopolitan factor of humanity basing itself upon the Biblical passage, 'Ye shall be unto me a kingdom of priests and a holy nation. . . .' The mission of the Jew is not only spiritual or religious in character, it is social and intellectual as well and the true Zionism demands of the Jews to be martyrs in the cause of truth and justice and peace until the Lord is one and the world is one."[12]

Others opposed it because they felt that such a movement would inevitably lead to an increase of anti-Semitic prejudice, for they felt that political Zionism was calculated to arouse antagonism. In Germany the notion that Jewry as a whole was a national entity was vigorously repudiated. The formal protest of German rabbis in 1897 holds that the attempt was contrary to Messianic promises, and that Judaism should demand of its adherents that they serve the state in which they live and in every way further its national interests.[13] In America the conference of American rabbis set themselves against it, one of them declaring "that America was the Jews' Jerusalem and Washington their Zion."[14]

Despite the opposition, Herzl pushed forward his plans for the movement. The great Zionist Congress at Basle in 1897 established the basis for the subsequent action. They declared:

[12] Quoted in *Jewish Encyclopedia*, Vol. 12, p. 672. This rapid sketch of the movement follows substantially the article on Zionism in the *Jewish Encyclopedia*.
[13] *Jewish Encyclopedia*, Vol. 12, p. 673.
[14] *Ibid.*, p. 673.

291

MODERN TENDENCIES

"The object of Zionism is to establish for the Jewish people a publicly recognized, legally secured home in Palestine. In order to attain this the Congress adopts the following measures:

"1. To promote insofar as it serves the above purpose the settlement in Palestine of Jewish agriculturalists, craftsmen and tradesmen.

"2. To select and organize the whole Jewish people in appropriate local and general bodies in conformity with the laws of the land.

"3. To strengthen Jewish national sentiment and national self-consciousness.

"4. Preparatory measures to obtain the sanction of governments required for attaining the objects of Zionism." [15]

Successive congresses were held every other year, each registering some advance of the movement, at least in numbers. Each national group was allowed a delegate for each 200 shekel-payers. Russia, as might be expected, showed the largest gain. England and America lagged far behind. By 1900 the number of societies had increased to 1,034 in Russia, in England to 38, in the United States to 135 and even in Bulgaria to 42.

Herzl's negotiations with the Sultan of Turkey failed to secure the conditions the movement was seeking, namely, a concession to settle in Palestine large numbers of Jews who should be locally self-governing. Other possibilities were considered; a portion of land in the Sinai peninsula, El Arish, but it was found impracticable; a region in East Africa was offered by Britain and the Congress went so far as to send an investigating committee to look it over,

[15] *Encyclopedia of Religion and Ethics*, Vol. 12, p. 856.

IN JUDAISM

but it was rejected as unsuitable. A group of seceders from the main movement, under the leadership of Israel Zangwill, interested themselves in certain sections of Canada, Australia, Cyrenaica, Mesopotamia and Angola, but without finding a suitable place. It was apparent that only Palestine could command the enthusiastic interest of the Jewish people as a whole.

Meanwhile a fund was being built up for financing the project under the Jewish Colonial Trust, Ltd., with an authorized capitalization of £2,000,000. By 1920 there were over 100,000 holders of shares of £1 each. In 1921 about 800,000 members of the Zionist organizations paid the annual membership fee known as the shekel, formerly one shilling or equivalent, but in 1919 raised to 2/6.

The World War gave a new impulse to Zionism at the same time that it interfered with the work of the international organization. The greatest impetus given it came in the famous Balfour declaration which reads:

"His Majesty's Government view with favour the establishment in Palestine of a national home for the Jewish people, and will use their best endeavors to facilitate the achievement of this object, it being clearly understood that nothing shall be done which may prejudice the civil and religious rights of existing non-Jewish communities in Palestine or the rights and political status enjoyed by Jews in any other country."

With the overthrow of Turkish power and the passing of Palestine into the hands of Britain, it seemed to the Jewish world that the great moment

MODERN TENDENCIES

had come. Enthusiasm ran high. To the peace conference at Versailles the Zionist leaders presented the following proposals which were ultimately accepted by the Allied Powers at San Remo. They read as follows:

"The sovereign possession of Palestine shall be vested in the League of Nations, and the government entrusted to Great Britain as the mandatory of the League, it being a special condition of the mandate that Palestine shall be placed under such political, administrative and economic conditions as will secure the establishment there of the Jewish National home and ultimately render possible the creation of an autonomous commonwealth." [16]

There have always existed two distinct types of theory with reference to the return of Jews to Palestine, so that today when one declares himself a Zionist it is necessary that he further define his position. One group is interested preëminently in political Zionism—that is, the actual formation of a Jewish commonwealth. Although highly desirable, this need not of necessity be independent. Herzl sought from the Sultan only local autonomy, but not independence from the national Turkish government. Even the post-war development has not contemplated entire independence, certainly not immediately, whatever their ultimate hope, but only local self-government under British mandate.

Herzl stood definitely for the political ideal but after his death there was a strong reaction to the "practical" or relief-cultural side. However, with

[16] *Encyclopedia of Religion and Ethics*, Vol. 12, p. 858.

IN JUDAISM

the coming of the Great War, the political emphasis again became predominant.

The other group which should properly again be subdivided into what may be called Cultural Zionists, and, for want of a better term, "Relief Zionists," both alike in their indifference—not to say, in many instances, opposition—to political nationalism. The Relief Zionists are motivated not by any desire to form a nation or primarily to preserve a culture by colonizing Palestine, but by a philanthropic interest in their fellow Jews in other parts of the world who are unhappy and under-privileged or oppressed, and to whom Palestine would offer a new opportunity to live and work under happier circumstances. This group may and easily does take on an added cultural interest, as the results on Jewish culture of the investment in Palestine begin to be seen.

Cultural Zionists are preëminently interested in Jewish culture, whether in Palestine or elsewhere. They hold that there are peculiar values in that culture which at all costs ought to be preserved. But the facts of Jewish disintegration in America, on the Continent, indeed wherever Jews are found in the diaspora, press in upon them and convince many that there must be some center about which Jewish cultural development may turn. Many have sought to discover such a center outside of Palestine. New York, or at least the United States, has been suggested, for, long since, the center of Jewish population and wealth has shifted to America. But the Old World Jew, himself part product of and sharing the general attitude of European culture toward America

MODERN TENDENCIES

as the land of the "nouveau riche" would find little to commend itself in such a suggestion. As a matter of fact, tradition, sentiment, and now the turn of political fortune, suddenly throwing Palestine into the hands of Britain, known to be favorable to a Jewish home, all conspire to point cultural Zionists to Palestine as the desired center.

So, cultural Zionists, while disclaiming any interest in the political status of the Holy Land, so long as a proper measure of security for peaceful development of their culture be guaranteed, are content to support liberally the colonizing movements which are slowly bringing back to the homeland groups in which may be preserved and enriched a genuine Jewish culture, and they are helping generously toward the creation of institutions like the Hebrew University at Jerusalem, designed to promote a true Jewish culture.

Under the new impetus given to Zionism by the action of the Allied Powers in entrusting the mandate of Palestine to Great Britain, the program of world organization and of actual occupation of Palestine by the Jews was greatly accelerated. Vast sums of money were contributed, not only by Zionists but by non-Zionists as well. Colonization projects on a large scale were undertaken. Large tracts of land were purchased from the Arabs and many Jewish communities were founded, some of them of a distinctly communistic character, others preserving the ancestral family organization but providing for a large measure of coöperation among the members. By no means all of the colonization was agricultural. A city of considerablet size, Tel-aviv, within a very

IN JUDAISM

brief period was built upon the sands back of the city of Jaffa, and became a flourishing industrial center. Altogether something like 150,000 Jews have returned to the homeland and are making a brave attempt to reconstruct Zion. The Jewish population in 1932 was 175,006 as over against 83,794 in 1922. Jews now constitute eighteen per cent of the total population of Palestine.

But after the first burst of enthusiasm, in which probably the efforts of the promoters and administrators were not always wisely directed, serious problems arose. The expense of the undertaking was proving to be heavier than had been calculated and questions as to the efficiency of the administration and the worthwhileness of the work that they were doing were raised in the minds of many of its supporters. Differences between the Zionist and non-Zionist groups became more sharply marked. Partly as a result of this fact there was organized what is known as the Jewish Agency in which Zionist and non-Zionist not only share as supporters but as administrators of the enterprise. Through the medium of this agency, Zionists of every shade—relief, cultural, and political—are enabled to work with a degree of real harmony toward the desired objectives.

A grave crisis to the whole movement was caused by the growing spirit of nationalism of the Palestinian Arabs, who saw their own position being progressively weakened in Palestine and perceived in this a threat of the eventual loss of their homeland. By reason of their many centuries' residence there they had come to think of Palestine as their home-

MODERN TENDENCIES

land, quite as fondly as do the Jews. The opposition finally flamed into open violence first in 1921, but much more seriously in the summer of 1929 in a conflict between Arabs and Jews over the Wailing Wall in Jerusalem. This served to crystallize the feeling of the Arab group. Thoroughly aroused and forced into concerted action they adopted a boycott of Jewish merchants and products to such a degree as seriously to cripple Jewish business and industry, since it restricted their market to their own rather meager numbers. A temporary solution of the difficulty was effected by the British government, but the problem is not yet solved, and it is difficult to see what the solution is to be, since pre-occupation promises seem to have been made to both parties. But while discouragement and some disillusionment has come to the promoters of the return, the leaders are steadfastly pursuing their way in the faith that Zionism will ultimately succeed.

Already, in addition to the colonies that have been planted, some really notable achievements in the cultural realm have been registered. More far-reaching in its influence than any other is the great Jewish university which is being developed in Jerusalem—great not in the number of students, for on this basis it would not rank high, but great in the ideal which it envisages of being the center of Jewish intellectual life for the world. Already it has gathered together a library of unique value to Judaism. To the university more than to any other single source is due the renascence of the Hebrew language as a spoken and literary medium. No more interesting or remarkable phenomenon has been observed in the pres-

IN JUDAISM

ent age than the rebirth of this language which for so long, like the classical Greek and Latin, survived only, or chiefly, as a ritual language, a part of the religious cult.

Other Movements

The present century has seen the rise of some very notable movements which are non-partisan and which therefore make for the solidarity of the total Jewish group. We have already spoken at length of Zionism. Probably no single movement has run across more barriers of partisan organization and tended more to fuse together the Jews of the world, both those of the synagogue and those without. But rather an impressive list of other organizations and movements may be culled from the *Jewish Year Book*. Among them may be noted "The Synagogue Council of America," organized in 1925, which states its purpose thus:

"To take council together for the sacred purpose of preserving and fostering Judaism, composed of representatives of national, congregational and rabbinical organizations of America for the purpose of speaking and acting unitedly and furthering such religious interests as the constituent organizations and the Councils have in mind."

The constituent organizations are:

Union of Orthodox Jewish Congregations (Orthodox).
Rabbinical Council (Orthodox).
Union of American Hebrew Congregations (Reform).
Central Conference of American Rabbis (Reform).
United Synagogue of America (Conservative).
Rabbinical Assembly (Conservative).

MODERN TENDENCIES

Another significant movement has been fostered by the B'nai B'rith Order, which has as one of its most important functions the maintenance of the Hillel Foundations at various university centers. Jewish students in large numbers are frequenting the campuses of the nation. In many centers Judaism is weak and wholly unable to care for or minister to Jewish students. The result is, of course, the drifting away from Judaism of many students. Subjected to an environment of research, inquiry and criticism, in which religion of any sort often enough is discredited, Jewish youth is hard put to it to maintain loyalty to Judaism either as a religion or a culture. The Hillel Foundation, closely similar to the Wesley Foundation of the Methodists and like organizations of other Protestant bodies, was the response. Its purpose is to surround the Jewish student youth with an atmosphere that is Jewish—social, educational, and religious. Most of the other Jewish campus organizations, of which there are not a few, have some limited purpose or appeal. The Hillel Foundation is non-partisan. It attempts to enforce no creed or set of practices upon students. It is not Zionistic nor anti-Zionistic, neither Orthodox, Conservative nor Reformed. It is all-inclusive. It welcomes every shade of Jewish thought and aspiration. "Nothing Jewish is or can be foreign to the Hillel Foundation," declares an enthusiastic admirer of the Foundation.

Among other recently founded organizations are the following:

Council of Young Men's Hebrew and Kindred Associations—organized 1913.

IN JUDAISM

Hadassah—Woman's Zionist Organization—organized 1912.

The Intercollegiate Menorah Association—organized in 1913 for the "study and advancement in American Universities of Jewish Culture and ideals."

The Intercollegiate Zionist Association of America—organized in 1915—To study and promote the Zionist Movement, especially in American Colleges and Universities.

National Federation of Temple Sisterhoods—organized 1913—for closer cooperation between the various sisterhoods.

United Synagogue of America—1913. Conservative.

One of the noteworthy trends in organizations, while not especially related to Judaism as a religion, has been the founding of numerous college Greek letter fraternities. The roster of national Jewish organizations in the year book of 1909 lists but one fraternity or sorority, that of 1919—six, while in 1932 there were thirty-one.

Trends within Orthodoxy

Within Orthodoxy itself changes are taking place, though to be sure these changes are not in fundamental matters. They lie chiefly in the realm of practice rather than theory. Of course if Orthodoxy be arbitrarily defined as theoretically rigid and incapable of change, then if theoretical change actually occurs it is no longer Orthodoxy, but Conservatism. But not all Orthodox Jews are willing to admit that their faith is wholly static, even in theory, and they are obliged to face the fact that modifications in practice are frequently discernible.

MODERN TENDENCIES

Suppose one discovers an occasional congregation which calls itself Orthodox and which has an Orthodox rabbi, but which does not segregate men and women in its services? The reaction of both the ultra-Orthodox and the Conservative is apt to be that such a synagogue is no longer Orthodox but Conservative. But the fact is that both the synagogue and its rabbis are members in good standing in the national Orthodox organizations. This to the writer indicates a distinct trend in Orthodoxy—that of the toleration, if not the approval, of departure from the regularly established norms. Cases of this sort are actually to be found.

With the rapid growth of the movement toward equality of sexes it becomes less easily possible to maintain a segregation which is basically a denial of equality. An entering wedge looking toward the abandonment of segregation is to be found in connection with another relatively common innovation of recent years, namely the late Friday evening service. The regular service falls at sunset. Many are engaged in business or industry and are unable to be present at that hour. The more liberal groups have long held late evening services. Orthodoxy has seen the need for something to enable them to hold their people. They have, therefore, developed a late service which offers a sermon or a lecture, in the language of the people, but in which the regular prayers and other ritual are omitted. To be sure, some of the younger rabbis see no harm in reading selections from the Psalms or other scripture, but do not repeat the prayers. Since, lacking this **feature,**

IN JUDAISM

the service is not a real synagogue service, there is no necessity for segregation, and men and women sit together as at the theater, the concert, or secular lecture. But they sit together *in the synagogue*. One wonders how long especially the rising generation of girls that are being educated in the public schools of America will consent to segregation—and remain in the synagogue. As one rabbi said, who had reluctantly been obliged to allow his women members to come down out of the gallery on to the main floor, "They simply came down. What can I do?" Of course, as another rabbi observed, he could have resigned and refused to minister longer to such a congregation—but here is a tendency in the rabbinate as well. Some concessions to the age seem to be necessary.

Concessions have been made of necessity in the matter of language in order to hold the newer generation, few of whom understand either the Hebrew or the Yiddish or other Jewish vernacular. The ritual is, of course, read in Hebrew, but increasingly the sermon is in English. Even on high feast days it is becoming fairly common to bring in theological students or others able to preach in English where the rabbi cannot himself do so. This is obviously necessary if the younger members are to be held, for many of them do not know the Hebrew. Preaching tends to become more important than formerly. The authority of one's ordination, i.e. by some renowned rabbi, becomes a secondary consideration to the preaching ability of a candidate when a congregation is seeking a minister. This was less true in an earlier

MODERN TENDENCIES

day. Older men, especially those who cannot preach in the vernacular, find it increasingly difficult to find places to minister.

There is a let-down notably in the observance of the dietary laws—the observance, note, not the official teaching. "Conviction is lacking among the middle aged and young," lamented one Orthodox rabbi. In the matter of sanitary laws there is likewise a breakdown, particularly among women with reference to the ritual bath. It becomes too easily an offense, to the more highly developed æsthetic senses of Jewish young women in particular, for the rabbi to discuss such matters or to insist upon strict obedience to the Law. One suspects that with the constant teaching of hygiene in the schools and in papers, magazines, advertisements, pamphlets and public lectures, it is simply a case of loss of belief in the authority of an ancient document, however holy, in matters so intimately personal, that accounts for this change.

Rabbi Goldman declares that while theoretically claiming that "The law does not alter," in practice Orthodox leaders and laymen

"seem to have abandoned much of the ideology underlying the *Shulhan Aruch* and by silent consent to have reduced its injunctions to a minimum . . . similarly orthodox leaders are guilty of most grevious sins of omission. In recent proclamations to American Israel within recent years, they have given considerable attention to sabbath observance and synagogue ritual. But there is an ominous silence concerning many very important laws which are trodden upon by all. . . . Why has the official code shrunk? Why maintain silence concerning shaving, the bare-headed woman, the curtain-

IN JUDAISM

less balcony, dancing, etc. . . . Is not this a silent admission that the Code can no longer be accepted as our guide in life?"[17]

Summing up the situation in Orthodox Judaism, an eminent professor in an Orthodox seminary has this to say:

"Theoretically, Jewish Orthodoxy advocates full observance of all Laws and customs prescribed by the codes, practically a large part of those that call themselves Orthodox Jews violate by force of circumstance not only minor laws, but expressed Biblical precepts—the Sabbath for example. In fact, of a large part of so-called Orthodox Jews, it can well be said that they differ in their private life but little from those who call themselves conservative or reformed Jews. Yet, in a number of cases, there is no conscious hypocrisy. It is merely a manifestation of the psychological phenomenon which is observed throughout life where men constantly make compromises, at the expense of their ideals and strivings."[18]

A distinct trend within Orthodoxy is toward a closer organization for the more effective pursuit of their distinctive aims. Curiously enough it has until very recently been almost without organization, while the more liberal schools have built up relatively strong national organizations. Concerning this matter, Dr. Waxman declared not long since in a public address:

"Unfortunately, Orthodoxy is poorly organized for the purpose of attaining its ideals and for the solution of its problems. The reason for this state of disorganiza-

[17] Solomon Goldman, *A Rabbi Takes Stock* (New York: Harper and Brothers, 1931), p. 6.
[18] Meyer Waxman, *Orthodoxy*, unpublished manuscript.

MODERN TENDENCIES

tion are many, and it would require too much time to enumerate them. We can only say, that of late there is evidence of a strong desire on the part of orthodoxy, especially the more Americanized element to organize its forces. At present, there is no organization which embraces all or even a great part of Orthodox congregations throughout the country. There is one organization known as the Union of Orthodox Jewish Congregations, with headquarters in New York. But this organization embraces only a small fraction of the number of Orthodox congregations. And what is worse, it meets in its work with some opposition on the part of the older type of Orthodox rabbis. Yet, it is expanding its work, and . . . it may become the leading organized party in Jewry." [19]

In the training of its young men for the rabbinate, there is a distinct advance over the earlier period. They have begun to provide over and above the specific training in the rabbinic lore, courses in the natural sciences, history, literature, sociology—in short a general cultural education. Rabbi Gup calls it a conscious attempt "to adapt American life and education to rigid orthodoxy. The Hebrew Theological Seminary of Chicago is an expression of this attitude. Its graduates are English-speaking rabbis who, in reality, have edged into a form of neo-orthodoxy, brushing with graduates of the Theological Seminary of America for the opportunity to serve in the same field." [20] The older Orthodoxy which trained its rabbis only in the Talmud and the codes deliberately omitted instruction in those sub-

[19] Meyer Waxman, *Orthodoxy*, unpublished manuscript.
[20] Rabbi Samuel M. Gup, *op. cit.*, p. 22.

IN JUDAISM

jects now being introduced on the score of their potential destructive effect upon Orthodoxy.

Finally in their attitude toward the restoration of Israel many of the Orthodox seem to have traveled far from the older position. If the testimony of a Reform writer may be trusted here, Rabbi Gup, apparently on the basis of a careful study of their own literature, declares:

"They regard Palestine as the central fact and supreme hope of Jewish unity, and labor for its reconstruction despite their belief in the personal Messiah. The miracle long expected and trusted for the restoration of *Eretz Yisrael* under the divine plan is superseded by the advocacy of practical, earthly, and human means." [11]

Trends in Conservatism

Are any trends noticeable within the Conservative group? Unfortunately only the last three annual assemblies of Conservative rabbis have published their proceedings so that it is difficult to discover any significant changes. One does not know for certain what was its spirit in the earlier part of the century. A discussion, however, regarding "Judaism as a Civilization," by Professor Mordecai Kaplan, in the assembly of 1929, and an address by a former president of the assembly on "A Reaffirmation of Traditional Judaism," reveal a line of cleavage within the group almost as sharp as that between Orthodox and Liberal Judaism. The latter holds firmly to the belief in Judaism as a revelation.

[11] Rabbi Samuel M. Gup, *op. cit.*, p. 24.

MODERN TENDENCIES

"We are asking our members to observe laws which entail sacrifices, we ask them to abstain from certain foods, thus causing them a great deal of hardship, we ask them to lead a life which will always expose them to the enmity of their neighbors. I for one feel that only at the behest of God could such a demand be made. Once we conclude that Judaism is man-made, there is no valid reason why the Jew should make so many sacrifices to maintain it outside of Palestine. As a civilization, Judaism can have no greater claim on the American Jew than German, French and Italian culture and civilization have on Germans, Frenchmen and Italians who have become American citizens. It certainly would not be worth dying for such 'a way of life.' "[11]

On the other hand, Professor Kaplan regards Judaism as a civilization,

"nothing less than the *tout ensemble* of all the elements that enter in what is usually termed the cultural life of a people, such as language, folkways, patterns of social organization, social habits and standards, spiritual ideals, which give individuality to a people and differentiate it from other peoples. According to this, Judaism is the funded cultural activity which the Jewish people has transmitted from generation to generation. It is the living dynamic process of intellectual, social and spiritual give-and-take of Jews in the course of their relationship to one another as individuals and as members of various groups."[12]

Elsewhere, by the way in which Professor Kaplan distinguishes folk religion and personal religion, and speaks of such theological concepts as God, immortality, etc., he clasifies himself with what we are

[11] *Proceedings of the Rabbinical Assembly of America, 1929*, pp. 48-49.
[12] *Ibid., 1928*, p. 117.

IN JUDAISM

accustomed to call the naturalistic humanist school. It suggests that here is something of a humanistic trend within the group. How numerous a following can be claimed for this position it is impossible to say. One of the leaders of the school estimated it as a very small percentage of the total group. A prominent member of this group related with great gusto an anecdote that is not without significance. Clarence Darrow once attended his synagogue service and followed carefully, with the help of a friend, the reading of the service, noting the changes and interpretations given by the leader to the ancient prayers and ritual. On leaving the synagogue Darrow remarked to his friend, "Tell the rabbi that I say he believes less than I do."

It is possible that here may be the beginnings of yet a fourth group in Judaism, to which some of the more advanced Reform Jews might affiliate themselves. To give tangible form to such an ideal a society was projected in 1920 with Professor Kaplan as president, called "The Society of the Jewish Renascence," the aims of which are set forth in a pamphlet by Professor Kaplan, published under the title, *The Society of the Jewish Renascence*.

The movement, there begun, resulted in no permanent organization. Perhaps it was prematurely launched. But the idea has not been abandoned. Within the past two years, according to advices given personally to the writer, a group of prominent Jewish rabbis, drawn not only from among the Conservatives, but from the Reform party as well, held a meeting looking toward the launching of a movement

MODERN TENDENCIES

not unlike that projected by Rabbi Kaplan. A second meeting was to have been held during the present winter, but preoccupation with the difficult problems raised by the financial depression has led to an indefinite postponement of further meetings. With the increasing liberalization of some of the Conservatives in matters of ritual and ceremony, and the revival of interest in cultural, not to say nationalistic Zionism, on the part of Reform Jews, a closer *rapprochement* between the two groups seems inevitable. Out of such a combination might come a party which would prove very attractive to a large number of Jews in the modern age.

Another tendency disclosed in the reports which represented something of a departure from earlier Conservative practices was the addition to the synagogue of the *Community Center idea*,[14] and numerous very expensive buildings have been erected containing social, educational, and recreational facilities, including the gymnasium and swimming pool. In this they were following a like trend in the Protestant Christian world as well. If one may judge from the rather slighting references to such equipment by speakers before the Rabbinical Assembly, it would appear that considerable disillusionment has resulted from this movement and that in the future there will be opposition to such a course. One hesitates to evaluate the strength or influence of such statements

---

[14] Of course the synagogue has for centuries been held to be the center of the Jewish Community. The term "Community Center" is here used in the more or less modern technical sense.

IN JUDAISM

in the absence of any evidence that the remarks represent general opinion. But the fact that not one but several rabbis mention it makes it worth while noting.

Trends in Reform

The trends within the Liberal or Reform group seem to be several. It will be observed that there is a two-way movement, one in the direction of greater liberalism in theological thought among some of the rabbis, the other a tendency toward the distinctively Jewish in matters of ceremonial. These express themselves among some as a movement in the direction of humanism among others as a movement toward Zionism; as a reëmphasis upon the use of the Hebrew language not simply as a language of scholarship but even for cult purposes; and as an increased emphasis upon the education of children and youth in Jewish tradition. One discovers among them likewise a tendency to redefine their mission to the world; a tendency toward a closer *rapprochement* with liberal Christianity, and among some a greatly increased interest in and admiration for Jesus as a Jew.

To document all of these fully is not easy, yet in conversation with leading Jewish rabbis all of them appear again and again. Fortunately it is possible to adduce evidence concerning the changing attitude toward Zionism from published official statements at different intervals. This is one of the most interesting observable trends. In 1897 Dr. I. M. Wise,

MODERN TENDENCIES

president of the Central Conference of American Rabbis, referred to the relatively new Zionistic movement, declaring:

"The honor and position of American Israel demand imperatively that this conference . . . declare officially the American standpoint in this unpleasant episode of our history." [25]

The conference thereupon passed unanimously the following resolution:

"That we totally disapprove of any attempt for the establishment of a Jewish state. Such attempts show a misunderstanding of Israel's mission, which from the narrow political and national field has been expanded to the promotion among the whole human race of the broad and universalistic religion first proclaimed by the Jewish prophets. Such attempts do not benefit, but infinitely harm, our Jewish brethren, where they are still persecuted by confirming the assertion of their enemies that the Jews are foreigners in the countries in which they are at home and of which they are everywhere the most loyal and patriotic citizens.

"We reaffirm that the object of Judaism is not political nor national, but spiritual, and addresses itself to the continuous growth of peace, justice, and love in the human race, to a Messianic time when all men will recognize that they form one great brotherhood for the establishment of God's Kingdom on earth." [26]

In 1917, on recommendation of the president, the Council passed the following motion, but it is worthy of note that a minority report had also been sub-

[25] *Year Book, Central Conference of American Rabbis,* Vol. 9, p. 12.
[26] *Ibid.,* p. 41.

312

IN JUDAISM

mitted and that the vote was only sixty-eight to twenty in favor of the resolution:

"We herewith reaffirm the fundamental principle of reform Judaism, that the essence of Israel as a priest-people, consists in its religious consciousness, and in the sense of consecration to God and service in the world, and not in any political or racial national consciousness. And therefore, we look with disfavor upon the new doctrine of political Jewish nationalism, which finds the criterion of Jewish loyalty in anything other than loyalty to Israel's God and Israel's religious mission." [27]

The Balfour declaration brought an expression from the conference which reads in part as follows. It will be noted that while still repudiating the political phases of Zionism there is a genuine expression of interest in the movement of Jews toward Palestine.

"The Central Conference of American Rabbis notes with grateful appreciation the declaration of the British Government by Mr. Balfour as an evidence of goodwill toward the Jews. We naturally favor the facilitation of immigration to Palestine of Jews who, either because of economic necessity or political or religious persecution, desire to settle there. We hold that Jews in Palestine, as well as anywhere else in the world, are entitled to equality in political, civil, and religious rights, but we do not subscribe to the phrase in the declaration which says, 'Palestine is to be a national home-land for the Jewish people.' This statement assumes that the Jews, although identified with the life of many nations for centuries, are in fact a people without a country. We hold that Jewish people are and of right ought to

[27] *Ibid.*, Vol. 27, p. 132.

MODERN TENDENCIES

be at home in all lands. Israel, like every other religious communion, has the right to live and assert its message in any part of the world. We are opposed to the idea that Palestine should be considered *the home-land* of the Jews. Jews in America are part of the American nation. The ideal of the Jew is not the establishment of a Jewish state—not the reassertion of Jewish nationality which has long been outgrown. We believe that our survival as a people is dependent upon the assertion and the maintenance of our historic religious rôle and not upon the acceptance of Palestine as a homeland of the Jewish people. The mission of the Jew is to witness to God all over the world." [18]

The conference president declined to send delegates to an extraordinary session of the Zionist organization to celebrate the action of the San Remo Conference in placing Palestine under British mandate. The conference upheld his position and declared in part as follows:

"With confidence in the free institutions of Great Britain, we rejoice in and recognize the historic significance of such a British Mandate for Palestine, in that it will offer the opportunity to some Jews who may desire to settle there, to go there, and to live full, free, and happy lives. And if facilities are offered for an appreciable number to go there from lands in which they suffer from religious, political, or economic persecution, they may be enabled so to shape their communal life that, inspired by the hallowed associations of the land in which Israel's Prophets announced world-redeeming ideas, they may become a great spiritual influence." [19]

Dr. Philipson, commenting on the action of the Conference, declares:

[18] *Ibid.*, Vol. 28, pp. 133-134.   [19] *Ibid.*, Vol. 30, p. 141.

IN JUDAISM

"It was abundantly evident in these resolutions on Zionism and on Palestine that the great majority of the members of the conference, though opposed to the political agitations of Jewish nationalists, are yet heartily in favor of cooperation in all efforts for the physical rehabilitation of Palestine." [20]

In 1924 the Conference again voted "to reaffirm its agreement to cooperate in the rehabilitation of Palestine."

Resolved "that we as a conference express our deep satisfaction at the extension of the Jewish Agency as a reuniting force in World Israel, and as an opportunity to the lovers of Zion who may not be Zionists, to serve Palestine restoration not only by contributions of money to the Jewish agency, the Hebrew university and similar undertakings and institutions but also by participation in the administration of these enterprises." [21]

Tracing thus the attitude of the Reform group through a period of years, it becomes evident that while they have not, and logically cannot support political Zionism, there is a very marked increase in the interest in the cultural phases of Zionism. From many verbal sources, though documentation is not possible, the writer was assured that the attitude toward Zionism of the Hebrew Union College, the educational center of the Reform group, had shifted to such a degree that whereas in an earlier time to become a Zionist was to invite dismissal from the faculty (indeed this seems to have occurred in two

[20] From David Philipson, *op. cit.*, p. 365. By permission of The Macmillan Company, publishers.
[21] *Year Book, Central Conference of American Rabbis*, Vol. 40, p. 129.

MODERN TENDENCIES

cases), at present probably half of the faculty are Zionists of one sort or another.

An illuminating declaration was made by Rabbi Felix Levy, an outstanding Reform leader, in a paper read before the World Conference of Liberal Judaism in 1930:

"Twenty-two years ago, when I joined the Central Conference of American Rabbis, and for a decade and a half thereafter, the word and concept Zion was to the preponderant number of members what a red rag is said to be to a bull, yet last month (1930), by a majority vote of this body, it was decided that the *Hatikvah* [22] shall be included in the Hymnal about to be published under its auspices. Is it sheer accident that by common acclaim the greatest Jewess in America, Henrietta Szold, a deep religionist unorthodox is a Zionist? Within my own Rabbinate, of less than a quarter of a century, I have seen changes made in our ideology of which we seem to be officially unaware. Our attitude toward Zion is purely a case of point; the old antipathy has been superseded by a reconciliation."[23]

Surely on the basis of such statements it is fair to say that the Reformed attitude toward Zionism is undergoing real modification.

Such a shift is natural if, as Rabbi Gup affirms, there is a growing awareness of the peoplehood of

[22] Reaffirmed in 1931. *Hatikvah* is the Zionist song.
[23] Felix A. Levy, *The Task of Liberal Judaism* (unpublished manuscript), p. 16. An exceedingly interesting article on "Trends in Reform Judaism Today," by Rabbi Levy, appeared in *The Hebrew Union College Monthly*, Vol. 14 (April and June, 1932), pp. 4-6 and 22-24. To this the reader is referred for a more extended discussion than space permits here. He will find particularly interesting Dr. Levy's characterization of what he calls the "right," "center," and "left" positions in Reform Judaism.

IN JUDAISM

the Jews among the Reform group. He quotes from Rabbi Silver, and other leaders, as agreeing in substance that "the group is of equal potency, with the religious idea in the fulfillment of the Messianic principle,". . . "that the center of gravity is moving away from the glorification of our mission toward the concept of peoplehood." "This bent," he further observes, "capitalizes loyalty, both to the community of Jews as Jews as well as our devotion to the Synagogue. It marks a slowing down of our proneness to become too much like the world, and a rearing of safeguards adequate for the preservation of the individuality of the Jew." [34]

There is evidently a tendency among certain of the Reform rabbis to a closer *rapprochement* with liberal Christianity. Evidence of this is to be found in a resolution submitted to the Central Conference of Reform Rabbis recently (circ. 1925). It reads:

"The purpose of the . . . Society is to find and demonstrate a common spiritual understanding and ground for Jews and Christians, and on this basis to formulate and propagate the principles of social and international justice; to propagate the two-fold fact that the enlightened leaders of Judaism through the centuries have followed in the footsteps of the Hebrew Prophets and that the *fundamental religious and moral teachings of Jesus are in complete harmony with the utterance of the Prophets and the traditions of Judaism.* There is, therefore, a common ground between the

[34] Samuel M. Gup, "Currents in Jewish Religious Thought and Life in America in the Twentieth Century," pp. 13-14. Reprinted from *The Yearbook of the Central Conference of American Rabbis*, Vol. 41, 1931.

MODERN TENDENCIES

Synagogue and the Church for the establishment of a permanent reign of social justice and universal peace." [15]

Presented to a committee of some twenty rabbis, it received no support and was not even reported to assembly, nor did it appear in the official *Year Book*. "Not because we were not in favor of social justice and universal peace but because we did not wish to accept the statement made about the relation of the teaching of Jesus to Judaism." [16]

The fact that the resolution failed to be reported out by the committee of twenty rabbis may and doubtless does mean that the tendency is not highly developed, but it is there. It will be noted that the opposition of the committee was chiefly at the point of the declared relation of Jesus to Judaism. The numberless conferences and commissions in which liberal Jews meet with Christians for the discussion of social, philanthropic, educational and even religious matters is a sure indication of this trend. To be sure, some of the Jews thus coöperating may belong to the Conservative group, but the Reform leaders are in the majority.

But while there was decided opposition to the statement regarding the relation of Jesus to Judaism, there has been a striking reappraisal of Jesus by many Jews of the Reformed School in recent years. The entire pamphlet quoted above, *Judaism, Jesus and the Decadence of the Reform Jewish Pulpit*, is

[15] S. Schulman, *Judaism, Jesus and the Decadence of the Reform Jewish Pulpit* (pamphlet), pp. 16 and 17.
[16] *Ibid.*

IN JUDAISM

against the tendency represented particularly by Rabbi Stephen S. Wise of The Free Synagogue, New York. Rabbi Wise, basing his remarks on Klausner's book on Jesus, had made these statements about Jesus: *Jesus was,* i.e. he was not a myth—*Jesus was a Jew, and Jesus was not a Christian.* Dr. Schulman thinks this is evidence that the Reform pulpit is decadent. They must go outside of Judaism to find subjects to draw a crowd. He continues:

"From one point of view, the Jewish pulpit may be said to have become during the years a footnote to the footlights. From another point of view, every Christmas and every Easter, it has become a soapbox from which to orate about Jesus. All this is indelicate and undignified and shows a lack of Jewish moral and spiritual vitality." [37]

It would be easy to bring together a long list of impressive utterances by Reform Jews with reference to Jesus. He has been the subject of noteworthy books by Jewish scholars in the last decade. One needs only to recall Klausner's *Jesus of Nazareth,* Trattner's *As a Jew Sees Jesus,*[38] Enelow's *A Jewish View of Jesus,* and Montefiore's recently published *Rabbinic Literature and the Teachings of Jesus,* to recognize the trend. Rabbi Stephen S. Wise, of the Free Synagogue of New York, has paid marvelous tribute to Jesus, asserting, however, that

[37] S. Schulman, *Judaism, Jesus and the Decadence of the Reform Jewish Pulpit,* p. 18.
[38] Trattner gives a most interesting Jewish bibliography on Jesus in Appendix D of his book *As a Jew Sees Jesus* (New York: Scribners, 1931).

MODERN TENDENCIES

he was not really Christian but Jew. James Waterman Wise, his son, in *Liberalizing Liberal Judaism*, has been quite as outspoken. Let the following quotations serve as examples of what might be extended almost indefinitely:

"Judaism is beginning to feel that in the life, in the teachings, in the suffering of this Jew, there was somewhat utterly Jewish, utterly human, of which it would no longer remain in ignorance. The modern Jew, separated by centuries from Jesus, begins to feel a very real kinship with him; not with Jesus the Christ, not with the Jesus of supernatural miracles, or of the resurrection, but with Jesus the Jew, with Jesus the man, with Jesus of Nazareth, who, in the word of Matthew 'went about the land doing good.'"[39]

"Figures enough can be found in the Old Testament and throughout Jewish history that have been upright and just and brave; prophets who like Jesus 'preached righteousness in the great congregation,' but there is no figure in all history whose nature was so compact of sympathy and of courage and of kindness; who was as firm as he, and yet as gentle, and who like him ministered to men in tenderness and love. The Jesus who went about the land doing good can be recalled today to serve greatly in the shaping of the character of Jewish men and women. He can again be made a living force in stimulating our generation to become, in some degree at least, like him."[40]

Praising the attitude of Liberal Judaism for this tardy recognition of the worth of Jesus he declares, however:

[39] From J. W. Wise, *Liberalizing Liberal Judaism*, p. 117. By permission of The Macmillan Company, publishers.
[40] *Ibid.*, p. 122.

IN JUDAISM

"Liberal Judaism has advanced far in its attitude toward Jesus. But it has not gone far enough. While it has recognized Jesus as a great Jew, Liberal Judaism has stopped there. It has made no effort to re-include him, in fact as well as in theory, among the long line of Jewish teachers, whose lives and works so largely determine what Judaism is today, and whose histories are impressed by rabbi and teacher alike upon the Jewish consciousness. Liberal Judaism admits freely that Jesus was a great ethical teacher, a teacher fully worthy of his forerunners, the prophets. But it fails to examine into what made Jesus a great ethical and spiritual power, what the doctrines were which he taught, and which of them, when tested by the standards of our own religious conscience and consciousness, can be of help to Jews today. In other words, Liberal Judaism admits that the personality of Jesus was a great and truly religious one, but it has so far failed to make use of that personality in shaping the lives and characters of the Jews of this generation." [1]

How far do these utterances represent Reform Judaism, and how far are they but expressions of individual opinion? The reaction of Jewish leaders good enough to read this chapter was that the statements are representative of but a very small group within Judaism. Yet all recognized that it does represent a present-day tendency.

Unquestionably the old reserve with reference to Jesus is rapidly passing. Modern scholarship is presenting an ever clearer picture of him in the setting of Judaism. As the theological trappings are successively stripped from him, he stands out more and more clearly as a great Jew, if not the greatest of

[1] From J. W. Wise, *op. cit.*, pp. 117-118. By permission of The Macmillan Company, publishers.

MODERN TENDENCIES

the Jews; certainly he is the most influential of his race. There would be nothing strange about it; indeed, sheer Jewishness and pride of race might logically lead to an increasing regard for Jesus. "For Jesus was born a Jew," writes a modern Jewish rabbi, "he lived on the ancestral soil of Palestine, never once setting his foot on alien territory; he taught a small group of disciples, all of whom were as Jewish as he; the language he spoke dripped with Jewish tradition and lore; the little children he loved were Jewish children; the sinners he associated with were Jewish sinners; he healed Jewish bodies; fed Jewish hunger, poured out wine at a Jewish wedding, and when he died he quoted a passage from the Hebrew book of Psalms. Such a Jew!" [42]

At any rate, whether of little or great importance as yet, here is a tendency among some modern Jews, most of them, as perhaps natural, of the Reform group.

Events have conspired to draw together, in recent years, the like-minded Reform Jewish leaders of the world. We live in an age of international organization. It would have been strange had there not developed some world movement among Jewish liberals. The recent formation in 1926 of the "World Union of Progressive Judaism" gives organized expression to the world fellowship of those who can no longer hold to ancient orthodox Judaism. The statement of purpose in the constitution adopted at the Berlin Conference in 1928 is as follows:

[42] Ernest R. Trattner, *As a Jew Sees Jesus* (New York: Scribners, 1931), p. 1.

IN JUDAISM

"(a) To further the development of Progressive Judaism; to encourage the formation of Progressive Jewish Religious Communities or Congregations in the different countries of the World; to promote cooperation between all such, whether now in existence or hereafter formed, and to stimulate and encourage the study of Judaism and its adaptation and application to modern life.

"(b) To make this adaptation without changing the fundamental principles of Judaism and to awaken an active interest in those Jews, who, for one reason or another, do not participate in Jewish religious life."[43]

That there is a swing-back among Reform groups in the direction of the more distinctively Jewish in ritual and practice, Rabbi Felix A. Levy declared before the World Congress of Progressive Judaism:

"We have restored Hanukah (Feast of Dedication) and Shevvrath (Feast of Weeks) to a prominent place in the calendar; we are doing the same for Sukkoth (Feast of Booths), and in America, Shemini Azereth (The Last Day) has been superseded in some communities by a real Simhath Torah. The cry today is for more and more peculiarly Jewish customs and observances."[44]

The Gentile reader will not fully understand what is meant by the Shemini Azereth and other technical terms. The point in the quotation is that these things which were once rejected are being brought back. Note: "The cry today is for more and more peculiarly Jewish customs and observances."

Rabbi Gup declares that "Liberal Judaism is

[43] From David Philipson, *op. cit.*, p. 432. By permission of The Macmillan Company, publishers.
[44] Felix A. Levy, *The Task of Liberal Judaism* (manuscript), p. 19.

MODERN TENDENCIES

evincing a revival of interest in Ceremonialism." [45] Many liberals, because of a sense of the relative barrenness of the Reform cult, would, in the interest of beauty, restore some of the rich symbolism of the older service. Others would reëstablish certain of the older ceremonial practices, because of their influence in "deepening the ties with the past and with Jews the world over," that is, as a means of fostering the sense of Jewishness, which Reform Judaism has been accused in the past of weakening.

Jewish friends have pointed out also that some of the practices of the Reform synagogues, which most thoroughly differentiated them from the rest of Judaism, have been dropped, notably the Sunday morning service. One informant declared that most of the Reform synagogues of Chicago no longer hold such services, and was of the opinion that the same thing had happened rather generally.

In an interview Dr. Levy further stated that Reformed Jewry was becoming increasingly convinced that mere secular education does not suffice and that there is a marked revival of interest in Jewish education, including emphasis upon the use of Hebrew. Many Reform rabbis are as intensely interested in the renascence of Hebrew as the language of scholarship as are the Orthodox and Conservatives. Reform Jews are contributing liberally to the building of the great Hebrew University in Jerusalem and evince the greatest interest in the revival and development of true Jewish culture in Palestine.

To quote Rabbi Gup once more:

[45] Rabbi Samuel M. Gup, *op. cit.*, p. 11.

IN JUDAISM

"New energy is being put into the educational efforts of Reform Judaism. . . . This accent on education in Reform Judaism is beginning to assume impressive proportions and is one of the most elegant patterns of its recently-woven cloth. We are bringing forward the old Jewish ideal of study, re-creating the spirit which prompted Ben Aggai to refuse the comfort of love when he said 'My Soul's passion is Torah.' " [46]

Perhaps no more notable trend has evidenced itself in Reform Judaism in the unfolding of the twentieth century than that in the direction of increased social-mindedness and active concern for social justice and international peace. Though by no means absent from the Conservative group, the trend, as might in the nature of things be expected, has been more vigorously and aggressively present in Reform Jewry. Those acquainted with the growing social emphasis in Christianity will find much the same emphasis among Reform leaders. Given their definite interest in prophetic rather than Rabbinic Judaism, it would have been strange if the vast social and economic problems arising out of the industrialization of modern life had not thrown them back upon the great social prophets of Israel. "In the Old Reform," writes Rabbi Gup, "questions of theology and ritual absorb the attention; now human values are crowding for a place in the sun. Then, Reform was inclined to accept the evils of society as unavoidable and to ponder their overthrow in the conception of a Messianic Age. Now, its tidings show an awakening faith in social progress and

[46] Rabbi Samuel M. Gup, *op. cit.*, pp. 10-11.

MODERN TENDENCIES

in the ability of life to elevate itself by attaining a mastery over its environment. . . . More and more we are coming to see that one of the most pressing problems of liberalism has to do with property and social justice." [47]

Summary and Conclusion

Thus, we have seen that Judaism, like every other religion, has, during the twentieth century, undergone significant changes to bring it into consonance with the modern age. While the three major groups were fairly well stabilized before or at the very opening of the century, all of them, even including rigid orthodoxy, give evidence of various trends, either by way of reaction or toward the new in thought and practice. All schools alike feel the effect of the environmental forces which are causing such notable attrition of the Jewish group as a whole. The drift from one school to another and the much more serious drift away from Judaism in any of its religious forms is the occasion of enormous concern to Jewish leaders, and has led, even in rigid orthodoxy, to significant compromises of a practical sort. For all the people the Zionist movement, in one form or another, has been perhaps the outstanding phenomenon of the century, and interesting modifications in the attitudes, both of Orthodoxy and of Reform Judaism, toward this movement have gradually developed. While there is not lacking a left wing liberalism, which to the rest seems to lead only to the ultimate disappearance of Judaism as a

[47] Samuel M. Gup, *op. cit.*, p. 10.

IN JUDAISM

distinctive force in the world's life, there has developed in all three of the schools a deepened interest in that which is distinctively Jewish, particularly their language and literature.

One wonders what the future holds for this people which, scattered for so many centuries over the face of the world, and living under the most adverse and diverse conditions, has nevertheless managed to maintain the vitality with which it still fronts the world. Confronted by probably a more difficult situation than even before in the cosmopolitanism and thorough modernism of the age, will they be able to maintain and pass on to posterity the values which Judaism has to the present afforded the world?

No one who has read sympathetically the history of their past, who has seen the determination with which they have met discouragement and opposition, and the courage with which they have met seemingly impossible odds, can doubt that they will prove equal to the present emergency, and will find some effective way to stem the tide of disintegration which is today upon them. One with historic perspective and a knowledge of the history of religions is apt to suspect that the key to the future lies not with the rigidly unbending attitude of the orthodox but with those Jews who have no less an abiding faith in the worth of their heritage, and at the same time the wisdom to discern what in it is of only ephemeral and what of permanent value.

APPENDIX

SUGGESTIONS FOR FURTHER READING

This list is in no sense a complete bibliography for each chapter, but will be found valuable as supplementary reading.

CHAPTER II, INDIA

Farquhar, J. N., *Modern Religious Movements in India*, The Macmillan Co., New York, 1918. Excellent for the beginnings of many of the modern trends, but reaching only to about 1914.

MacNicol, Nicol, *India in the Dark Wood*, Edinburgh House Press, London, 1930.

Underwood, A. C., *Contemporary Thought of India*, Williams & Norgate, London, 1930.

Gandhi, Mahatma, *The Story of my Experiments with Truth*, 2 vols., Madras, 1930.

Radhakrishnan, S., *The Hindu View of Life*, G. Allen and Unwin, London, 1928.

The Indian Social Reformer, a weekly periodical published at Hyderabad.

The Modern Review, a monthly periodical published at Calcutta and comparable for the Indian world to *The Review of Reviews*.

CHAPTER III, CHINA

Rawlinson, Frank H., *Revolution and Religion in China*, Kwang Hsueh, Shanghai, 1929.

Lo, R. Y., *China's Revolution from the Inside*, Abingdon Press, New York, 1931.

Peffer, Nathaniel, *The Collapse of a Civilization*, Day, New York, 1931.

APPENDIX

Monroe, Paul, *China, a Nation in Evolution*, The Macmillan Company, New York, 1928.

Lew, T. T., *China Today Through Chinese Eyes*, Geo. H. Doran Co., New York.

The Chinese Recorder, a monthly magazine ably edited by Frank H. Rawlinson. Thoroughly alive to the changes taking place in China's religions. While a Christian periodical, its columns are frequently open to expressions of religious thought by non-Christian leaders.

CHAPTER IV, JAPAN

Anesaki, Masaharu, *History of Japanese Religion*, Kegan Paul, Trench, Truber and Co., London, 1930.

Kato, Genchi, *Shinto, the Religion of the Japanese People*, Tokio, 1926.

Kennedy, Captain, M.D., *The Changing Fabric of Japan*, Richard R. Smith, New York, 1931.

Pratt J. B., *The Pilgrimage of Buddhism*, The Macmillan Co., New York, 1928.

CHAPTER V, ISLAM

The Moslem World Today, John R. Mott, Editor. Doubleday, Doran and Company, New York, 1925.

Edib, Halidé, *Turkey Faces West*, Yale Univ. Press, New Haven, 1930.

Titus, Murray, *Indian Islam*, Oxford U. Press, London, 1930.

Cash, W. Wilson, *The Expansion of Islam*, Edinburgh House Press, London, 1928.

The Moslem World, a quarterly magazine edited by Dr. S. M. Zwemer. No other periodical keeps so closely in touch with the entire world of Islam. It is necessary to have in mind that its interest is missionary, and thorough objectivity is not to be looked for in most of its articles of a propaganda character. However, its survey of the whole field of current literature, both books and periodicals,

APPENDIX

dealing with Moslem questions makes it an invaluable aid to the student of Islam.

CHAPTER VI, RUSSIA

Spinka, Matthew, *The Church and the Russian Revolution,* The Macmillan Co., New York, 1928.

Hecker, Julius, *Religion Under the Soviets,* Vanguard Press, New York, 1927.

Eddy, George Sherwood, *The Challenge of Russia,* Farrar and Rinehart, New York, 1931.

Chamberlin, W. H., *Soviet Russia,* Little Brown & Co., Boston, 1930.

Hindus, Maurice, *Humanity Uprooted,* Jonathan Cape, New York, 1930.

Fülop-Müller, René, *The Mind and Face of Bolshevism,* A. A. Knopf, New York, 1930.

CHAPTER VII, JUDAISM

Hertz, Joseph H., *Affirmations of Judaism.* Oxford U. Press, London, 1927. (Extreme orthodox.)

Goldman, Solomon, *A Rabbi Takes Stock,* Harpers, New York, 1931.

Philipson, David, *The Reform Movement in Judaism,* New and revised edition, The Macmillan Co., New York, 1931.

Gup, Samuel M., *Currents in Jewish Religious Thought in America in The Twentieth Century.* (Pamphlet.) Central Conference of American Rabbis, 1931.

INDEX

Ablutions, 209.
Abraham, 210.
Achad Haam, 272.
Addison, J. T., 154, 164.
Adhikary, R. C., 22, 23.
Afghanistan, 22, 187.
Agnosticism, 192.
Agreements, 203.
Ahmadiya movement, 224.
Ahmed, Syed Maqbool, 205.
Akita, U., 138.
Al Azhar, 184, 211, 214, 215, 222, 223.
Ali, Syed Amir, 202, 210.
Allah, 261.
Allied powers, 296.
All-India depressed classes conference, 75.
All-India Untouchable League, 75.
All-India women's conference, 66, 84.
Altar of Heaven, 113.
Amanullah, 187, 221.
Ambala, Punjab, 228.
Amon-Re, 12.
Ancestor worship:
  China, 133, 134.
  Japan, 140.
Andrews, C. F., 46, 49.
Anesaki Masaharu, 143, 164.
Angora, 183.
Anti-Brahmin movement, 76.
Anti-Christian movement:
  China, 95, 100.
Anti-priest movement:
  India, 32.

Anti-religion movement:
  China, 94, 95-100.
  India, 30.
  Japan, 138, 139.
Anti-religious campaign:
  Russia, 247.
Anti-Semitism, 288, 290.
Apologetic in Islam:
  New, 207.
Apprehension of Goodness Society, China, 129.
Arabia, 182, 221, 222.
Arab-Jewish conflict, 298.
Arabic, 196.
Arabs, 297.
Argentine, 289.
Arya Samaj, 42, 43, 86, 228.
Asceticism, Communist, 268.
Ashram, Sabarmati, 53.
  Santiniketan, 53.
  Sat Tal, 55.
Asia, 247.
Atheism, Russian, 247.
Australia, 41.
Avatar, 58.

Babbitt, Irving, 120.
Babylonia, 12.
Bajaj, Jamnalal, 71.
Balfour declaration, 293, 313.
Balkrishna, 48.
Baptists, Russia, 246.
Baroda, 65.
Behaviorism, 8.
Benares, 78.
Bengal, 63.
Bengalee, Sufi M. R., 226.

INDEX

Bhakti-Marga, 58.
Bible, 3, 50, 190, 261, 275.
B'nai B'rith Order, 300.
Bolsheviki, 235.
Bolshevism, 188, 264.
Bombay, 35.
Bo-tree, 159.
Boy Scout, 271.
Brahman, 45, 57, 58.
Brahmanism, 33.
Brahma Samaj, 36, 37, 45.
Brahmins, 67, 76.
Brotherhood in Islam, 225.
Buddha, 45, 155, 159.
  birthday of, 159.
Buddhism, 3.
  in China, 94, 95.
  in Japan, 143, 144, 145.
  revival of in China, 122-127.
  social note in Japan, 160, 162.
Buddhism and Science, 124, 154.
Buddhist Church, the, 122.
Buddhist hymns, 157, 158.
Buddhist Mercy Association, 126.
Buddhist missionaries to West, 166, 167.
Buddhist monthly, 123.
Buddhist revival:
  China, 122-127.
  Japan, 152-168.
Bukhara, 197.
Buksh, Sir Kuda, 208, 210.

Cairo, University of, 210.
Calendar, Moslem, 200.
Caliph, 183, 184, 185.
Caliphate, 183, 199.
Cash, W. Wilson, 227.
Caste, 38, 40, 67.
Caste-Hindus, 74.
Catholicism, 3.
Central Conference of American Rabbis, 299, 312.
Ceremonialism in Judaism, 324.

Chamberlin, W. H., 256, 257.
Charvakas, 30.
Chastity, 218.
Chengtu, 113.
Chicago, 224.
Chien Huen Chang, Dr., 115.
Child marriage, India, 37, 62-63.
  Persia, 187.
Children's Communist movement, 247.
China, 18.
  anti - Christian movement, 100-103.
  anti-religion movement, 95-100.
  Buddhist revival in, 122-127.
  Communism in, 97, 132.
  intellectual and social revolution, 91-93.
  nationalism and religion, 103-109.
  Neo-Confucianism in, 117-122.
  political revolution, 89, 90.
  religions of, 94.
  religious liberalism in, 109.
  Syncretism in, 128-132.
Chinese Buddhist Association, 124.
Chinese students, 14.
Chinese *Tripitaka*, 164.
Christ, 54, 58.
Christa Seva Sangha, 53, 54, 55.
Christenings, Russian, 250.
Christianity, 2, 13, 53, 58, 276.
  in China, 90, 94, 97, 106.
  in India, 68, 70.
  in Japan, 140, 143.
  in Russia, 231.
Christianity, social emphasis, 13.
Christmas, Buddhist, 159.
Church, the, 10.
  and the Revolution, 233-235.
  and Soviets, 235-246, 254.
  and State, Turkey, 200.
  in Old Russia, 232, 233.

334

INDEX

Church property, Russia, 239.
Civil registry, Russia, 237.
Class strife, Russia, 264.
Clergy, in Russia, 241.
Cochin, 84.
Columbia University, 115.
Commercial interchange, 14.
Community center, 310.
Communism:
　in China, 90, 98, 101, 132.
Communism—a religion?, 259-269.
Communism, missionary activity of, 265-266.
Communism, orthodoxy of, 261.
Communism vs. religion, 256-259.
Communist ceremonials, 267.
Communist party, 247.
Confiscation of church ornaments, 242-244.
Confucianism, 3, 94, 95, 112.
Confucian society, 115, 116.
Confucius, 96, 262.
Conservative Judaism, 278-284, 307-311.
Constantinople, 183, 189, 198.
Constitution, Soviet, 240.
Coöperation of religions, Japan, 170-172.
Council of Young Men's Hebrew and kindred associations, 300.
Counter-revolutionary activity, 245.
Creed of Communism, 260-261.
Criticism of Koran, 203.
Cromer, Lord, 193.
Cultural interchange, 15-16.
Cultural interpenetration, 5.
Cultural Zionism, 295.
Czar, 232, 233.

Das, C. R., 21.
Das, Govinda, 33.
Decalogue—Tao Yuan, 130.
Dedication, 80.
Dietary laws, 275.

Democracy, 12, 199.
Denationalization of Jews, 286.
Dependence, 9.
Depressed classes, 72, 75.
Devadasis, 78-84.
Dharma, 22, 57, 83.
Divorce in India, 64, 65.
　Persia, 187.
Dyananda, 42.

Easter, 250.
　Buddhist, 159.
Eastern Buddhist Association, 164.
Economic change, 10, 11.
　China, 88.
　Islam, 178.
Eddington, A. S., 17.
Eddy, George Sherwood, 247, 254.
Edib, Halidé, 201.
Education, 18.
　Buddhist, Japan, 161.
　China, 91.
　Japan, 141.
　Persia, 186.
Egypt, 12, 182, 226.
El Arish, 292.
Emperor worship, 150.
Enlightening Association, the, 122.
Evangelical churches, Russia, 246.

Fakir, 26, 32, 34.
Famine, Russian, 241, 242.
Far Eastern Buddhist Conference, 165.
Farquhar, J. N., 41.
Father India, 83.
Federation of Buddhist organizations for children, 164.
Ferment in China, 93.
Field, Harry H., 63.
Forest dweller, 33.
Frankel, Zacharias, 279.
Freedom of worship—China, 115.

335

INDEX

Free thinkers, China, 97.
French Revolution, 288.
Fujin, Howakwai, 158, 159.
Fülop, Müller, René, 257, 264, 270.
Fundamentalist Hinduism, 41.
Fundamentalism, 2.
Future life, 9.

Gandhi, Mahatma, 28, 32, 45, 46.
and outcastes, 69, 72, 75.
fast unto death, 72.
Gautama, 155.
General trends in Judaism, 284.
Ghetto, 284.
God, 1, 2, 7, 10, 26, 32, 38, 45, 55, 58, 96, 147, 150, 170, 172, 193, 203, 206, 208, 213, 219, 222, 225, 247, 257, 258, 260, 261, 263, 275, 278, 290, 308.
Godless universities, Russia, 248.
Goldman, Solomon, 279, 280, 281, 304.
Great Britain, 27, 188.
Gup, Samuel M., 280, 307, 316, 324, 325.

Hadassah, 301.
Hankow, 101.
Hanukah, 323.
Hatikvah, 316.
Hawaii, 168.
Headley, Lord, 208.
Heart Cleansing Society, 116.
Hebrew language, 281, 298.
Hebrews, God of, 258.
Hebrew Theological College, 280, 306.
Hebrew Union College, attitude to Zionism, 315.
Hebrew University, 296, 298.
Herzl, Theodor, 289.
Higher criticism :
of Bible, 210.
of Koran, 210.

High Procurator, 232.
Hillel Foundations, 300.
Hindu, 22.
Moslem problems, 51, 52.
Scriptures, 61.
Temples, 82.
Hinduism, 1, 3, 39.
definition of, 20-22.
liberal or reformed, 35.
orthodox, 64, 66.
tendencies in, 25, 26.
unrest in, 23, 24.
Hindus, Maurice, 270.
Hodous, Lewis, 116, 119.
Holtom, D. C., 146.
Holy Land, 296.
Holy Man, 26, 32, 85.
Holy Synod, 232.
Hongwanji sect, 168.
Hu, H. C., 110.
Humanism, 120.
Japan, 169, 173.
Judaism, 283.
Humanists, China, 112.
Hu Shih, Dr., 109.
Hussain, Sir Ahmed, 208.
Hussein, Taha, 211.

Ibn Saud, 184, 188, 222.
Idealization of Prophet, 207.
Idolatry, 37.
Iglehart, C. W., 139, 146.
Ikdam, 198.
Immortality, 265.
Incarnation, 57.
India, 18, 20.
caste in, 38, 40, 67.
influences on, 27, 28, 29.
social change in, 59-84.
syncretism in, 44-59.
Indian Christians, 25.
Indian social reformer, 22, 23, 25, 34, 36, 61, 69, 71.
Intellectual awakening :
Japan, 153.
Intellectual change, 4.
China, 88, 89.
Intercollegiate Menorah Association, 301.

INDEX

Intercollegiate Zionist Association of America, 301.
Inter-cultural contact, 12, 13.
China, 88.
Interest, 205.
International Buddhist Institute, 125.
Iraq, 182, 184.
Irreligion, India, 30.
Ise, 147.
Ishmael, 210.
Islam, 3, 14, 276.
in China, 227.
tendencies in, 177.
Islamic Church, 199.
Islamic review, 202, 213, 224.
Izvestia, 255.

Japan, 15.
Buddhist Revival in, 152-168.
Christian Year Book, 162.
Humanism in, 169, 173.
Industrialization of, 136, 137.
Jazz of religion in, 143.
National Committee for Promotion of International Peace through Religion, 172.
Syncretism in, 172.
Jedda, 206.
Jeffrey, Arthur, 216, 223.
Jerusalem, 184, 291.
Jesus, 45, 46, 47, 48, 58, 101, 155, 225.
Avatar, the, 27.
Jewish attitude to, 317.
Liberal Jewish attitude to, 320-321.
Moslem idea of, 216.
Jewish:
Agency, 297.
art, 281.
Colonial Trust, 293.
Company, 289.
National Home, 294.
organizations, recent, 300, 301.
Theological Seminary, 279.

Jewish—continued:
Year Book, 299.
youth in college, 287, 288.
Jewishness, 272.
Jewry, American, 282.
Jews, 261.
Jihad, 182.
Jodo sect, 156.
Jones, E. Stanley, 56.
Journal of Religion, 35.
Ju Chiao, 117.
Judaism:
Conservative, 278-284, 307-311.
Definition, 272-274.
Orthodox, 277-278, 301-307.
Reform, 274-277, 311-325.

Kagawa, Toyohiko, 162, 163.
Kali, 69.
Kaplan, Mordecai, 307, 308, 309, 310.
Karma, 38, 77, 78.
Kato, Genchi, 150, 151.
Kawashiri, Seishu, 139.
Keng, Dr. Lin Boom, 117, 118.
Kepler, A. R., 99.
Kerensky, 233
Khadija, 217.
Khilafat, 52.
Kiang Kai Shek, President, 99.
Kiev, 248.
Kingdom of God Movement, 163.
Kingdom of God—Communist, 265.
Klausner, J., 319.
Kohler, K., 290.
Komsomol, 247.
Koran, 190, 196, 203, 204, 206, 207.
a living book, 206.
criticism of, 203.
higher criticism of, 211.
inspiration of, 212, 213.
reinterpretation of, 205.
translation of, 214, 215.

INDEX

Korea, 108.
Korean Methodist Church, 108.
Kosher, 285, 286.
Krishna, 57.
Kshatriya, 67.
Kulaks, 253.
Kuomingtang, 90, 95, 105.

Lao-tze, 94, 130.
Law, the, 282.
Laymen, Buddhist, 122.
League of Nations, 294.
Lebanon, 188.
Legislative Assembly, India, 61, 62.
Leisure, 11.
Lenin, Nicolai, 138, 233, 257, 261.
  corner, 263.
  veneration of, 262, 264.
Leningrad, 240, 248.
Levonian, Lootfy, 198.
Levy, Felix A., 316, 323, 324.
Lew, T. T., 123.
Liberal Buddhist Association, Japan, 164.
Liberal Hinduism, 35.
Liberalism in Islam, 201.
Literary renaissance:
  China, 92.
Lo, R. Y., Dr., 97, 98, 101, 103, 111.
Loyalty, Communist, 267.
Lumbini festival, 159.
Lunacharsky, Commissar, 256.
Lyon, D. Willard, 121.

Machinery, 28.
MacNicol, Nicol, 30, 31, 32.
Madhi, 224.
Madras, 75, 84.
  presidency of, 81.
Magic, 5.
Mahasabha, 43, 44.
Mahayana Buddhism, 123.
Manchus, 89.
Manhood Suffrage Act, 138.

Marduk, 12.
Margoliuth, Dr., 209.
Marriage, Russia, 257.
Martyrs, Communist, 267.
Marx, Karl, 138, 257, 261.
Maurois, André, 273.
Mayo, Katherine, 62, 69.
Mass education, 18.
"Meaning of the Glorious Quran," 215.
Mecca, 184, 206, 222.
Mei, K. T., 120.
Mendicants in India, 33.
Mennonites, 254.
Messiah, 290.
Messianic hope, 276.
Messianists, 283.
Mexico, 266.
Middle East, 186.
Mikado, 173.
Militant Godless Society, 247.
Millikan, Robert A., 17.
Ministers, Russia, 254.
Mission of Jew, the, 291.
Missionaries, 14.
  Christian, 13.
Missionary:
  activity of Communism, 266.
  movement, Moslem, 223.
  propaganda, 28.
Missions:
  Buddhist, 166-168.
  Christian, India, 43.
  Islam, objectives of, 229.
Mission Schools, China, 102.
Modernism, 2.
  in Egypt, 211.
Modern Review, 30, 80.
Mohammed, 179, 206, 213.
  as example, 218.
  character of, 216.
  wives of, 217, 218, 219, 220.
Mohammedanism, 23, 45, 48.
  in China, 127, 128.
Montefiore, Claude, 319.
Morality, 198.
  Communist, 270.
Mori, M. G., 144.

INDEX

Mosaic legislation, 277.
Moscow, 240, 248, 263.
Moslem sunrise, 226.
Mother India, 62, 79, 82.
Mo-Ti, 119.
Moving pictures, 16, 29, 190.
Muhammad Ali, 217.
Museum of Religion, 249.
Mussolini, 185.
Mustapha, Kemal, 181, 186.
Mysore, 80, 84.

Nationhood, of Israel, 282.
National Christian Council:
  China, 108.
  Japan, 175.
National Christian Council Review, 57.
National Federation of Temple Sisterhoods, 301.
Nationalism, 44.
  China, 90, 95.
  Indian, 28, 41, 42, 70.
  Persia, 186.
Nationalism and religion:
  in China, 103.
  in Japan, 174-175.
Near East Relief, 189.
Nehru, Motilal, 31.
New Testament, 58, 261.
New Thought Movement, China, 98, 109.
Nichiren, 156.
Niebuhr, Reinhold, 260.
Noguchi, Yone, 140.
Non-Brahmin castes, 76.
Novgorod, 248.

Ober-procuror, 234.
Old Testament, 57, 261.
Omotokyo, 147, 148, 149.
Opium of the people, 257.
Orthodox Church, 233, 237, 238, 244, 245, 252, 253, 258.
Orthodox, Hinduism, 81.
Orthodoxy, 283.
  Jewish, 278, 281.

Orthodoxy—*continued*:
  Jewish trends in, 301.
  lack of organization, 306.
  Other-worldly religion, 197.
  Outcasts, 67, 68.
  and Hindu temples, 69-72.
  and Mahatma Gandhi, 72-74.

Pai, A. K., 33.
Palestine, 182, 276, 294, 296.
  colonization of, 296.
Pancharatra, 81.
Pan-Islam, 180, 182.
Pan-Islamic Congress, 183.
Patriarch, 242.
Patriarchate, 235.
Peace, 225.
Peasants, Russian, 249.
Peking, 115.
Penance, Tao Yuan, 131.
People's Party, China, 99.
Persecution, Russia, 253-255.
Persia, 184, 186, 196, 221.
Philipson, David, 277, 314.
Philosophy, 198.
Pickthall, Marmaduke, 215.
Pieters, A., 150, 151.
Pilgrimage, 222.
Pioneers, 271.
Pittsburgh Conference, 275.
Planchette, 129.
Polygamy, Moslem, 217.
Political change, 11, 12.
  in China, 88.
Political evolution, 4.
Political ferment, Moslem lands, 180.
Poona, 53, 228.
Pope, 185, 254.
Pratt, J. B., 161.
Prayer, Moslem, 208, 213.
Preaching, Buddhist, 156.
Preaching in Orthodoxy Judaism, 303.
Presidency of religious affairs, Turkey, 200.

INDEX

Priests:
  Brahmin, 35.
  Russia, 238.
Processions, Russia, 267.
Prophet, the, 196, 201, 203.
  back to the, 207.
  character of, 207.
  idealization of, 207.
  wives of, 216-219.
Proselytizing, 50.
Prosperity, 9.
Prostitution, 79, 80.
Protestantism, 3.
Psychology, 7, 8, 17, 18.
Publications, new, China, 93.
Pudukottah, 84.
Puranas, 81.
Purdah, 65, 66.

Qur'an. See Koran.

Rabbinical Assembly, 299.
Rabbinical Council, 299.
Radhakrishnan, Professor S., 21, 38.
Radical reaction, India, 29-35.
  Islam, 192.
Radio, 17.
Ramakrishna Mission, 30, 85.
Ramohan Roy, 36, 60.
Rapprochement between liberal Judaism and liberal Christianity, 317.
Rasputin, 270.
Rationalism, 202.
Razek, Abdul, 211.
Reactionary Islam, 212.
Reactionism in Islam, 221.
Rebirth, 38.
Reddy, Dr. Muthulakshmi, 83.
Reform:
  in Germany, 274.
  Judaism, 274-277.
Reform movement in Hinduism, 36.
  trends in, 311-325.
Reichelt, Karl L., 125, 126.

Religion:
  attitude of Communism to, 258.
  definition of, 259.
  change-producing factors, 1-20.
  future of, in Russia, 269.
Religious education, 171.
  Buddhist, 156.
Religious instruction:
  in Russia, 240.
  of children, 241.
Republic, China, 90.
Research Union of Buddhism, 124.
Resurrection, 101.
Review of Religions, 224.
Revival, Buddhist:
  in China, 122.
  in Japan, 152.
Ritual, Moslem reform of, 213.
Robert College, 189.
Roberts, J. M., 105.
Russia, 97.
  anti-religious campaign, 247-256.
  Church and Revolution, 233-235.
  Church and Soviets, 235-246.
  Communism vs. Religion in, 256-259.
  future of religion in, 269-271.
  is Communism a religion?, 259-269.
  Orthodox Church in Old, 232, 233.
  religion in, 231.
Russo-Japanese War, 28, 137.
Rutter, Eldon, 222.

Sabbath, Jewish, 286, 305.
Sadhu, 34.
Saint's days, Russia, 250.
Salvation Army:
  Buddhist, 158.
  Japan, 140.

INDEX

Salvation, Communist, 264.
Samsara, 33.
Sangathan, 31.
Sannyasa, 31.
San Remo, 294, 314.
Santiniketan, 53.
Sarma, Professor, 22.
Sati, 60.
Sat Tal Ashram, 55, 56.
Satyagraha, 69.
Schulman, S., 318.
Science, 5, 6, 40, 87, 96, 202.
  Russia, 265.
Scientific discovery, 4, 7.
Scientific method, 7.
Scientific progress, 8.
Scriptures, Hindu, 41.
Sectarian societies, Russia, 252.
Secularism, 172.
  in India, 31.
Segregation of sexes, Jewish, 302.
Self, 8.
Self-respect Conference, 76.
Separation of Church and State:
  China, 114-115.
  Russia, 236.
  Turkey, 199.
Sermon on the Mount, 46, 47, 50.
Servants of India Society, 85.
Shah, Ikbal Ali, 187.
Shanghai, 100.
Shastras, 64, 81.
Schechter, Solomon, Dr., 279.
Shemini Azereth, 323.
Sheriat, 199, 207.
Shevvrath, 323.
Shingon, 154.
Shin Sect, 156.
Shinto, 140, 141.
  Shrine, 146.
  State, 146.
Shuddhi movement, 228.
Shulhan Aruk, 278, 304.
Sikhs, 3.

Silver, Rabbi, 317.
Six Sages Union, True Tao Society, 128.
Sobor, 234, 235, 238.
Social change in India, 59-84.
Socialization of Buddhism in China, 1, 25.
Social revolution in China, 91.
Social work of churches, 246.
Society:
  for enlightening the people, 122.
  of the Jewish Renascence, 309.
  for religious liberty, China, 114.
Soul, 8.
  of Judaism, 276.
South America, 266.
South Sea islands, 168.
Soviet government, 255.
  Church and, 235-246.
Spinka, Matthew, 240.
Spirit of Islam, 208.
Stalin, 255.
Stamboul, 204.
State Shinto, 146.
Study of Morality Society, 128.
Substitutes for Christian festivals, Russia, 249-252.
Sudra, 67.
Sugimori, K., 172.
Sukkoth, 323.
Sultan of Turkey, 184.
Sunday, 286.
Sunday schools, Buddhist, 156, 157, 158.
Sun goddess, 152.
Sun Yat Sen, cult of, 95, 104, 105, 106.
Supernatural, 3, 6.
Swadeshi 48-49.
Synagogue, 303.
  Council of America, 299.
Syncretism:
  China, 128-133.
  India, 44-59.
  Japan, 172.

INDEX

Syria, 182, 188.
Syrian College, 189.
Syncretism in China, 44, 128.
Synod, 232.

Tagore, Rabindranath, 50, 57.
Tai, Hau, 124.
Takakusu, Dr., 155.
Talmud, 278, 306.
Tao, 130.
Taoism, 94.
Tao Yuan, 128, 129, 130, 131.
Teachers, Atheist, 256.
Tel-aviv, 296.
Temple entry, 69, 70.
Temple prostitution, 27, 43, 78-84.
Tendai, 154.
Tenrikyo, 147, 149.
Thebes, 12.
Theology, 39.
  Shinto, 151.
Theological Seminaries:
  Moslem, 199, 200.
  Russia, 236, 240.
Theosophy, 44.
Tikhon, 235.
Titus, Murray, 203, 207, 210.
Tokyo, 165.
Tradition, 39.
  Moslem, 209.
Trans-Jordania, 182.
Transmigration, 77.
Trattner, Ernest, 319.
Travancore, 84.
Trotzky, 233.
Tsai, Dr., 110, 111.
Tsu, Y. Y., 118.
Turkestan, 197.
Turkey, 18, 180, 184, 204.
Turks, 198.
Twice-born Hindus, 33.
Twinem, Paul D., 128.

Uesugi, Dr., 151.
Ulemas, 214, 216.
Union of American Hebrew congregations, 299.

Union of orthodox Jewish congregations, 299.
Unitarian, 45.
United Buddhist University, 164.
United Christian Church in China, 108.
United Goodness Society, 128.
United provinces, 84.
United Synagogue of America, 279, 299, 301.
Universities, 15.
University of Cairo, 210, 216.
"Unsynagogued" Jews, 281.
Upanishads, 48, 81.
Untouchables, 70, 72.

Vaishnava, 48.
Vedanta, 41, 58.
Vedas, 21, 38, 42, 86.
Versailles, 294.
Village schools, 18.
Virgin birth, 101.
Virgin Mary, 262.
Vishnu, 58.
Voice of the surge, 124.
Volga, 241.

Wahhabis, 184, 221, 222.
Wailing Wall, 298.
Washington, 291.
Waxman, Meyer, 280, 305.
Widow, 60.
  in India, 61, 63.
  re-marriage, 37, 43, 60.
Wise, Isaac M., 311.
Wise, James Waterman, 320.
Wise, Stephen S., 319.
Wives of Mohammed, 217-219.
Women in Islam, 225.
  seclusion of, 219.
Women:
  status of, in India, 58, 60.
  unveiling of, 219.
Woodburne, A. C., 35.
World Buddhist Conference, 165.

INDEX

World Conference of Liberal Judaism, 316.
World Moslem Conference, 184.
World Moslem Congress, 203.
World Union of Progressive Judaism, 322, 323.
World peace, 171.
World's Christian Student Federation, 100.
World War, 28, 137, 293.
   in Turkey, 181.
Worship of Heaven, 113.

Yaroslav, Metropolitan of, 244.
Yellow Swastika Society, 126.
Yen, Hunter, 110.
Yerravda pact, 73, 74.
Yoga, 57.
Young East, 159.
Young India, 46.
Young Men's Association of India, 69.
Young Men's Buddhist Association, 158.
Young Men's Moslem Association, 227.
Young Women's Buddhist Association, 158.
Youth, China, 72.
Yuan Shih Kai, 90, 114.

Zakat, 226.
Zangwill, Israel, 293.
Zen, Buddhism, 156.
Zionism, 283, 288, 310.
   attitude of Hebrew Union College, 315.
   cultural, 294, 295.
   object of, 292.
   political, 294.
   reform, attitude to, 312.
   relief, 295.
Zionist Congress, 291.
Zionist movement, 184.

Printed in the United States
by Baker & Taylor Publisher Services